Stilwater

~~ Stilwater ~~

Finding Wild Mercy in the Outback

Rafael de Grenade

milkweed
editions

The names of animals, people, and places in this book have been changed to protect privacy.

Published 2014 by Milkweed Editions
Printed in the United States of America
Cover design by Brad Norr Design
Cover photo and interior photos by Rafael de Grenade
Author photo by Jaime de Grenade
14 15 16 17 18   5 4 3 2 1
First Edition

Milkweed Editions, an independent nonprofit publisher, gratefully acknowledges sustaining support from the Bush Foundation; the Patrick and Aimee Butler Foundation; the Driscoll Foundation; the Jerome Foundation; the Lindquist & Vennum Foundation; the McKnight Foundation; the National Endowment for the Arts; the Target Foundation; and other generous contributions from foundations, corporations, and individuals. Also, this activity is made possible by the voters of Minnesota through a Minnesota State Arts Board Operating Support grant, thanks to a legislative appropriation from the arts and cultural heritage fund, and a grant from the Wells Fargo Foundation Minnesota. For a full listing of Milkweed Editions supporters, please visit www.milkweed.org.

Library of Congress Cataloging-in-Publication Data

Grenade, Rafael de, 1980–
    Stilwater : finding wild mercy in the outback / Rafael de Grenade.
        pages   cm
    Summary: "Set on an abandoned cattle ranch in Queensland, Australia, this memoir explores the power of a beautiful coastal landscape, contrasting this place with the brutality of modern ranching, and exploring the tension between wildness and human efforts to create order from it"—Provided by publisher.
    ISBN 978-1-57131-314-0 (pbk.) — ISBN 978-1-57131-888-6 (ebook)
    1. Ranching—Australia. 2. Feral cattle—Australia. 3. Grenade, Rafael de, 1980—Travel—Australia. 4. Australia—Description and travel. I. Title.
    SF196.A8G74 2014
    994.3'8072092—dc23

                                                                    2013043098

To Soraya, with love.

Stilwater

Stilwater Station

~~

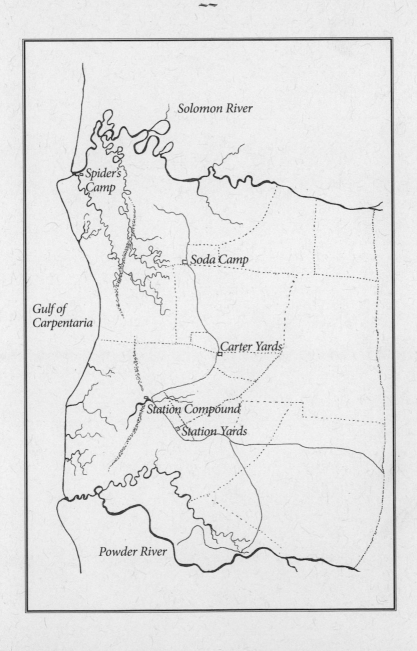

I

Gulf Country

I LANDED ON STILWATER in the dry season. I arrived by air, sweeping across white savanna mottled with sand ridges and the speckled green of vegetation. From above, the upper reach of the gulf country was a painting—tracings and patterns with vivid colors and no distinct shapes, the future and past laid out below all at once, temporal paths cut by countless spirits on walkabout, here and gone.

Trees took shape as the plane descended, tall, with blue-green willowy canopies, and then a small station rose up, a compound with a few rectangular scattered buildings, a few corrals at the end of a long white line of road leading in from the east. The pilot veered, dipping one wing, and then a long dirt strip appeared and there was no avoiding the ground. The small wheels jolted against hard-packed earth and yellow grass blurred past the windows.

When the pilot opened the curved door, I climbed down over the wing. I had arrived alone, the sole passenger. The searing white earth rose to meet me.

~~

Australia is an island between two oceans, a landmass isolated for some fifty-five million years. Most of the twenty million people there today choose the tranquilizing lip of deep blue water at the eastern rim. But farther inland, farther north, red earth and black earth, hot savannas of eucalyptus trees and bronze desert reveal the continent's heart. This subtle expanse reaches for days of flat nothingness, the creases of thin drainages like wrinkles of skin—parched, leathered, endless.

Hours from the cities on the coast, across the barren sweep, a horn juts upward on the northeastern corner: the spiked protrusion of the Cape York Peninsula, which reaches almost to Papua New Guinea. Here the earth begins to green again, just the palest tinge of tropics clawing onto the flattest land on earth. In its farthest domain, the horn cuts between the Arafura Sea in the Indian Ocean and the Coral Sea of the Pacific Ocean. Retreat a little to the south and west and the Arafura Sea bleeds into the Gulf of Carpentaria. Stilwater Station is a rectangle that borders the sea and covers a swath of the coastal plains.

The gulf country is alternately, and sometimes all at once, a rippling savanna, a salt flat, and a scrub whose edges endlessly change and play at the wide silk of the sea. Rivers snake across it in broadening oscillations, resisting the moment they become one with the glittering ocean, trying to slow down time. Shallow channels cut between the major conduits, where, depending on rain and the direction of storms, water can flow in either direction. Salt arms reach inward like the limbs of an octopus, their tentacles fringed in mangroves.

This land is a body without boundaries, filled with veins that transgress and regress, feeding and starving its different organs with impunity. In other places, rivers are dependable, land is dependable. This is a landscape where anything can happen. A place that defies human nature, and even seems to defy nature itself.

Few places on earth have a single tide each day, but in the gulf, two oceans collide in what feels like a conscious rebellion against physics and gravity, and the combined forces cancel a tide. Rivers flow out to the gulf for half of the day and the gulf flows into them for the other half. The tide pushes upstream, miles inland, blending salty and sweet.

The gulf is not inviting. More like luring—full of sharks and jellyfish and silver barramundi. Crocodile eyes follow any creature that ventures to the shore, but not many do. Most know to give the coastline a wide berth, and the waters ripple alone. Low tide exposes white beaches and sandbars with shallow water spreading in translucent, jade-green fins between them. The crocodiles sleep on the warm sand just above the surf, deadly and serene.

Inland, forested bands of sand ridges dissect the grasses and flats. Low ridges appear and disappear across the plain, sections of old waterways left a few feet higher than the surrounding country after millennia of erosion. Tall waving grasses sweep several feet high in faded gold between open forests, brackish lagoons, and murky bogs. Saltwater mangroves line the coast and saline rivers; freshwater mangroves grow on stick legs along the swamps. Water lilies raise white and purple palms in the lagoons in rare, delicate gestures. Sea wind blows in from the coast, cool on the winter mornings. Sea eagles haunt the line between sand and sea while wallabies fidget and nibble and bounce, a foot tall and easily frightened. Huge lizards—goannas—prowl the scrub and snakes trace wandering lines into the sand.

Deeper still, the forest country begins, a savanna of tall bloodwood trees, weeping coolibah, broad-leaved cabbage gums, white-trunked ghost gums, and shorter tea trees. A year turns the grass between them from a lush green to a bleached brown.

There are only two seasons here, and there is no mistaking which is which.

The wet thickens the air with heat and moisture until it bleeds into drops, the pounding monsoon storms turning the country into a hammered sheet of water—half flood, half ocean. Thundering herds of clouds give the sky more topography than the land has known for eons. As the rain falls, the sea invades as far as it can reach, and the crocodiles follow. Animals crowd onto the jungled sand ridges, which afford them only a few inches of protection above the surface of the water. Violent cyclones crack the trees, and animals huddle against the rain. Many don't escape. Roads become impassable, and the mail plane can rarely land. Mangoes ripen and fall in rotting layers on the lawns. Heat turns viscous and the shallow sea of rain and gulf rises under the metal stilts of houses, isolating the inhabitants for months at a time.

Eventually the rains stop, and not a drop falls for nine months. Water recedes and mud hardens slowly, along with remnants of dead vegetation and animals. For a shuddering moment, the country blazes in neon green. Small flowers bloom. Then the green follows the water, receding, the sun bleaching the savanna. Grasses dry into a dead sea. Dust releases from the clay-hold, ready to scatter with any hint of wind. The sky reaches an unobstructed, piercing blue and haze rings the edges. The sun shifts imperceptibly, warmth and light losing their tone. A subtle chill invades the night. Few clouds tear against the thorny crown of stars or temper the incessant sky. Months in the dry, like those of the wet, stretch on and on, demanding either patience or surrender. All weather intercepts and seems to pass right through the skin.

꒐

When I was twelve I quit school and began working as a ranch hand on rough-country mountain ranches in Arizona. More than a decade later, when I learned of North Australian cattlemen and their strange lives on the edge of an edge, I thought that my years on horseback might have prepared me for the extremes of wilderness they call home. At the least, they sparked a longing in me for a place that was wilder and more remote than what I had known. And because I was more at home in a sleeping bag under the stars than among people and had a driving motivation to be away, beyond borders clear to me then, I decided to travel to their country.

I wrote to my great-uncle's wife's stepmother's cousin, who lived in Central Queensland. Tara responded, eventually, with enthusiasm. She was pregnant with her first child, and her husband needed help in the "muster," or roundup, of cattle. I could ride her horses and stay as long as I wanted.

I flew to Central Queensland and landed in the land of kangaroos and billabongs and coolibahs. I worked there for a month, and in exchange, the small family bought me a plane ticket to Cairns to see the Great Barrier Reef. This plane was a tiny passenger plane that serviced the Aboriginal towns in North Queensland. On the return trip I simply got off in one of these towns, Normanton, and from there kept moving north, farther toward the edges of that harsh flatland. I was female and not yet twenty-five, and I traveled alone.

The path I took would eventually lead deep into that world at the edge of wildness. It would forever crease strange lines into my skin. I made arrangements to work for a season as a ringer, or ranch hand, on a thousand-square-mile cattle station called Stilwater that lay northwest of Normanton on the Gulf of Carpentaria. Stilwater Station would be the beginning of the end of my journey.

Stilwater Station

THE PLANE WAS A SMALL PIPER that made weekly runs to several outback stations carrying mail and sometimes passengers. The desert we had just crossed still rose and fell within me as the pilot handed my backpack across, riding boots strapped to the outside. The moment I turned away, dust, heat, and light assailed my body and my mind. I stretched my neck to ease the tightening in my throat, blinked, and saw a cluster of buildings not far away. A figure in a stockman's hat climbed out of a truck that was apparently waiting for me. This was Angus, the station manager. Short and heavy on the hoof, he ambled over and took my hand in his grip. He had a wide wrinkled face, and he eyed me with reserved suspicion.

"Angus Sheridan," he muttered.

"My name is Rafael. Nice to meet you."

He indicated I should get in the truck, and took a sack of mail from the pilot in exchange for a few gruff pleasantries. I turned back to watch the plane gather speed, lift, and take with it my only chance of escape. Angus did not bother to say anything more as we crossed the short distance to the station compound kitchen and Claire, the other half of management. She had wispy graying hair cropped against her neck and wore a plain blue denim shirt and skirt. She nodded and turned back inside with the mailbag Angus handed her. I would be their responsibility for a few months at least, and they had little sense for my use. I too was unclear about what I could do, so far from anything I had ever known.

Angus showed me to a small yellow house facing the lagoon at the edge of the compound—a gesture of subtle, unannounced generosity: a space to myself. I arranged my clothes in a drawer, dusted the spiderwebs, rubbed rust from the sinks with a rag, and called it home. My meager belongings didn't even take up the space of one room in the two-room bunkhouse: boots, a few pairs of jeans, and shirts. A wooden veranda, perched just off the ground with the rest of the house to keep it above the summer floods, extended out back, overlooking the brackish lagoon.

I lay down on the old mattress, which released a faint smell of mice, and stared up at the low wooden ceiling. Faded blue paint flecked from the sheeting. Claire would be serving a meal in the kitchen, Angus had said, though at that moment I had no desire to meet any of them. I had little enough to protect me from what would happen next, and, though I had chosen to come here, I was stuck in the middle of the outback. Stilwater Station lay beyond me on all sides, reaching for what might as well have been forever in all directions. The immensity I had sought out brought nothing like solace now.

~~

A section of coastline thirty miles long between the mouths of the Powder and Solomon Rivers defines the western boundary of Stilwater. But in summer, when the ocean moves inland and the flooding freshwater pushes a slurry of mud and land out to sea, who is to say where that line really lies? The eastern end is more clear-cut: a rusted, barbed-wire fence, worn through in places by the corrosive tea tree branches, running a semi-straight course from one river to the other.

The rivers form the other boundaries, the Powder to the south and the Solomon to the north—the S of its name a suggestion of the river's track across the flat landscape. Stilwater lies in suspense between, its borders ephemeral as the rivers seek out more intriguing courses through the flat savanna. They loop and twist and eventually touch the gulf, two steely blue serpents, so perfect in their meandering that from the air they suggest an artist's hand at work. Maps show them running straight courses directly to the sea. I decided that the cartographers in this country had never ventured this far; no river here had such a focus, no river in this country was so honest. The result is a hypothetical rectangle of about one thousand square miles.

Stilwater has been a cattle station as long as anyone can re-member, but its history has the same ambiguous character as its borders. It was probably part of other stations at one time, and before that known by Aborigines who had better judgment than to draw straight lines across a dynamic landscape. But the British divided the territory and introduced laws of land ten-ure and enterprise; colonization ran its course and continued to frame existence on the continent. The land still nourished many,

but it was owned as a set of resources and operated as a business for the sake of profit.

More recently, a company had used the station as a remote destination for outdoor enthusiasts and Japanese tourists. They built a large kitchen and several bunkhouses for the guests, made a few misspelled signs for the strange geometry of graded tracks across the station, and tried to make a little money off brave and foolish tourists who caught big fish and put stiff saddles on half-wild horses, then struggled to bring in a few cattle. Or so the story came to me.

Eventually they put the place up for sale, left it untended, and waited for years. Drug runners forming a link between Indonesia and Melbourne took over a few fishing camps on a secluded section of the coast and made their own dirt runway. Otherwise, most of the station was left to the wild, and the wild took it back.

At times it seems as if the farther a place is from civilization, the more people try to impose order there. The wild of the outback takes over as soon as anyone stops working. It disintegrates fences in a matter of a few years. Salt water and the oil in the tea trees turn the barbed wire into thin flaking strands, until they rust completely and become part of the soil again. Weather, rot, and termites dilapidate buildings and other structures, whole pieces of them washing away with every flood. Cyclones take down anything still standing and not rooted in deep. Cattle turn feral and old station horses run with the brumbies. Dingoes chew on the water lines. Fires scourge the dry grasslands and sweep away all that remains.

A thousand square miles, flat but forested enough to make seeing more than a few miles impossible. This is Stilwater Station, such a definitive name for such an undefined place. I lived on Stilwater for a dry season, melded and became part of it, until I wondered if I was half salt water too.

--

The Sutherland Corporation purchased Stilwater a year before I arrived. Gene Sutherland was a self-made man who had created the largest privately owned, vertically integrated beef business on the continent. The Sutherlands were a sharp-thinking, hardworking, intensely loyal family. One daughter and two sons shared management responsibilities for the operations, which produced and shipped Australian beef to the far corners of the globe. They owned farms and pasture in the South, feedlots in Queensland's Darling Downs, a meatworks, and millions of hectares in properties spread across the eastern half of the continent. Such geographic diversification of cattle properties provided more options for drought management, cattle dispersal, market flexibility, and access to export markets—meaning they made money regardless of the weather or the market.

They purchased Stilwater to make a profit. As in most enterprises, the wild corner of gulf country represented natural capital: grass grew there, which meant food could be produced to feed thousands with relatively little alteration to the landscape. But before that happened they needed to create an inventory of the stock, clean out the worst animals, and put the station back in operating order. They calculated the costs, the risks, and the needed returns, then proceeded.

No one knew how many cattle still ran on the station, but the guess was somewhere around eleven thousand. No one knew where these cattle were, or if they could still be called domesticated, but the initial plan was to take the station back and make it functional again.

The original buildings stood in the station compound along with the newer kitchen-dining complex, complete with windows and porches to admire the expansive country. Several houses and bunkhouses, an office, outbuildings, barns and shops—all in various stages of decay and disrepair—comprised the human encampment. Many of these sat on the same large lawn: the kitchen, houses belonging to the manager and head stockman, the ringers' quarters, and a covered barbecue area; between them grew several shade trees, mangoes, and a fig. Beyond the fenced lawn, two long sheds had been constructed for a random mix of machinery that spilled over into two other equipment barns. The station had four cranes. Excess of some things and scarcity of others had yet to find the most efficient combination on the place, or maybe they just made up for each other. A diesel generator throbbed steadily to provide power.

Sutherland Corporation delivered a new tractor and paid for the repair of the old cranes and road grader. They put their personal security man in charge of hiring and firing, finding a manager, and arranging the mustering contractors.

~~

Angus and Claire Sheridan were the first true station managers on Stilwater in more than a decade. They had lived many of their married years on an Aboriginal-owned, two-thousand-square-mile cattle station a few hours to the south along the gulf: a property that ran thirty-seven thousand cattle and took in $4 million a year. The gulf country was etched into their skin and coursed through their blood. They were perfect for the job.

They came to Stilwater Station in mango season, the dripping heat and water immediately isolating them. For six or seven months, Angus had been trying to figure out the bores—wells drilled into the artesian aquifer—and pipelines to water the cattle, the tangle of old fences, the few electric lines running off the generator, the rusting equipment, and the well-being and location of thousands of cattle.

Angus wasn't tall, and he wasn't thin. His forehead was engraved with a series of deep wrinkles, and he pulled his brown felt hat low over his eyes. He ambled about with a stiff gait from a previous injury, barefoot sometimes, or in sandals, with his little terrier, Frankie, not far behind. He didn't get into the brawl and ruckus of cow work much. Instead, he tinkered with equipment, toured every road in his dusty utility vehicle, deciphered old maps and records and developed strategies for the work to be done, and tried to overlay his previous experience with the way things actually were. Once the world began to dry, his first order of business was to find a mustering crew who could handle the cow work, and a station crew to repair the infrastructure and build new fences and corrals.

The mustering crew could be hired as one mangy lot, contained and self-sufficient; they migrated like Gypsies and charged a flat daily rate for drafting, branding, and vaccinating all of the cattle on the station, and then for turning back out the keepers and shipping the rest for sale or slaughter.

Assembling the station crew, on the other hand, was a piecemeal job. Angus knew many of the free-floating men who crossed that northern swath of outback, and it was a matter of finding a few good hands who would be willing to join the operation and take on the not-so-glamorous work of general station maintenance. Angus would oversee both crews and be responsible to the station owners for their work. He would be responsible for seeing that the place eventually turned a profit.

Angus had a way of spreading out the day, making it move slowly so he could keep up with it. He drifted across the lawn from the manager's house toward the kitchen with a slow rocking gait, carrying his flashlight, or torch, in the full dark of morning, careful as he placed his steps to miss the cane toads and slithering brown snakes. He gravitated to the same place at the table on the veranda at breakfast, midmorning smoko—a smoke and coffee break—and dinner, that old chair his throne. He had a small, white-china cup for his tea, stained with faint rings of tannins in the bottom.

Every morning he sat with Ross Porter, the new bore man, in the yellow bulb light of pre-morning for a prolonged cup of black tea and a cigarette or two while he ordered and reordered the operation in his mind. By the time he decided on the best tactic for the day, light would be turning the sky milky where it touched the horizon. He then had several hours to drive to some remote set of water troughs, or check on the cattle around lick tubs. Long solitude would swallow him, but he could arrange the hours to emerge from it in time for lunch. If he was in the office, he crossed to the kitchen again for a midmorning cuppa. Later, or sometimes earlier, when he'd had enough, he poured a rum-and-Coke and lay lengthwise on one of the couches, facing the television in the kitchen to watch the horse races.

Claire sorted the books, accounted for the details and kept the compound in order, cooking and cleaning, watering the gardens and lawns—her own way of defying the inherent wildness of the place, and drawing out elements of femininity wherever she could.

The generator kicked on at five every morning when Claire walked across the lawn beneath stars and turned on the lights in the kitchen. On most mornings she served up bacon, eggs, and stewed tomatoes and onions, setting platters out on a table in the large dining room. Knives, forks, plates, and coffee cups filled one end of the long table, and the electric hot-water pitcher, tea bags, milk, instant coffee, jam, butter, bread, and a toaster filled the other. Above the table, a picture of a sinuous river meeting the blue gulf served as a reminder of the surreality surrounding this refuge of human reality.

The crew would filter in, fill plates, and stir hot drinks in ceramic mugs. Afterward they washed their own plates and cutlery and, without rinsing off the soapsuds, dried them and placed them back on the table. Later in the morning, they filed back into the kitchen for smoko, kicking off manure- and mud-covered shoes on the veranda and walking in socks across Claire's freshly mopped floors. They devoured her baking: Tupperwares of jam-filled biscuits, vanilla cupcakes, chocolate slice. Every evening for tea, the crew piled plates high with beef, potatoes, slices of baked pumpkin, and, on special occasions, mud crab or barramundi caught in the river or salt arms reaching inland from the sea.

Claire occupied the rest of the day with bookwork, keeping tallies of expenses on the computer database in the small office. She knew how many cattle had been shipped and the prices they might bring at market. She kept track of supplies and groceries, paychecks, mail, machine parts, medicine and supplement shipments, money in and money out.

She ordered in her mind the cluster of houses and buildings surrounded by the three-foot chain-link fence for keeping out wallabies and wild pigs. Perhaps she had the details of the place memorized already, the young mango trees, the hoses she stretched to water the lawns, the giant fig tree filled with white, screeching corellas, the palms along the fence near the kitchen.

Beyond the rivers, the neighboring station was twice as big, another to the southeast half as big, another three times as big, and Claire knew the wives of some of the other managers. They talked on the phone every so often. The dirt roads traced between them were thin lines of white chalky soil that boiled into potholes of bulldust, dropping three feet down to swallow entire trucks. The long way leading from the station to anywhere else had burned itself into her memory too. She and Angus were no strangers to the elusive nature of the outback. They both had a quality of resigned patience that would weather just about anything.

They knew that like most cattle stations, Stilwater would function as a world unto itself: mail services were provided by plane and school for the children living on the station, called School of the Air, was taught via radio. Doctors left kits of medicine coded with numbers for protection so they could make diagnoses and recommend treatment over the radio. Equipment and supplies too large or expensive to send by air came in by way of the dirt roads. Cattle were shipped out of the stations on road trains, or by rail or ship.

Angus and Claire's job was to make the station a hive of domestic, mechanic, and livestock work, with the crew operating across the extensive territory in spokes extending from the compound. The structure of daily chores provided a framework for sanity; the livestock and waters had to be fed or checked, the crew fed at regular intervals, the lawn watered, the generator turned on and off, minor and major problems addressed. In the absence of these chores, in the absence of maintenance, disorder would rule.

Seasonal cycles offered higher order. Cattle had to be mustered and handled, some shipped away, some returned to their paddocks until another season. The wet and the dry negotiated in their turn, one leading inevitably to the other, the promise of a predictable future making life slightly easier to manage.

When cyclones smashed against the coast, the crews would wait for the storms to pass and then repair the damage. When floods stranded them for a month or two at a time, they would ration the fresh food and hunker down to wait. They understood the way place and work cultivate a culture in which humans and the environment mutually shape one another, becoming, despite the modern amenities of air conditioning, good satellite television, telephone, and Internet, two manifestations of the same entity.

Station Horses

I WOKE THAT FIRST MORNING on Stilwater to the metallic ribbons of cricket song outside the window, left open to let in night breezes as the world turned to dry. The smell of rain lingered even though it hadn't rained and constellations receded into the deep blue of dawn. I stepped out of the bunkhouse, pausing before abandoning its cocoon to face a strange world that now included me. I turned toward the weak gleam of a porch light across the compound and risked the thin lawn and mango trees as I crossed to the kitchen in the dark. The distance was alive with possibility: slithering, thin, deadly brown snakes, taipans, black snakes, and whatever else might have sought out the cool of the grass for shelter. My toes crunched only mango leaves and one squishy brown lump, a cane toad.

As I neared the kitchen, I saw the figures of two men in the pale orange light of the veranda, seated at the small outdoor table. When I came up the stairs and into the light, Angus nodded at me. The other man, with silvery hair and a wide smile, greeted me—"How are you, sweetheart?"

"Fine, thank you."

"The tea's inside, hit the button on the kettle to heat up the water again; it's been a while since it boiled." This was Ross, the bore man, offering some hope that Angus' gruffness wasn't endemic to the people of this place.

When I returned with my tea to sit across the narrow table from Angus, he waited a while before saying, "We're getting in some horses, reckon we'll sort them out today." He looked over at me then for a moment, assessing me in the yellow bulb light. "You ride?"

"Yes sir."

We sat there, the three of us at a table with our cups of coffee and tea, waiting a good hour for the sky to brighten. They both seemed disinclined to learn any more than the few tattered pieces of information they had already received about me. I didn't get more out of Angus, except that he had ordered a load of twelve horses from one of the Sutherland properties several hours to the south. The current station horses were either old, completely wild, or both.

~~

They unloaded the new horses at the yards. A mismatched bunch if I ever saw one: a mass of manes and dust, tumbled and shaky and roughed up from jolting hours on the road. Some were monstrous animals, half draft horse, and others bony and small. All of them were stock-horse blood—thoroughbred, Arabian, and pony descendants of the earliest horses of Australia—made for distance, agility, harsh conditions, and cow work. I didn't know whether to be enthusiastic or concerned. These were the horses that had fallen to the bottom of the barrel, scraped from other stations and trucked north to the farthest, newest Sutherland station, which had yet to gather credibility. But at the same time I didn't feel quite so out of place as I swung the heavy pipe gates closed around the stirring, biting tangle of animals. After all, they would not have any more experience on the outfit than I did.

Angus introduced Wade Hamilton, the head stockman, who had arrived with the load of horses. Short, in his early thirties, with close-cropped dark hair and a coffee-brown stockman's hat, he had a strong grip and a shadow of a grin. With him was Dustin, Wade's young brother-in-law and my fellow station crew member. He was a kid, not yet eighteen, and he gave me a lopsided smile as he stepped forward and said, "How ya goin', mate?"

Angus indicated to Wade that he was passing off responsibility for me, and he climbed back into the ute—a utility vehicle with a cargo tray—and left us there at the corral without another word.

"Well mate," Wade said, "let's sort out these horses."

He carried a saddle and saddle pad out from a shipping container serving as a tack storage that sat just beyond the pens.

He swung the saddle to rest on the cross-rails of the rusty pipe fence and stepped inside the corral with a halter. Dustin and I followed into the smoke of agitated soil.

As the head stockman, Wade had first choice of the new mounts, and he didn't waste time laying claim. He didn't even turn to us, just quietly said, "I'll take the white gelding and the tall bay." We would each need a change of horses, two or three for the cow work that lay ahead.

Wade moved forward, and the horses pressed against the farther corner of the corral. "We'll ride 'em and you can choose a couple for yourselves."

We didn't argue with his choices, the most handsome horses in the motley herd. I had silently chosen another two horses, but I'm unsure how they caught my eye. One was a tall dark horse, almost as regal as the bay, and the other a smaller black horse with a quiet eye. Maybe it was the same magnetism that draws people to recognize each other without having met before. I knew those were the horses I wanted to know, to approach quietly and lay a hand on the dark withers, to slip a lead rope around the neck, feel the nostrils quivering, and look into the liquid eye.

Wade stepped into the milling band and eased the white gelding apart, slipping the halter strap around his neck and leading him back to the fence to be saddled and bridled. Dustin and I opened the gate to let the others into the next corral, should the gelding get wild. Wade held the reins close to the horse's neck as he swung into the saddle, ready for anything. The white horse arched his head and pranced the first few steps, but moved off into a fast high trot without revolt.

Wade had arrived at Stilwater a few months prior, bringing his wife, Cindy, and their two young children—Wyatt, who was five, and a newborn daughter, Lily. Wade had grown up on cattle properties in Central Queensland and spent his early life around horses and cows. He had also been a bull rider.

He'd met Cindy in the rodeo circuit—she was a professional

barrel racer, and she kept her brumby-cross chestnut barrel horse close to the house to ride. Some days she took her horse and Lily out to the round yard, set her sleeping daughter in the pram, and galloped dusty circles around the innocent child. I'd heard stories of some mothers carrying their infants in slings while they mustered and hanging the babies in trees when they had to gallop off after an unruly cow. Cindy helped Claire with the cooking, pulled the sprinkler around the lawn, and started lessons with Wyatt via School of the Air, struggling like most mothers in the outback to haul her little son into the house and keep him there until he had finished his schoolwork.

Wade surveyed the horses in the pen, no doubt considering the mess he had been handed and the work that lay ahead. If he was equally uncertain about his new station crew member, he did not let on.

Dustin chose his favorites next, both younger, unsettled broncs who could give a wild ride. A rider is only as reliable as his horse, and good crew members ride good horses. I nodded.

Wade and I closed the gates behind Dustin and stood warily to the side while he saddled his first choice, the young horse's white eye rim signaling a forthcoming explosion. Dustin had blond locks that fell from underneath his silverbelly stockman's hat, covering his long eyelashes. He took his hat off and slicked his hair back with his hands, replaced the hat, and gathered up his reins.

Dustin swung quickly into the saddle and within two steps the horse hit the air in panic. Dustin rode him through several high jolts and came out astride, riding at an unsteady canter around the small corral.

Wade turned to me, coated in fine white dust. "Your turn, mate."

To a rider, a horse is a second spirit, and riding is like becoming one being with two minds, two beating hearts, four legs, and two arms that must join into a seamless whole. The secret is to strive to become the horse while it yearns to become human; then the elusive ephemeral being comes into momentary existence.

Imbalance between horse and rider, combined with movement, leather, and terrain, make it hard to follow a line forward. But with the right spirit, a good horse could mean I had a chance on this station.

I took a bridle and filtered into the herd, letting the horses slide past until I had the smaller, black, quiet-looking stock horse caught against the corner. He surrendered with a sideways look, a flick of the ear, and did not move as I approached, murmuring quietly, and looped the reins around his black neck and the bridle over his ears. He had a white blaze that flickered to a tip between his nostrils and he lowered his head, acquiescent. Leading him out of the herd, I nudged him to a trot in a small circle on a long rein before tying him to the fence. I carried over the pad and he waited while I swung on the saddle and eased the cinch tight.

I rubbed the roughened hair of his neck and then held a closer rein while I pressed at his muscles, slid a hand down his leg, and lifted a front hoof. Though he kept one ear pointed at me and his eye open, he didn't flinch. I ran my hand over his withers, his straight back, his flanks. Wade had instructed us to check each horse for formation, hooves, teeth, lameness, and injuries. But, when they all turned up lame and knock-kneed, we didn't have much choice in the matter. My two companions hadn't seemed overly concerned about a thorough assessment anyway, not pausing for a second before they swung into the saddle.

I stepped in close to his shoulder, gathered the reins, and gripped, the fingers of one hand wound into the mane, the others on the smooth leather pommel. I placed a toe in the stirrup and swung my other foot off the ground. The first contact of seat to saddle leather, legs to ribs, fingers to leather reins, is all it takes to feel the exchange of electricity. Riding is not the domain of the mind, more an intuitive tactile engagement. The horse moved off in a walk without resistance. I took a few turns around the pen, then pressed my legs into the saddle leather and his flexing ribs until he stepped into a trot. I sat gently back and propelled him into a lope. He was quick to turn, light on the bit. He moved between gaits with agility. I pulled him to a stop several yards from Wade and said quietly, "I'll take this one."

I waited until Wade had ridden and affirmed both of his choices and Dustin his, then haltered the regal brown horse who had caught my eye in the beginning. He kept one ear flicked toward me, his eyes like black lakes. He blew hard through his nostrils a few times while I saddled, but once I was up, he stepped out in a long stride and eased into the movements. He was the tallest of the horses, less sensitive to the bit and my leg, but he was young and eager. I now had a set of companions with whom to face the onslaught of the days ahead.

Wade, Dustin, and I rode the rest of the horses one by one. Some were young broncs barely broke, a few were feedlot horses who could turn quickly but tripped in the deep melon holes left from the wet season, and some were old station horses who conveyed with their eyes that nothing would surprise them or prove too demanding. Even in the dust of the yards, in the rough survey of horses, subtle tinges of chemical response caught in my chest and pricked at my skin. With some horses I felt fear flooding my body, with others a more confident familiarity; some were scared and had perhaps been handled roughly or mistreated; some were obstinate, heavy; others flared their eyes and reared to get away.

We shuffled through papers that had come with the horses, a few including a photo, name, age, markings, brands, and comments by ringers who had ridden them. I took the stack of yellowing pages after Wade and, by process of elimination and the tracing of markings, found my two horses. The first stock horse's name was Crow. His papers said he was seven years old. The tall gelding was a five-year-old named Darcy. Wade gave me two more horses whom neither he nor Dustin wanted: a massive stocky bay and a little filly. We turned the horses into a larger pen to cool down and water, then walked together, the three of us,

across the corrals toward the truck they had parked by the loading chute, leaving the dust cloud behind.

Angus later brought out an old Brekelmans saddle that he'd
found in the tack shed for me to ride. The dark leather had seen
many years of riding, but I found each piece well riveted and
sewn. The saddle was small and light like most Australian saddles, with the low, rounded, single arch where the horn would
be on an American saddle. The stirrup fenders—the leather
holding the stirrup—were cut wide, like an American Western
saddle, and swung easily. They were burned into a polish where
the last rider's knees had rubbed.

I wanted to know the horses intimately before the muster
work began, and so I caught Darcy later to ride him again. I
led him out of the corrals where the new station horses still
milled and tied him to the fence near the shipping container.
He snorted and raised his head high, his neck stiff. He was taller
than any horse I had ever ridden before, his shoulder at the level
of my eyes. With his narrow withers, the saddle fit him well. I
adjusted the bridle carefully, so that the rings of the snaffle bit
pulled a couple of wrinkles at the corner of his mouth. Then I
walked him out past the paddock gate and into the open bunchgrass clearing, took a deep breath, and swung into the saddle.

He tensed immediately, and I let him step out in long strides
to release his nervous energy, riding with my legs pressed in al-
ternate rhythmic motion against his ribs to establish control, my
hands exerting light but firm pressure on the reins. He was a
thunderstorm ready to roll across dry grass. I let him break into
a fast trot and we covered the ground across the clearing, then
passed through forest and yet another clearing in moments.
A horse prefers a rider with focus, feels more comfortable if
he doesn't have to make decisions other than where to place
his hooves. I chose an invisible point in the distance, feigning
confidence for the sake of the dark horse beneath me, and rode
straight ahead, into the unknown landscape.

I kept riding and almost didn't return. We broke our course forward only to dodge around deep melon holes and fallen trees. The country unfurled like bolts of linen, forest and clearing, without any distinguishing characteristics or landmarks. If it were Arizona, I would have ridden for hours, climbing ridges when I needed to reset the compass of my mind or remember elements of the terrain described to me at one point or another, the internal lay of the land, maps drawn from story and memory. Here I had no such assets, no history, no stories, no outback formation.

I reined Darcy in and we stood there, quietness filling in the space around us. I would go no farther. A light wind erased our tracks in white tendrils of dust and eucalyptus leaves. If I were to die, it would take them a while to find me. I felt an unsettling in the pit of my stomach, an intuitive warning that this was not my landscape, and I had little right to be here. I shifted in the saddle to ease my discomfort and saw only the same close screen of weepy eucalyptus trees. So easy to get lost out here. Darcy flicked his ears. He was standing still anyway, the tension released from his muscles and neck. I turned back in the direction we had come and, choosing my angle carefully, let Darcy pick up speed for the ride home. I would saddle Crow and venture out another day.

Stephen Craye

MIDMORNING A FEW DAYS LATER, a stocky gentleman I didn't recognize approached me and offered a ride around the station in his pickup truck. He had short silver hair and a beard and wore a clean, pressed, button-down shirt, jeans, and dusty leather boots. He was not tall, but his shoulders were so broad he looked as if he could have wrestled an ox to the ground, and he stood, unconcerned, with a steady and ambivalent gaze. I said I would need to ask permission to abandon my chores, wondering silently what sort of danger he might present. He indicated then that he was the boss, and I could do as he said.

"You are the security man," I said. He was supposed to have met me when I arrived.

"Yes."

"Nice to meet you then." I climbed up into his white Hilux. Stephen nodded. Then, almost apologetically: "I get busy."

He headed east, driving past the yards into the successive waves of forest and clearing. I stared out the open window, at times able to see for a ways. After a while I became intensely aware of the security man at the wheel, guiding this foray into some reach of the station.

I overcame my sense that small talk was not his forte, and asked, "What is it that you actually do?"

His face was impassive as he replied, "I protect the family's interests."

He sped down the straight dirt track. The landscape around us was, I presumed, the family's property, or a piece of it anyway. Stephen had appeared at the station apparently without notice or being noticed.

"What does that mean, exactly?"

He waited before answering. "I am in charge of overseeing all their operations."

He continued after a while in measured, unhurried sentences. He worked directly with the owner, Gene, and his children, driving or flying to all of the many stations the family owned across two states in Australia. I gathered that his work was to haunt the remote reaches of the properties and know what was going on at all times. He was ultimately responsible for directing the overhaul of Stilwater. He was the one who had placed new managers and a new head stockman on the property.

We encountered occasional swamps, lagoons with crocodiles, and stretches of coarse grass too thick to walk through and almost unpalatable to the stock. The types of plants changed dramatically over short distances, and yet the overall look was almost the same: white slender trunks and stretches of grass, in repeating patterns.

"Can you tell me more about the owners?"

"Gene and his family?"

"Yes."

"They are a good group." He added, "They take care of me, and I take care of them."

The few cows we passed threw up their heads when they saw us and disappeared into the scrub. Sarus cranes hefted up from swamp grasses on great gray-blue wings, masks pulled over their heads. Ibis clung to dead tree branches, their long hooked bills like sickles. Whistler ducks huddled at the edges of the murky waters. Wild boars rooted along the swamps, one sow with squealing piglets, one male with his head buried in the water, eating water-lily tubers and freshwater mussels. Paperbark tea trees wept along rivers and water holes while the bloodwoods bled down their shallowly ridged bark stained black with sap. Carbeen gums with white trunks and broad leaves; ghost gums with white bark and narrow leaves; ironbarks with poisonous leaves and dense heavy wood; black tea trees, low and almost bushy-topped; broad-leaf tea trees with elongated wide leaves and sparsely foliated short branches. Kapok trees grew almost naked with a few yellow flowers.

"What were you before you were a security man?"

"I was a cop. I was also a livestock inspector. I didn't have such a benevolent reputation."

As the hours of our station tour passed, he offered more information. He described different stations in the region and wove stories of people and families who had lived for generations in the sparsely populated wilderness, raising and stealing cattle and horses, slipping in and out of human tangles. He had a family in Cairns, a wife who waited for him through all his escapades and four sons who were better off when he was gone, he said; they were about as independent and strong-willed as he was. He preferred long intervals of solitude with short respites in the ocean air and civility of the eastern coast.

He started asking me a few questions then. Where had I worked before? What were my plans after Australia? I could see for myself, even as I began to answer his questions openly, how he gathered his information. He made me feel a sense of camaraderie, showing me his favorite places on the station, talking about his family, telling me what it was like to work alone and apart, to be a sea hawk over a long stretch of open plain. He said he knew everyone and was a friend of no one, preferring the distance afforded by an air of enigmatic malevolence. He liked Stilwater because it was the farthest away, the quietest. He liked inhabiting a world where urban laws of social interaction had no place and weren't tolerated anyway.

We drove to a point on the Powder River where it was joined by another creek, the plain opening up suddenly into a wide tidal flux that carried jellyfish and crocodiles clear from the gulf. The water cut high along the banks, still swollen from the previous wet season. A white sandy beach and a band of trees on the opposite side separated the blue of the river from that of the sky. Stephen knew a crocodile that haunted this confluence. We crawled down the mudstone ledges sculpted with patterns of watermarks and onto an outlook of rocks that jutted into the river to look for it, but the monster never surfaced. Then Stephen drove me to another place, where a freshwater seep flowed into the brackish water. He'd seen crocs there numerous times, he said, waiting to prey on the wallabies that came down for a drink.

"Walk up quietly," he murmured.

We did not see any crocodiles lying on the bank, so we climbed down to the water's edge. He picked up a big stick in case of a sudden attack, though I wondered if it would only provide the beast with a bit of fiber in its lunch. I followed him to the seep, where he pointed out a carnivorous plant, lime green with sticky hairs exuding a droplet of sap, to which ants and

bugs had become glued. He showed me a print in the mud—
tail, body, nose, feet, and all—just under the high-tide line, with
only the nose out of the water. I could see the entire story of the
ambush pressed like hieroglyphs into wet clay. As soon as we
had climbed the bank again and turned back to look, Stephen
pointed to a crocodile that had lifted its head above the water.
The croc followed us as we walked upstream along the high
bank, keeping low in the murky water and surfacing one more
time. Stephen called it a cheeky bastard. "Sly," he said, "those
crocs are sly." I couldn't believe we'd actually walked to the water.

He showed me a water hole, dammed to keep fresh water in
and the inquisitive tide out. He said it had hundreds of crocs.
We saw five or six lift their heads—just bulb eyes and nostrils
above the water's surface—and sink again. Long-stemmed,
multiple-petalled white water lilies made the water hole seem
like a Japanese tea garden, gum trees dropping long leaves toward the water, the setting serene. Then the outline of a crocodile head would appear and the water would seem suddenly
murky and deadly. We headed back late in the day, churning up

dust while the repeater, retransmitting a signal weakened by distance, announced itself over the CB radio.

As we neared the station compound, I asked Stephen how far we had driven.

"About two hundred kilometers."

"Have we seen most of the station then?"

"Not even a corner."

Stephen deposited me at the station compound with mild warning and encouragement: "They don't get much drama out here, so they have to make their own; you'll be fine."

The Mustering Crew

AT THE BEGINNING OF FALL, just before I arrived, Angus had devised a plan to muster the entire station. He would start with the paddocks close to the house and bring all of the nearby cattle in to be worked—drafted, branded, vaccinated, and tick-dipped—at the house yards. This permanent set of pens for working and shipping cattle lay several miles up the road from the station compound. He would then send the mustering crew out to a middle set of yards, called Carter Yards, an hour or so away on a dirt track. They would commute from the compound each day with their motorbikes, vehicles, and horses, working the middle swath of the station. He would need a big cattle-hauling truck, called a road train, to bring the shippers—all of the cull cows, weanlings, orphan calves, steers, and old bulls—back to the station. Finally, he would send the mustering crew out to Soda Camp, a makeshift camp at the far northern reach of the station. A set of portable panels there could be made into an operable yard. The crew would have to move their camp entirely for the month or so he thought it would take them. He hoped that by the time they got out there the weanling calves, young steers, and cull cattle would be bringing in the needed income and the outlook would be favorable.

Angus found a mustering crew to begin the cow work and

livestock inventory of the station—gathering, working, sorting, and shipping the cattle. A mustering crew sets up portable yards and camps and moves from paddock to paddock. They come in, they work the cattle, they leave. The head stockman of a mustering crew brings his own ringers and supplies them with food, petrol for their motorbikes, and horses, or horse feed if they bring their own. When they arrive, their world arrives with them: makeshift tents, strung-up tarps, forty-gallon drums of petrol and diesel, large stock trucks, packs of dogs, a herd of horses, motorbikes, four-wheelers, bull-catching vehicles, extra tires and wheels, long chains, short chains, saddles, guns, bridles, halters, catch ropes, bags of dog food, small generators, refrigerators, a portable sink, a portable washing machine, horse trailers—called floats—pots, pans, billycans, swags—bed rolls—unrolled on foam pads or rusty folding cots, spare batteries, truck parts, cans of fruit and vegetables, peanut butter, Vegemite, bags of white bread, and a folding table and chairs. All these items appear suddenly at the camp and then disappear when they move on. A cook usually comes along too.

On many stations, crews work with experienced efficiency, covering thousands of miles twice a year, living out with the heat and flies and remote expanses for months before returning home to other stations or small towns. But Stilwater hadn't been properly mustered in at least a decade, and the remnant cattle included cleanskin, or unbranded, bulls ten years old, cows twice as old still wobbling along, and a mess of calves, yearlings, young bulls, and heifers—many without tags or brands and almost all, not surprisingly, feral.

~~

Miles Carver ran the mustering crew, a large bear of a man with black hair and a thick beard. He wore coarse work shirts— usually torn or smeared with cow slobber, manure, or blood—a big hat that drooped a little in front and back with a small roll up on the sides of the brim, and heavy stockman's boots. He was from a small town on the eastern coast, where his father had raised horses and where most people knew him, knew of him, or knew his father. Thirty-seven years old that winter, he seemed to have a good heart, and he rode good horses: a tall black stallion named Snake, and a black gelding called Reb. The mustering contractors called him "the big fella."

Miles used his mass and brute strength to muscle through work—throwing cows around, lifting fallen cattle up by the horns, and ramming his stallion into cattle to push them through gates. His pack of scrawny, motley, kelpie-cross dogs clung close to his horse's hock and were keen at cow work. He called them by name—"Down Killer, sit Ruby, come Roo, *sit* Ruby"—and he sent them slinking around milling, charging, snorting cattle with a few whistles and verbal commands. He could signal one dog to drop on his belly in the dust, another to lunge at a cow's throat, another two to surround a deviant calf, and three to come back to his horse, clucking at them in reward. As he rode, his horse arched his neck down under the bit and Miles' big hands imperceptibly tensioned the reins until the stallion ducked his head further, moved off sideways with a subtle pressure from spurred heels, and—followed by the ghost shadows of dogs—stepped forward toward the mob of cattle.

Alongside his impressive pack, Miles mustered a few people he knew with several months open and dogs, horses, trucks, and motorbikes of their own. Together they hauled a caravan of gear up to Stilwater. Most of them knew each other and each other's families and had worked together before, but it was still a mishmash of a crew, some experienced, a couple thrown in out of sympathy or on a gamble.

They set up camp at the end of the lagoon in an old portable tin building called a donga. Manufactured in the shape of an L and rested up on stilts, this structure had some ten rooms and a narrow walkway. The crew quickly filled it with swags and gear, which they hung from the railing of the narrow veranda

that ran the length of the building. In front they parked their
vehicles, trailers, and motorbikes, and unloaded spare batteries
and fuel drums. Drying pants and work shirts hung from a wire
strung between the veranda posts, and three blackened tin cans
full of water for tea and coffee and dishes sat on a small fire that
seemed to burn perpetually.

A short distance from the quarters, the crew tied their packs
of dogs—more than thirty altogether—to old machines, trac-
tors, trailers, fences, and vehicles. Every other day each animal
received a small cup of dog food, a little water, and a few scraps
of meat. A couple of curly-haired lap dogs ran around the camp
as pets, but the rest of the mongrel lot stayed tied up unless
there was cow work to be done or a couple feral bulls that just
needed some chewing.

~~

The sky glowed a shade of orange umber when Miles drove up
to the station compound one morning. I was seated at the small
table on the veranda with Angus and Ross, awaiting a list of
chores for the day. Miles pulled out the chair opposite me and
gave a brief "morning" to the table before he sat down. I had met
him briefly before, but he didn't acknowledge me. Lamplight
threw shadows from his silver hat onto his face, darkening his
black beard. Ross offered coffee, but he shook his head.

"What time you reckon the road trains'll show?"

"Early, they're coming up from Normanton."

Miles waited a moment before he replied. "We should have 'em
ready to load." After another silence he said, "Maybe I could use an
extra hand." The crew had mustered two paddocks and had about
a thousand cattle in holding, waiting to be drafted, branded, and
shipped or released. When Miles needed an extra person or two,
he borrowed them from the station.

I tried not to notice the look of relief that crossed Angus' eyes; he'd be free of me for the day. While Wade often took Dustin with him on long station runs, Angus had been finding odd jobs for me around the compound.

"That'd be fine," he replied.

Miles rose to leave and Angus nodded for me to follow. I climbed into the rattling yellow ute with its wire dog crates on the flatbed against the cab. Starting the truck and turning on the headlights, Miles said it wouldn't matter if I didn't know much, I could work the gates while they hassled the mess of livestock in the yards.

He gave me a ride down to the donga, where they had a fire going, water heating in billycans to wash the breakfast dishes in a makeshift sink, laundry strung up along the veranda, and dogs everywhere. There was one other woman, tall and blond, pulling on a pair of boots.

"My name is Victoria—you can call me Vic," she said with a white smile. The rest rose from the cluttered table or moved in and out of the lamplight, gathering a few things, passing comments. We piled into several vehicles and headed up the road to the cattle yards.

That first day, I had a hard time remembering the names of the new crew in the melee of feral cattle as I tried to maintain my place at the gates. I knew livestock from childhood, how to handle them, move and manage and predict them, and a little of the Australian traditions of stock work. But that morning all I had learned blurred and disappeared in the noise and battle, and it was a struggle to stay upright and alive. Dust stirred so thick that every breath felt like a gritty drink. Cattle bawled and moaned, agitated and distressed. Calves separated from their mothers wailed in disbelief, loneliness, and fear. Mothers called back to locate them, to reassure them, to register their protest. The commotion made a pandemonium of sound, tones that filled the air and ears and overflowed into the brain and nervous system. Gates clanged and banged and the ringers called out, swearing, urging, answering, whooping. Cattle filled pens and smashed through fences, so many that they trampled the dirt and pummeled each other and the crew.

One of the ringers, Ivan, worked near me, slamming the sliding gate of the race—or chute—shut behind a line of heifers. He was working full force; dust coated his skinny legs and arms, and his angular face. I could see only that he had three tiny gold earrings in one ear, and that he wore a T-shirt, shorts, and a once-red ball cap. We were waiting for the road trains Angus had indicated would be arriving soon, the huge trucks hired to haul loads of cattle south to the meatworks.

Ivan took a break in a spare moment to lean against the pipes of the railing and said, "I wonder where that trucker is." He smacked a young heifer through the rails with a battered piece of poly pipe.

"Had too much goey and just kept on going," he barked, answering his own question with a jolting laugh.

Outback truckers often took methamphetamines to conquer the enormous distances.

"Or not enough," I said.

From Normanton alone, it was 155 miles, four hours of potholes and bulldust. Beyond that, who knew how many hours to the next biggest town? Twenty, fifty, with a load of cattle that had to be unloaded along the way to water and feed, and then loaded again, many getting injured or dying en route.

Some cattle are still driven along by a crew of horsemen for weeks, or months, just as we did in the United States before barbed wire divided the landscape. But in this tradition, called droving, the cattle have to be moved slowly enough that they can graze and not lose too much weight along the way. Entire crews of patient stockmen spend months trailing the dust of thousands of cattle from home pasture to their final destination at the meatworks. When they eventually arrive, they might be asked just to turn around and do it again in the reverse direction, taking young or new cattle to stations farther on. Most landowners afforded a half-mile track to the passing mobs of stock. Lined up, these spaces turned into what they called the long paddock. Now stockmen often lease stretches of grass along the margins of highways to fatten cattle as they pass.

Ivan worked too hard and was too familiar with cattle to be a random junkie off the street, but he didn't have the arrogance of a horseman or the solemnity of a stockman. Another four year-lings banged into the pen, and he reached through the bars with his piece of poly pipe and whacked a couple of them on the nose to turn them into the race. The cattle spun and jumped, frantic between the metal paneling. Ahead, ringers moved them through the race into the crush—a squeeze chute—to be branded and ear-tagged. Heifers bawled as the brands hit them. One of the crew took a pair of dehorners to the small nubs on their heads.

Ivan called over his shoulder, "You get into that stuff much?" Meth, I guessed.

I responded, "Me? No. You?"

Between the crammed and bawling heifers, the dust, and the almost reckless work of directing cattle into the race, he gave a quick, unnerving, and infectious laugh, before yelling back, "I reckon, work hard, play hard, party harder." Ivan sagged his long lean frame against the rails of the race, propping one boot up on the lowest bar. One of the heifers slammed a hoof through the bars, and he stood up. The crush gate banged open, and we stepped forward to move the heifers up the race.

The road trains finally arrived and the truckers lined up monstrous vehicles, massive semi trucks with two trailers, on the dirt road. Each deck could hold thirty cows. These rigs were called type-ones because they had five decks in all; a truck with two double-decker trailers and six decks was a type-two, and those were restricted from the highways except in Western Queensland. They looked like American rigs used to haul cattle, except that the top deck on each was open to the sky.

The crew shuffled to load the cattle bound for the slaughter-houses. Tanner, another ringer, nodded hello as I passed to take a place in the pens. A tall strong man with a drooping mustache, he worked one of the drafting gates. He walked with a stiff arched back, his broad chest thrust forward a little, and wore Wrangler jeans, black sunglasses, and a big black stockman's hat. Sometimes, I noticed over the following weeks, he traded his black hat for a white hat, a change that seemed to match his mood. He rode a tall white horse for the cow work when he wasn't riding his motorbike, and rolled the sleeves of his work shirts up past his elbows, as many did, his forearms thick, red-brown, and freckled.

I learned later that he had broken his back in several places riding bulls, and that he had steel pins holding his spine together, which was why he walked and perhaps why he acted the way he did. Who knew how he ended up at Stilwater? He raised his own bulls for the rodeo circuit, but maybe he needed money, or just a job out far from town, where his life might find meaning again.

Cole, who worked nearby, was shorter but just as strong, with dark curly hair. He wore work shirts cut off at the sleeves to reveal sun-browned, muscled arms, and he was so composed that I wondered if he wasn't immune to the pandemonium. Sometimes he wore a bright purple shirt with his white stockman's hat and wraparound sunglasses that made him stand out, though in all other ways he was the quietest. He was second in command on the mustering crew, perhaps because he was the most amiable and imperturbable.

Vic was Cole's partner. Her leathered hands conveyed the truth of her spirit, which was fierce and emotional, though she kept the skin of her high cheekbones smooth and wore small silver earrings. She and Cole were both thirty years old and the anchors of the crew, making it more domestic and civilized than it would have been otherwise. They had a seven-year-old daughter back at home, somewhere to the east, with the child's grandmother, along with several young thoroughbred race-horses and a house and property of their own. A licensed jockey, Vic brought her tall, well-bred horses out to do the mustering work after they had won several races and retired from the track. She had a wispy blond braid, and she exercised a mostly charming but firm tyranny over the crew. Even Miles took her opinions seriously and considered her part of the already top-heavy strata of management on the station. He was also in love with her, as was almost everyone else.

Vic took the numbers down on the small tally book, making hash marks for the cattle as they ran up the race and into the trucks. She stood by the rails, her braid tossed back and her black hat dusty.

Max worked in the pens near Vic. He was the youngest member of the mustering crew, eighteen or nineteen, lanky with close-cropped blond hair and a red face. He worked hard at times, but he was also the first to whinge or complain. Max was the first one to leap into the pen with rank bulls and chase angry cows to get them to charge him through gates and into the proper pens. He would climb the rails and drop his long legs around the back of an old cow and ride it bucking across the pen until he could scramble off and over the fence again. I once saw a cow kick him down and smash his head against a heavy metal post; he recovered his feet and slipped through the bars with a bloody nose and a swollen black eye, then returned immediately to the work.

Cattle crammed onto the decks of the large road trains. The branding furnace roared, and the truck driver and Cole used yellow electric jiggers to jam cattle up the ramp and onto the top deck of the truck. When the last skinny cow caught in the race climbed up, Tanner pushed the slide gate closed and I opened the other gate to send another ten cows into the pen and up the race. They slammed their horns against each other and blew snot. Miles loomed by the rails of the race to check each cow for a brand as she passed. If the cow lacked a brand, meaning she hadn't ever seen the civilization of a corral, he pressed the glowing-hot branding iron to her side as long as he could before the cow jumped forward and the iron slipped, leaving a burned pattern on the hide.

I would get all of the crew's names eventually and see how each fit into the felting of that strange fabric, but for the moment it was a hurricane of dust and holler, bellowing and bodies, stockmen and cattle and a ramp into a big semi with a double-decker trailer. The cows were loaded onto the truck and headed south, to their deaths perhaps, or to better pasture.

One cow climbed over the railing of the top deck somehow and fell more than fourteen feet. She had leaped over the gates of the pound earlier, clearing the seven-foot rails, and it had taken a few of the crew to get her back. Amazingly, after her fall from the truck, she rose up and ran away, and Miles, who didn't seem like he would intentionally harm anything, said she could use some lead—a bullet, in other words. He thought she might be a little chewy though, with the heat and stress and all. The rest of the cattle would have a long hot ride on that narrow strip of bitumen across endless red clay, no matter the ending.

Then a cow suddenly slammed headfirst into the gate and slumped to the ground. Max stepped in and slapped her on the neck and back, but she only jerked a few times.

"Reckon she's broke her neck?" he asked.

"Hmm," replied Vic.

Vic grabbed the cow's tail and Max grabbed her ears and they dragged her until she was free of the race. Vic patted the dying cow and then sat down on the animal's rounded side to rest by the sliding gate of the race while she waited for another pen to be drafted.

Troy limped over. He was supposed to be the cook, but he didn't seem well suited to the job. Miles had adopted him as part of the crew after a stroke left his left arm and leg impaired and sunk him into a bout of depression so severe he wouldn't eat or speak. Miles thought the open air and work might do him some good.

Troy didn't cook much, but he rolled cigarettes of loose-leaf tobacco and another easily distinguishable herb, hung his limp arm in a sling, and came out to the yards to slide open gates and brand cattle with his one good hand. His drooping hat almost covered his eyes. The hat had once been a good silverbelly, but now it was tattered, sagging and stained, and the rest of him had followed suit. He sat down on the dead cow beside Vic while the crew drafted a load of bulls and prepared to run them into the trucks. The monstrous, mad, testosterone-charged Brahmans almost smashed them all several times. I didn't even try to help them load and was quick to jump the fence any time one of the beasts charged in my direction.

Smoko

WITH TWO ROAD TRAINS LOADED and the crew sweating and mad, Miles finally hollered that it was time for smoko. The ringers set down their poly pipes, turned off the branding fire, and gravitated to the shade of the old shipping container that had been dropped by the edge of the yards to serve as a tack shed. A line of dogs whined at our approach from where they had been tied up along the fence behind the shipping container. We washed our hands of dirt, sweat, blood, manure, and cow hair with the rubber hose outside the pens and slumped on metal and plastic chairs. The day had grown hot in the sudden stillness, and we sweltered there among the flies. A few of the crew pulled out plastic bags of tobacco they kept tucked in their shirt pockets and rolled cigarettes.

Miles had a beat-up tin coffee can to put the billy on, a plastic bag of cups, tea, and sugar, and a plastic bucket full of cookies that his mother had baked for him before he left the east coast with the crew. He filled the sooty can with water from the bore hose and put a match to the blower from the branding pen. He hung the can by a wire handle from a rebar over the blasting flame. When the water boiled, Miles shook a small heap of black tea leaves into the tin can and splashed a little cold water from the hose into the black liquid to get them to settle and cool off the handle. Then he carried the old tin back to the shade, where he poured dark-reddish tea, offering me a pink pannikin full of it.

The billycan was blackened on the outside from years of wood fires, and it smeared his big hand with soot. The crew drank tea with breakfast, at the midmorning break, at lunch, and sometimes in the afternoon. They even called their dinner "tea." Miles also had a couple of thermoses that sufficed when the branding blower wasn't around and they didn't have the muster to light a fire.

He poured the rest of the cups.

"Tea? You like two spoons of sugar?"

"Thanks, mate," replied Cole.

In the wake of the drafting this civility was beyond strange. But it lasted only so long.

Ivan picked up his mug and asked, "You plugged the hole in the billy?"

Miles didn't even raise an eyebrow. "Yeah mate, with my finger."

"The hole in the side or the bottom?"

"Both—you could braze 'em for me, mate."

"You could get yourself another can."

"I've had this one nearly ten years."

"Just tie a new one behind the truck for a while, and it'd get beat up like that one," Ivan retorted.

"Then it'd get covered in cow shit," Miles said.

"That one's seen worse, I reckon."

Ivan tipped up the old can and poured himself another cup, mixed in a little sugar, and sat back down. We sweated there for a while, with hot black tea in pannikins, pants smeared with manure, faces and arms coated in dust, boots caked and lying heavy on the packed earth. A wind picked up, sweeping most of the flies away and veiling the cups of tea with a film of dust. Ivan smashed an ant with the bottom of his pannikin and pointed to another, carrying a huge crumb. He pinched two off the ground, laughing, and said, "Ready, set, go." Then he set them down, and the ants scrambled off in different directions.

Max said, "They do that with cane toads, draw a circle and make bets, and the first toad out of the circle wins."

Max threw his puppy a part of his biscuit, but she was tied to the fence nearby and couldn't quite reach it.

The heat gave all these moments an unpleasant weight, though the prospect of heading back to the din and adrenaline of the pens was equally uninviting.

I felt weak and a little shaky, my hands trembling along with the cup. The crew didn't seem to notice, and I took a careful breath, resting my nerves. The morning had pitched everything in me to overdrive. The bulls weighed more than a ton; the mad-eyed cows could have gutted any of us with a sideways swipe of a horn—all this surrounded by hard iron posts and constant movement, shouts, hooves, and dust.

Cattle are prey animals, and they respond to humans appropriately, as predators. There are correct positions and distances to maintain with respect to a cow, and correct timing—when to press toward a cow's shoulder or head, when to back away, when not to look a cow in the eye, when to move back and forth to stimulate reactions in the herd. And while the madhouse of the pens had made chaos and brutality of the art of livestock handling, the same rules applied. If they were flouted, the work would never be finished, or one of the crew could be injured or worse. My old instincts told me when to leap forward and move back. For that I was grateful, but everything beyond was stimulus almost entirely unfamiliar to my being.

Miles finally gave a nod and said, "We've got a pen full of cows we should put through the tick dip and draft up before we finish loading."

He tossed the butt end of a rolled cigarette, shook his empty cup upside down, and set the bucket of biscuits and cups in the front seat of the yellow ute before walking back to the pens of cattle. The rest of the crew followed.

Tick Dipping

TICK DIPPING WAS A REQUIREMENT only for cattle loaded onto a road train, but all of the cows brought to the yards went for the black swim. That afternoon, we dipped a set of five hundred cattle, running the drafted mob through the race until they plunged into a putrid trough of chemicals that was supposed to kill the small ticks they'd picked up from grazing in the bush. Any cattle leaving the station and bound for destinations across the tick-range perimeter had to be dipped and later checked. It was standard government protocol for the stations in the North.

The cattle had to swim through the chemical liquid until they reached the opposite end, where the concrete sloped up to a set of pens with concrete floors. The cows behind pressed and pushed the lead cows forward over the drop-off and into the acrid pond, and it rose in a surging splash as the line of cattle plunged in, swam across, and climbed, dripping, up the other side. They glistened black in the sun, standing on the wet concrete to dry for a few minutes.

The ringers worked the chutes behind to cut off the ends of the tail hair of the cattle headed for the tick dip. It was a process called tail-banging, to mark which had been dipped and which hadn't and maybe save a few from being run through the brew twice. The small black handle of the bang-tail knife fit easily in the palm, and with one hand pulling the cow's tail and finding the last joint of the tail bone, a ringer placed the blade facing up, twisted the stringy hairs around it, and pulled hard.

Miles held the knife in one hand and a fistful of tail hairs in the other. When he reached the end of the line, he nodded to Cole, who pulled the slide gate and hollered at the cattle to move forward. Ivan moved another group into the race, cramming the end cow to slide the gate shut behind her. A heap of tail hair lay on the ground like a pile of discarded wigs.

Dust stuck to the wet cattle at the far end of the trough, and the murky liquid pooled on the concrete. Another mob lunged forward, cattle jamming together and getting stuck between the narrow panels, slamming forward and backward and pushing legs out through the railing. After one group had plunged through the tick dip, dried off on the other side, and run into another pen, the ringers walked to the back of the yards to draft another.

Ivan said later he reckoned we all did as we were told because the government said so, and then because the station owners said so, and then the manager and the head stockmen and whoever reckoned he was in charge at the moment. We thought we operated under our own free will, he said, but it wasn't that way, and the cattle took the brunt of it through no choice of their own. They tried not to, with all of their wily savanna fire. They smashed and cleared metal pipe fences, broke the welds on the rails, tore up each other and tore down wires, but in the end, most of them emerged tick-less, or at least should have.

Tanner swaggered up and down the race, checking whether each cow was full of milk or not, calling out "Wet" or "Dry." They directed cows with full udders into a pen to be reunited with their calves after they had been drafted and branded. The dry cows would be loaded onto road trains.

Tailing the Mickies

WHEN THE DAY STARTED TO STRETCH OUT into afternoon, Miles got me to help walk the young bulls out—tailing the mickies, they called it—to the dried coastal plains to graze for a few hours. He let me ride his black gelding, Reb. The dark horse moved easily, giving his head to the bit. Miles and I rode in the lead, letting the young bulls find their way into the wide lane. A hundred yards out, we reined in and turned in our saddles to watch the slow herd. We sat on our horses in white sun in the dead swamp grass for an hour and a half while the dogs kept the mob together and the bulls had some time out of the mud and dust of the yards.

Savanna stretched in a choppy sea, and the low-angled sun leaned across scrubby paperbark tea trees. A nearly imperceptible breath of wind rolled off the gulf, gently sweeping away the dust and the daring, releasing the tension of cattle and crew. Pale grasses tossed their drooping heads among the gum trees.

Deep within us, cows and workers alike, lived the urge to breathe the moist air, inhale the expanse and feel just as wide and unbridled and quiet, away from the tumult and ruckus of the yards. The wave of noise, commotion, and pent-up anxiety slid from me and disappeared into the waving grasses. I was not sure how to take in all that had passed in the morning hours, as if it were perfectly natural to find oneself in with a lot of maddened cattle and an equally brave and rough crew. These were not domesticated cattle. They were wild animals, pressed into pens of heavy iron rails, from which they had little chance of escape.

I could not make sense of how I had been accepted in this situation, as a foreigner of no known ability in the intimate chain of human interaction needed for livestock handling. And yet I had not died. I had not even found myself hurt. And there I was astride a borrowed horse, a big dark horse I might only have dreamed of riding, waiting in quiet sunshine. Like the others, Miles didn't seem to care about asking questions, or knowing anything more about me. I wondered briefly if there was a series of unspoken tests for me, and whether I could just as suddenly be shunned and dropped from the crew. Then I gave up trying to understand the situation and closed my eyes, feeling, through the leather reins, the dark horse lower his head and chew a few mouthfuls of coarse grass.

Miles sat his stallion a short distance from the young bulls to keep them from moving too fast. The mob of mickies spread in the lane, shadows stretching against the tall bunchgrass before them. Miles rode over and asked if I wanted to trade horses for a while.

He swung out of the saddle and gave me a brief glance before adjusting the stirrups. Ordinarily a cowboy would never trade out his best horse, even for a short ride, or adjust his stirrups, or trust anyone he didn't know, especially with a good horse like Snake. I nodded, swung down out of my saddle, and took the reins when he offered them. I was less than half of Miles' size, and I felt quite small astride the big stallion, unsure how to ride a horse with such supple power. I rode back slowly, letting the horse beneath me pick his way through hillocks of grass and melon holes and old water channels.

In the pens Miles showed me how to fill bags of grain for the horses. Each bag was made of a feed sack folded down to half size with a thin twine knotted into the corners so that it could be hung around a horse's head. We put nose bags on the herd of biting, milling horses and waited until they had finished eating before leaving the yards at dusk, leaving the bawling cattle behind, the dead cow by the race.

Mudflats and mangroves patterned the gulf country, and we each had our own, less visible, emotional topography. I thought the reason the red cow had died in front of me, with one quick slam into the gate, was that I needed to write of her death. I needed to pause in the raucous tumult of loading and find the words of poetry that would be a strange prayer for this one death among thousands. I needed to brush one hand on the red swirled hair of her forehead before turning back to the cattle in the race. The wild wasn't tender when it came to life and death. This cow had been born beneath some gnarled bloodwood in the gulf-country forest to live among the heat and flies of the coast, only to die suddenly in a chute because people wanted their will imposed where they thought there was none.

But she wouldn't have been there to begin with if it hadn't been for some human dream of order long ago. And she would have died anyway. A croc or a pack of wild dogs would have had less mercy. That it had happened before my eyes made it neither sacred nor profane. The kites would clean her completely. The wind and sun, bleaching bones and carrying away the dust of her living, would somehow purify her, or wrap her into the cycle that existed above and beyond human dilemmas. As it was, I would have to let go of my sadness, to learn, like the mangroves, to filter the salt out of my blood, or cry like seabirds do to flush out the sea, or release salt through my tongue like a crocodile. Vic had sat on the cow's turgid lumpy belly and tallied cattle in a small green book. Later, when the road trains pulled away for long hours of dirt road and highways farther south, when dust had cleared from the air and the cattle milled quiet, one of the guys would drag her out to the mudflats to give the wild pigs and dingoes something to eat for the night.

Stock Industry

MUSTERING IN THE MODERN OUTBACK entails a large operation. Long stretches of barbed wire, several strands of it held up at intervals by metal and wood pickets, divide the property into paddocks. The entire expanse is cross-fenced into these smaller parcels, each a few hundred to a few thousand hectares in area. The herd of cattle, whether it numbers five hundred or fifty thousand, is split into several mobs, a mob being any subset. The different mobs graze year-round in the large paddocks. Twice a year, crews muster all of the paddocks, one at a time, walking or hauling the cattle into a set of yards to brand the young calves, wean the older calves, sort out the cull cows and bulls, and then vaccinate, doctor, tick-dip, tail-bang, and sometimes preg-check the cows that will be turned out again. During drought years, the owners or managers might sell off a larger portion of the herd, keeping only the best genetics—young healthy cows for breeding stock.

The stock industry—cattle, horses, and sheep—has long defined the outback. The land proved too harsh for most agricultural endeavors, but sheep in particular found ways to survive and even flourish, their numbers expanding from a hundred thousand in 1820 to over a million a decade later. In another three decades, the numbers had swelled to thirteen million. Yet in those years, the settlers were no more than four hundred thousand, and the tracks of settlers, squatters, and herdsmen could only be followed with uncertainty.

No one knew how far into the interior the settlements reached, or how far each man traveled with his herds. Maps that might have assisted would-be settlers and stockmen had yet to be drawn up. The continent was to them a blank stone, scratched only along the edges with a few lines running inward, the Great Dividing Range holding all of the newcomers back for a quarter century. Then, in a haphazard, each-man-for-himself rush, the psychological barrier crumbled. The government sent out surveyors and issued land grants and titles, but herdsmen quickly spread beyond the farthest surveyed limits, beyond the known world, and beyond the reach of the law. Livestock were pushed into new areas across the continent, and released to find their own ways of surviving.

Great herds reached the northern state of Queensland, and the far north of the gulf country, in the 1860s. Livestock were shipped by boat, then waded through mangrove swamps to reach dry land and find water holes that weren't full of tide. In some cases they were driven across the desolate inner swaths to the farthest reaches of the continent. The tough—the stock that didn't get smashed to death by hurricane winds and swells, or sucked into mud, didn't sicken from bad water or disease, or die of exhaustion and lack of water or feed—made it to the interior and beyond. Sheepmen sheared and shipped the wool back to England, to be spun and woven into blankets and garments. Cattlemen shipped out beef on the hoof. The industry became the foundation for wealth and sustained the continent during the first century of its colonial occupation.

When stock prices dropped too low and livestock herds grew too large for the arid land to support them, a few thought they would recover their costs and turn a profit by boiling millions of sheep and cattle until they turned to grease. They called it boiling down, a sickening image, but tallow made soap to cleanse the country of its overindulgence. This was the story. The people who stayed endured every manner of depression, drought, and setback, layer after layer.

Cattle gradually replaced sheep as the wool market plummeted and refrigeration techniques were developed on cargo ships to transport beef back to Europe. Cattle also proved more durable in the long run. English breeds of Shorthorn and Hereford adapted well to the more verdant fringes and the South, but the interior demanded other blood. So in the early part of the twentieth century the North American-bred Brahman cattle—heat-, tick-, and disease-resistant—changed the entire herd of

Australia. Over time the stockmen adapted too, developing their own traditions and heritage, born of Australia, written into songs and the creases of their hands and faces; carried with pride, patience, and the requisite rugged recklessness. The process resulted in a coevolution of stock, stockmen, and the environments of the immense island continent.

A Quiet Muster

DAWN SEEPED IN AT THE EDGE of the clearing beyond the kitchen, offering its pale glow as a halo over our world. We gathered and left in the dark, piling into utes to drive to the yards. I had silently joined the mustering crew, following after Miles when he left the kitchen after a brief consultation with Angus. No one told me to do otherwise. If I kept quiet and almost invisible, I might be able to slip in, as I had in the yards, without much disruption.

The crew had split up to divide the work, and just a few of us—Miles, Victoria, Cole, and I—would ride together that morning, bringing in cattle that had been mustered to a holding paddock to be worked at the house yards. Cole, with his vest zipped up but bare arms exposed, started the big diesel horse truck that stayed parked at the yards and pulled up alongside the loading ramp. Vic opened the door to the shipping container that served as the saddle shed. She and Cole had brought a pile of saddles, bridles, pads, shoeing tools, and veterinary supplies along with their truckload of thoroughbreds. The inside of the shipping container was so dark I couldn't distinguish the saddles, but I found mine by feel, and the other ringers seemed to know by instinct which rack held their saddles and bridles. Vic and Cole gathered halters and bridles and entered the pens through metal gates, their figures moving in among the shadowy forms of horses.

I caught Darcy and slipped the snaffle bit into his mouth and the headstall over his ears. He followed me on a loose rein through the pale filtered dawn. The ringers tied their horses and hauled saddles out of the shed. We brushed the horses' backs with our hands, placed blankets and saddles, and pulled up cinches. The little Australian stock saddles were lightweight, easy to toss up onto the horses' backs. The latigo—a strap used to adjust the cinch—was just a piece of webbing, instead of the thick band of leather I was used to. Following the others, I led Darcy carefully up the loading ramp to stand packed close and parallel with the other horses. The horses lined up in the back of the big truck, their hooves braced against the metal grid welded to the floor to give them extra footing.

Miles tied his horse at the front so he could unload his mount last, after he mustered the paddock with the motorbike. Cole closed the heavy iron doors of the truck crate and slid the ramp back into place. The ramp was hard to lift, and harder to slide under the bed of the truck. Cole said a bull had smashed it a few weeks back and bent it out of shape. He spoke quietly, gently, his tone defying the meaning of his words. Miles left ahead of us with the motorbike; he would gather cattle together in that small paddock and work them toward the watering area.

Cole drove carefully, downshifting to slow the vehicle so the horses would have a smooth ride. He sat silent for the most part. Vic had a few things to say about the muster, how she wasn't so sure about the whole prospect, how the crew seemed a bit disorganized. The radio broadcasted a quiet stream of American country music. The flat landscape made for good radio reception even hours from the transmitters.

We parked out in the middle of the paddock near a water trough, and the three of us unloaded our horses and waited in the early morning heat. The plains seemed larger away from the yards. The first light blasted us, Vic with her button-down shirt and tight black Wranglers, her black hat and blond braid, Cole in his vest and faded jeans, a pair of old tennis shoes. His face, arms, and hands were burned a deep red and brown.

We watched as cattle began to arrive from different directions and gather at the concrete troughs. They came in as if pulled

by a magnet, bawling for calves and raising enough dust to obscure the rim of the morning sky.

Miles eventually pulled up with the motorbike, dirt covering
his bulk. His pack of little dogs hopped into the water trough,
displacing cattle. The dogs eventually leaped out, shook, and
came over to drop to their bellies in the dust beside him.

"A bit stirred up, that mob. Thought they'd've worked out
the salt in this holding paddock."

Vic said, "Wouldn't surprise me if they'd run 'em with the
chopper just to stir 'em up for us." She tightened her cinch and
swung up, one hand gripping the horn of her Western saddle, one
hand on the neck of her horse. She headed off toward the mob.

"They'll settle in once we get moving," Cole said.

Miles nodded. He stepped off the motorbike, cast a worried
glance toward the cattle, and climbed the metal ramp up to the
truck to unload his horse. Some had already begun to disappear
back into the scrub, and Vic took off after them. I tightened my
cinch, pulled on my gloves, and followed Cole, who had loped
out to hold the stirring mob that remained. Vic brought back
her little dissidents and then she blocked and redirected others
back until we could form a better net around them.

Miles joined us on horseback, followed by his pack of dogs.
"Cole, if you'll take the lead, Vic and I'll ride the wings, and
Rafael, you can take the tail? Guess we'll walk them to the gate
in the corner?" The corner of the paddock lay somewhere to the
southeast, invisible in the distance. I rode away with a pounding heart. The tail was the easiest place to ride, usually assigned
to the newest or greenest of a crew. A thrill flooded my chest,
knowing Miles was considerate of what I could and could not
do. Darcy seemed pleased with the task and stepped out with
ears forward and a lift to his stride.

Cattle circled up and moved away from the troughs, calves
running to their mothers and the cows in the lead drawing away
and filing out on paths. Cole loped easily to the front and rode
out ahead, orienting the lead cattle southeast. Behind him the

smoky herd moved in a river of backs and heads. Heat gave a surreal cast to the plains as we rode. We whistled and hollered at the trailing cattle, rode up to turn breakaways, and trotted back to our places beside the mob.

The lead rider sets the pace, and turns back only if the cattle veer off to one side or another. Wing riders ride wide to the outsides, the horses walking quietly unless the herd spreads. A wing rider will point his horse to redirect the strays, but most often his presence is enough to keep the cattle in line. The rider on tail has more work to do, urging cattle forward, turning wayward cows, and breaking up fights between fractious bellowing bulls.

The cattle did settle in. Many had been worked earlier by the crew and, in some memory of the process, filtered out and down the trails, called pads. The Brahman blood in them lent the beasts a distinctly elegant appearance. Some were white or gray, with honey-colored points on the tops of their heads; others were light red, with drooping dewlaps and ears, dark eyes, and long lashes.

Vic dropped back to ride with me for a short distance. "How ya' goin' mate?"

"Good, you?"

"Yeah, good." She let her tall thoroughbred pick his way through fallen branches. She added conversationally, "These cattle are going all right." And then with a glare toward her horse's ears, "Wait till they bring in the choppers though; they'll rile 'em up and make us all crazy."

In country so immense, with cattle spread far apart, motorized vehicles work more efficiently than horses. Many stations own their own helicopters or employ pilots to help muster the cattle. Choppers cover large expanses of paddocks and drop down to scare cattle toward a corner or a water hole. People on motorbikes or horses work beneath them, keeping the cattle directed, congregating the mobs, and lining them out toward the yards.

Vic rode with both hands holding the reins. Cattle threaded across a dry watercourse ahead of us and up the bank on the other side.

I asked, "What's the largest mob of cattle you've mustered?"

She thought for a while. "Four thousand head. It's a pretty picture, a big mob crossing a river. If you're in the lead, you can see the whole thing full of cattle." She turned her horse to ride ahead, saying over her shoulder, "You'll get your chance, mate."

The grass was a sea that bore us, vessels with sorrel sails aligning and realigning by the compass of the yards, navigating the flat waters and occasional swells of the gulf country. The skyline swung a flat 360-degree circle beneath the arcing blue. The thin current of fifty or so breeders, calves, and a few bulls stretched ahead, moving toward the corner gate with the early sun dropping shadows beneath them, to be trampled beneath their rhythmic hooves.

When we reached the gate, we held the cattle there until they quieted, and then Cole pointed his horse out along a track, riding into the horizon, and the cattle followed instinctively. Like many of us creatures, they were willing to follow if the lead was strong. I rode behind the last cow, sweeping back and forth to keep the mob moving. The work was familiar, but disconcerting in a foreign landscape.

I tried to read the braille of the place, the texture of wide expanse, heat, and bright sun, the Australian saddles and the lean, athletic horses. The horizon was my only reference to begin mapping the lay of the land in my mind—where channels ran, the fences, water holes—and I wondered which direction the storms would emerge from, if it would change depending on which ocean sacrificed its surface to the sky, which winds undertook the pilgrimage.

We reached the small paddock that was closer to the yards, defined only by lines of long wire fences. As cattle filed into the lane leading toward the yards, flocks of gray parrots with bright pink throats thronged overhead. Galahs, the silver and

wild-rose birds of the tropical savanna interior, flourished in agricultural settings, and hundreds of them clung to the rims of the water troughs. Cattle flowed seamlessly into a large pen called the cooler. I swung the heavy iron gates closed behind the last of the trailing calves.

Drafting

MILES SAID WE WOULD GO AHEAD and draft the mob. Drafting entailed shifting the cattle through a series of pens to a pound, a small enclosure with gates opening to six different pens. If one wanted to divide hundreds or thousands of cattle, the pound worked like a human-run threshing machine—one set of cattle this way, another that way, a third this way. We could make six different divisions if we chose, and sometimes even that wasn't enough. Vic and I moved cattle forward through the succession of pens up to the pound, where Miles worked on foot with a length of rubber tubing he used as a pointer to separate the cattle individually. Cole worked the pound gates to direct each solitary animal.

Miles called "Bush" for cows, "Calf" for unbranded calves, "Weaner" for branded calves, and "Cull" for cattle to be sold or checked for pregnancy. They sorted cattle into their different pens, the sound of Miles' voice barely audible above the din of bellowing cows and clanging gates. Bulls mashed each other against the fences until we could separate them. Cows dodged the black tubes we swatted them with to urge them through the gates. The heavy metal pipe gates clanged against fences as they swung open or closed. Miles called "Hold!" when too many escaped into the pound, and he and Cole had to direct them through separate gates. Only Cole's black hat and wraparound sunglasses, face, and shoulders were visible above the mob. Vic and I waited for the mess to clear before we opened the gates again.

Dust was the incense burned before the ritual. Our shouts were chants, but we spoke quietly for the most part, urging and clicking and tapping the animals with the black plastic lengths of tubing. We crowded the calves into a smaller pen with a narrow race that led up to the cradle used to hold the calves for branding.

Branding

MILES PULLED AN ORANGE PLASTIC CRATE of branding supplies from the tack shed and swung the crate across the high pipe rails of the race so he could carry it to the calf cradle. Miles and Cole brought a bucket of antibiotic liquid to paint on each calf's head after dehorning, two branding irons, and a few bags of ear tags. Miles picked up one end of a large propane tank, and Cole grabbed the other. They lit the torch to heat the branding irons, poured some of the antibiotic liquid into a small coffee can holding a paint brush, loaded the steroid gun with small pellets that would be placed in the ears of the male calves, placed a tag and button in the ear tagger, and sharpened the castrating and dehorning knives. They slid the gates of the race open and pushed a line of calves up toward the cradle. When a calf leaped forward into it, Cole, Vic, and Miles squeezed the cradle shut. The calf immediately flopped sideways onto the ground, exposing its left hip or "near side" to be branded. A large tire cushioned the calf's weight.

As soon as the calf flipped, Cole called "Bull" or "Heifer." Miles held the small castrating blade in his mouth while he worked, and kneeled down on the flanks of bull calves to castrate them. He stood up when he finished and threw the testicles out to the dirt where the fork-tailed kites dive-bombed the bloody yard. Then Cole held the hind leg steady and reached for the branding irons. He pressed an iron briefly into the thin hide on the left flank. The hair flamed for an instant. With his other hand, Cole pressed a number brand to identify the year the calf was born. The hides of the calves were thin and their hair sleek with summer, and after only a second the hot irons made a clean, tan impression lined by burned hair. At the head, Miles snapped an ear tag in the right ear, clipped out the earmark from the thin skin of the calf's ear with a separate device, and sliced the horn buds off with a large pair of dehorning shears. Blood leaked over the side of the calf's face while Miles took the purple brush to paint antibiotic liquid over the patches. He slid the steroid gun into the flesh of one ear of each of the steers to implant a small cylinder of growth hormone. The entire operation took mere minutes. I had taken part in this ritual many times before, but the smell and textures—the scorched hide, the smeared dust, blood and manure together, the silkiness of calf hair—always jammed in my mind.

The calf bawled a complaint at the unfairness and sudden brutality of its world. Months of sweet sunshine and grass, interrupted only by a dingo or two, and then a roaring helicopter, a sweltering chase for several miles, motorbikes, humans on horseback, the crowding in the yards, separation from its mother. And then came the onslaught of pain, the stench of its

own burning flesh and blood. This imprinting of human interaction was neither benign nor gentle.

The two men nodded, stepped back, and Victoria reached to
release the catch and lift the top half of the cradle. The stunned
calf jumped up and cleared the branding area in a few frantic leaps to join his bleeding mates. When the cradle was ready,
I prodded another calf forward, and it clanged into the cradle
and hit the ground. The three of them muscled the heavy cradle,
pushed and pulled the calves forward, and moved through the
rhythm all over again.

They worked with sweat streaming down their faces, coated
in black dust. The pile of ear tags lay on a tipped-over barrel
beside the crew. Miles had a bloody smear across his once-
white shirt from the head of one of the calves. Manure and dirt
streaked their pants. Calves crammed up the race and bellowed
in the cradle, straining their sleek long-eared heads out the
front for the few minutes that they were under the duress of
the branding. The propane blasted a steady roar, adding to the
heat, and the ends of the irons glowed and flickered translucent
orange. One lived this experience completely, or not at all.

Flies stuck to anything alive. They covered hats like a mul-
titude of hatpins and crawled up underneath the brims to bite;
they clung to shirts like a black cape and worked their way under
clothing to leave burning welts.

Ringers wore their hats pulled low, their hands and faces
dark from work outdoors. During the first few weeks, I wore
gloves and a scarf across my face to keep out the sun and dust. I
soon abandoned the useless precaution. We finished the branding and worked the mob of cattle through the smoky pens again,
the sound of our voices mixing with the screaming of galahs
and the bellowing of cattle.

The horses drooped their heads in another pen, backs lined
from a morning of riding and coated in mud where they'd rolled
after being washed. They waited for the drafting and branding
to reach its end, when they would be used again. Saddles, wet
blankets, and bits lay in haphazard piles in the shade of the

loading chute just outside the pens, caked with froth and sweat and a good coating of gulf-country clay.

Walking Out the Mob

WE SADDLED THE STREAKED MOUNTS again to walk the cattle out to the holding paddock. In the distance the clouds released virga—thin veils of rain that evaporated before it reached the ground. A few drops fell on our hat brims.

"You'd have to ride fast to keep up with that storm," Cole murmured.

The rain wasn't enough to settle the dust, but the flies seemed to bite less, and wind cut through the dense heat. After many months without rain, the grasses had crumbled and almost disappeared, the plains wide flats of dusty bare earth. The sun broke out intermittently. Clouds cut the light at intervals, teasing. This was winter.

As we rode, the mob lined out across the grasslands, shadows rippling as if the grass itself were moving along. Horses responded to the liquid spread of cows as if they were parts of the same thought, a symphony in which each echoed the other. Cole rode the left flank, backlit. His mount leaped into a powerful lope as the cattle spread to the side and dropped to a walk when they returned to the herd. Vic rode the other wing, one hand holding the reins crossed just above her horse's neck, the other resting lightly on her jeans. Miles rode toward the lead, sitting easily in the saddle, his big frame just a silhouette at times.

We left the cattle at the water troughs and retraced our tracks. Dusk fell as we unsaddled the horses, washed hardened sweat from their backs, and turned them loose in the horse paddock. Evening pulled the scarlet sun down, leaving the shades of violet and blue that draw back just before the entire sky darkens. We rolled large round bales of Flinders-grass hay from stacks to feed weaned calves. The sky cleared of its circling kites and flocking galahs. Silhouettes of trees banded the horizon. We all pulled off sunglasses and sweaty hats, called to the scraggly dogs, and piled into the trucks for the ride home.

At dusk, alone again, I dragged myself up the stairs to my bunkhouse by the lagoon. Night had already darkened the water, and it glinted shards of silver moon. I scrubbed my face in the sink with a bar of harsh white soap and watched the water run black with dirt. I felt weak enough to collapse, mostly from the stress of trying to stay in the right place in the crew and not make mistakes, to work hard and stay attentive enough to be unnoticed yet helpful.

I stepped out onto the veranda with its few broken wooden slats. The liquid eye of the lagoon stretched long and wide enough that it looked almost as if the sun had set in the water to hide through the night. It would be weeks before I saw the lagoon in the light of day. I wondered each dawn if I would emerge from this cocoon a slightly different person, perhaps more lean, more sun-darkened, with more eucalyptus oil in my blood. The crocodiles in the black water would be witness to my metamorphosis, if I made it through alive.

The Choppers

I DIDN'T HAVE TO WAIT LONG to experience the choppers. Two flew in from Karumba, a town on the gulf a few hours flight to the south. I heard the roar of engines and saw the metal dragon-flies land on the flat at the end of the airstrip. The pilots walked toward the station compound carrying duffel bags and a case of beer.

Flynn Cooper owned the chopper company. He wore a plaid shirt and a brown cap over short sandy-gray hair, and had fair but gulf-weathered skin. Rich was one of the pilots with whom he contracted. They climbed the stairs to the kitchen veranda to join Angus, Ross, Mike the mechanic, and those of us on the station crew who drifted in at dusk to sit at the table and make light conversation over a few beers before dinner.

In the age before helicopters and motorbikes, the mustering crew waited for the floods during wet season—usually the months of November, December, and January—when most of the land turned into a sea. In those months, the livestock that escaped being swept out to the gulf sought refuge on the sand ridges and waited for the water to recede, and this made them easier to locate. Ringers set up temporary camps and endured the heat and sand flies for months, riding in the boggy country and spending long days to cover hundreds of thousands of hectares in the muster.

In those days, many of the ringers were Aboriginal men, property of the station. They were provided with places to live for themselves and their families, along with bread, meat, coffee, tea, chewing tobacco, and, on some of the stations, limited alcohol. They did not receive payment. They were kept away from the grog and gambling of the towns because they didn't own vehicles or have the money to get them. Every so often the boss would let them go for a few weeks and then pick them up later, hauling them home in whatever state of mind and body they had ended up in and sending them back to work. They rode long days and were chained if they tried to escape.

In 1967 the government decided to give the Aboriginal citizens rights and passed a law that stated they must be paid station wages. The move backfired for those it meant to assist, as the station managers fired most of their Aboriginal ringers and station hands, leaving them and their families unemployed and homeless, with no place to go. The dole handed out by the government did little to assuage the condition, and for many, the situation grew worse. This scarred human history, these practices akin to slavery in a shockingly recent past, appeared very rarely in the romantic tales of the Australian stockman.

Diminished cattle prices in the seventies narrowed the margins of station profits, and many went under, unable to afford the costs of maintaining the stock camps and paying employees. Wives and children and neighbors replaced many of the permanent station employees, regardless of their race, on the smaller properties. And mustering contractors who didn't require the benefits of full employment replaced many of the station men on the larger properties. The mustering contractors worked on bids, or by numbers of cattle mustered, stayed a few weeks or months, and then moved to another station.

Helicopters, motorbikes, and bull-catching vehicles began their gradual takeover. Despite costs of $500 an hour, the time and expenses saved with the choppers made economic sense in most cases. In the flat country where mechanization proved effective, the traditional methods have been all but abandoned in favor of propeller-powered steeds. But the price paid in stock damage can be as high as fuel costs: Calves are often separated from their mothers in the hectic escape. Cattle become anxious, stressed, and wild. Some even acclimate to the menacing machines and don't bother to leave their shady hollows beneath the trees, where, try as they might, the choppers can't reach them. A few thousand cattle either panicked and fleeing or stubbornly resisting expulsion make for a tumultuous muster, no matter the skill of the pilot. Over a few decades, though, the stations adapted and the new muster found its own system and efficiencies, machines replacing a century of intimate cattle and landscape savvy, horsepower replacing horses, and noise and speed replacing the slow pace of station life. To most owners, the benefits far outweighed the costs.

The idea was that cattle could be mustered with helicopters in order to save crews time and energy. The crews would simply walk the animals several miles to the yards, hassle, brand, draft, vaccinate, and doctor them, and then walk them out again. On the bigger stations, pilots might bring in two thousand head of cattle in a few hours. On Stilwater that day, Flynn and Rich, with Wade riding along, would find and muster only five hundred head of unruly cattle from one of the immense paddocks before early afternoon. Miles rode the motorbike out to work the country beneath them. They communicated via two-way radio, covering the paddock and its fifteen thousand hectares of forest country in a fraction of the time it would have taken with horses.

The rest of both crews rode on motorbikes and in the stock truck with horses to meet the helicopters. We unloaded our horses and waited, dust from the distant struggle settling over us, sun streaking through trees as if we were in its graces.

One of the helicopter pilots radioed, and said he was bringing cattle down the fence line.

Cole answered, "Right-o. We'll move up a little."

Cole and Vic rode their chestnut thoroughbreds in the lead. The road grader had bladed a path alongside the barbed-wire fence, and horse tracks covered the cow tracks in the dust. The pilot worked back and forth over the trees, cutting a grid pattern toward the corner of the paddock, the sound of the chopper alternately fading and then growing louder. When the pilot spotted cattle in the forests of the sand ridge, the engines whined as he dropped down directly over them. The roaring propeller almost cut the trees as he dipped in and out of the thick stand. Soon a small mob of five or six cattle emerged, high-headed and wide-eyed. We set a fast pace to keep them pressed along the fence line to the corner. Cattle poured in before buzzing helicopters as the sounds of the roaring engines, bawling calves, and hooves crazed the air.

Five hundred cattle bunched in the corner like hornets milled in a circle, still riled, white-eyed, and slobbery-mouthed from their wild escape. Ringers and horses worked to keep turning them back as they tried to break, first in one direction and then another. Cattle moved in a whirlpool of grit, where moments before had been the still, streaked shade of narrow-leaved bloodwood. Miles called instructions over the radio, working his motorbike around streaming escapees.

We held them in the corner until they settled a bit. The pack of dogs worked double-time. When Miles eventually called, "Move on out, Jo," Cole and Vic rode their red horses to point the cattle through the gate in the corner, but the animals refused to follow. They started up again, ready to break, and it was almost impossible to put pressure on the lead cattle from behind the milling group. We worked back and forth with the horses, plowing a fire line. Eventually the current of beasts started rotating in a coherent circle and they all funneled through the gate and down the fence line.

The mob settled—not quickly, but eventually—with the entire crew bordering them along the fence in a net of horses and motorbikes and cow dogs. The river of cattle in the dust and the open grassland trampled beneath a few thousand hooves reached before me. Above was the endless blue of the Australian sky. The sun burned black highlights on the shoulders of the cows and threw shadows from their hipbones and heads. Calves trotted, high-tailed, in the rear. The dust blew thick enough to obscure the herd, stinging in my nostrils, plastering a fine grit to my face and sticking in my eyes. At one point a group of cattle pressed hard enough against the fence that one jumped over and got caught in the wires. About fifteen more followed and spilled into the adjoining grassland before we could move the mob past the broken wires. The strays followed the main mob down the fence until a helicopter brought them together again at a fenced trap around a water hole.

We followed the last of the cattle through and walked the horses into the milky pond to drink. They sank in the mud and plunged their nostrils into the murky water amid green algae and water lilies. Wade pulled up the Toyota Land Cruiser, loaded with a barrel of aviation gas for the helicopters. Both pilots waited with Wade and Miles by the truck, eating sandwiches and drinking cups of coffee and tea. The pack of scraggly cow dogs lay in the shade.

We dismounted, loosened cinches, and tied the sweaty horses to the fence. Most of us took out plastic-wrapped sandwiches from the esky in the truck and crouched in the dusty shade of a few short coolibahs. A few lit cigarettes. Rich said he would fly back to Karumba and Flynn would stay the night to muster a holding paddock in the morning. Rich set his coffee cup in the esky and walked toward the little helicopter, giving a wave before he climbed into the cockpit bubble. We waited while the engine started and then roared, and in a tornado of leaves and grass, the chopper rose and cut a line toward the horizon of trees.

Miles brought us back to task. "We'll follow the fence a couple of kilometers through this open stuff, then hit a sand ridge and follow it for maybe five or six kilometers, and then head back out in the open for a while."

Miles and I took up the tail. He didn't have much to do on the motorbike but creep along, stop, idle, and then move forward, so he stopped to light a cigarette and drove with it held in his mouth. Meanwhile the ridge closed around the cattle and the soil turned to fine-grained sand that made the storm even thicker than before. The trees became dense and more diverse, several species of tea tree, wild plum, wild pear, nonda, and wattle forming a forest through which the cattle parted and merged. The male individuals of the broad-leaf tea tree bloomed green flowers shaped like bottlebrushes, while the female trees sported purple-tipped buds at the ends of their short branches. Nonda trees drooped thick foliage of dark green, rounded leaves, and a few had small yellow fruit. Wild plum trees dangled hard, brown, elongated fruit that left my mouth parched and chalky when I sank my teeth into one.

Crow picked his way over fallen branches, and I reined him back and forth to keep the cattle moving. He stepped gingerly on the hardened and pocked mud left from the wet season. I did not catch any glimpse of the lead ringers, who were separated from me by the herd and the thick trees of the sand ridge. I felt alone again. Swamp grass pressed and cut against my horse's chest, brushing my thighs and making a gold sea through which we rode.

~~

Flynn took me up in the chopper to muster the next day. He offered in the same uninterested way that Miles had given me a place in the crew, and he too refrained from any conversation. I followed him to the helicopter and climbed into the seat as if doing so were normal. He reached over to show me how to fasten the shoulder harness and seat belt and handed me a set of green plastic headphones that completely covered my ears. He put on his own headphones and showed me a lever and a press-to-talk button on the control panel. Then he turned on the VHF radio, checked the gauges, and started the engine—four cylinders roaring at increasing rpms. I took a deep breath, my heart thudding as it had often done those first days, my body strapped in to the open-sided machine. The roar was deafening, the craft seemingly so insubstantial it might crumple with the force of wind. Flynn pulled up the lever, and we left the ground.

Grass whirled around us as we defied gravity, flying skyward, suddenly and curiously separated from the earth. My stomach dropped as we tilted sideways and swung in a lifting circle. The earth simultaneously grew smaller and expanded, reaching, spreading, details diminishing out of focus far below. The helicopter was like a white metal bug with two glass eyes, so small that the openness of all the air pressed against me. The country revealed its full breadth, the tree-covered flatlands stretching until they blurred into a blue horizon line.

Flynn angled northwest, flying across the forest waterways, the winding sand ridges, and the wide-open areas between. Spotting cattle required almost 360-degree vision, and my eyes took a while to identify them: the dots beneath the green smudges of trees. Wind burned cold on my shoulder, and I tugged on my shoulder harness to make sure I wouldn't fall out the open side when the helicopter tipped sideways.

The ride reminded me of being on a boat, the tossing and turning and complete absence of anything like earth beneath me. The experience was a freefalling, dropping, tipping, diving, rising, and hovering that left my body reeling. I was held in a storm, ungrounded, freed of the order of gravity, it seemed.

When we did start seeing small mobs of cattle, Flynn ducked the helicopter right over them, dropping quite close to the ground, and they took off running. Dust rose up from their trail as they lined out on the pads. He called over the radio to a ringer he had spotted and knew was Ivan, "I've got four cows coming to you."

"What?"

"I've got four cows heading toward you."

"Right-o."

Two ringers, Ivan and Tanner, emerged from the trees below us on motorbikes and made a circle behind the galloping cattle. The ringers knew when the chopper had located a mob by the way the rpms shifted as the helicopter dropped to begin working them out of the trees. The muster hummed noise, a symphony or cacophony of motors, a chopping propeller, static, and radio communication. Flynn saw another mob and dropped the helicopter into the trees. The sudden plunge and the proximity of branches to the propeller blades made me sit a little straighter in the seat. Branches and leaves swirled around us and Flynn elevated the craft again as cattle emerged from the trees. I yelled into the headset, "Aren't you worried about hitting the trees with the prop?"

His voice, mixed with static, returned. "I don't worry about anything."

I raised my eyebrows but didn't reach forward to press the talk button and respond. The headset cupped my ears in warmth, the engine vibrating the chopper. The ride was tenuous enough without any added anxiety. Flynn had been flying the little mustering helicopters for twenty years, working all over the Australian outback. He owned his own helicopter mustering company and employed a few other pilots. The pilots would fly in to the stations the evening before a muster and spend the night there. They knew the landscape better than many, having the benefit of an aerial perspective. Flynn had a room in one of the bunkhouses at Stilwater, and at dusk, when he arrived, he would cross the end of the landing strip with his duffel bag and a case of beer, only later joining us in the kitchen for dinner.

Flynn turned the chopper and scoped the grassland. The sun angled in suddenly, searing, as he pivoted. He pointed out a wild pig, scared from the swamp, loping in a choppy run beneath us. Wallabies took off through the grass like little bouncing stuffed animals, tails hooked into question marks.

Ancient creek drainages meandered across the landscape, the surrounding savannas eroded down and the sand beds slightly elevated. Cattle pads striated the grassland. Endless miles of dirt roads linked different dams, bores, water holes, and yards on the property, but it was only when I lifted above the trees that I grasped the expansiveness of the landscape. The fence lines, dams, and scattered mobs of cattle gave evidence of human impact, but the gulf country was a wilderness far greater than this. The land seemed to have no boundaries, the forests fading to blue on the horizon, merging into the sky.

We swooped back and forth in the helicopter, high above tree-speckled plains, looking for smoky dots that were cattle amid trees and along creek drainages. We lifted and plunged for hours, until I lost track of both time and space above the endless landscape.

Flynn drove with one hand on the center stick attached to the overhead propeller and one on a lever between us, with which he raised and lowered the helicopter and controlled engine speed. Twin foot pedals enabled him to turn using the rear propeller. He told me how quickly the helicopter would drop if the engine were to die, but added that it would get you to the ground alive. I asked what would happen if the tail propeller failed.

"You would go straight to heaven."

Flynn dove the chopper down between branches, micky bulls turning to fight the machine with its roaring propeller. He called their bluff and dropped the skids onto their backs, then pulled up hundreds of feet for an aerial view, the cattle miniature and running, red and brown and white against the burned brown of the plains. We talked back and forth over the two-way, but his radio was acting faulty so he plugged in a hand-held. He needed two hands to fly when the cattle got wild, so he gave me directions over the roar of the engine and prop, and I passed them on to the crew. The cattle gathered and dispersed, giving the ringers a hard time on the flats.

I felt my stomach rise again as we descended into the dense trees along a drainage and I caught a flash of red animals beneath the canopy. Flynn leaned out the side and hollered at them above the din of the engine and propeller. The wind from the blades racked the branches back and forth and twisted leaves around us, a storm of our own creation that we rode in unscathed. The cattle didn't know which direction to run to avoid the madness above, some confused, some scattering, and Flynn couldn't get close enough to them in the trees, so he buzzed the helicopter above them until they all started running, then dropped down, almost to the ground, to push them in the direction of the dam. Helicopter skids scraped the bristles of grass and squeezed the sky thin between us and the careening earth before he deftly defied gravity again to find a broader view. He left a few lame cattle and a bull that he said had three-day sickness, transmitted via mosquitoes.

"Did you see where those two bulls went?" He spoke through the headset and the angry whir of the propellers.

I answered, "I think they're behind us."

I could see Miles, Tanner, and Ivan on motorbikes below us now, covering a lot of ground to bring the smaller mobs together into the flood heading toward the dam. Working in sync, the helicopter and the motorbikes made long runs across the paddock, and the cattle strung out down the trails. The lines of cattle looked like parallel snakes, reaching for miles. They swarmed and parted and merged in viscous formations. The other ringers waited on horseback, holding up the lead cattle and keeping the

mob together as more came in from the far-flung arms of their barely bounded territory. A fence line gave the milling sea one flat edge as they moved down to the corner.

~~

I stepped out of the helicopter and onto the hard-packed landing strip, the landscape rising and falling around me. This was no ordinary stock experience, this was pure madness. Nothing, not a thousand days spent with horses or cows on any number of ranches, would have prepared me for the insanity of a muster in the Australian outback. I set out in a weaving course across the stretch of cropped grass toward the station compound, heat adding to my nausea. A silver haze veiled the buildings in the distance. This was more than an out-of-body experience, this was a world turned, almost literally, upside down. To be lifted from the ground, to herd cattle from the air in a sheet-metal steed that knew no orientation, to be pitched sideways hundreds of feet in any direction with only a seat belt strap holding me in, to have a thousand miles of country unfurled, to work with a reckless, unfathomable crew and wild cattle, many of which had never seen humans, was more than I could comprehend.

Fencing

WHEN ALL THE NEARBY CATTLE HAD BEEN mustered, drafted, and shipped or turned back to their paddocks, Wade and Miles sent the station and mustering crews on fence repair. While fence work was not usually in the contract of a mustering crew, they reasoned that trying to work cattle on a station of failing fences was inefficient, ineffective, and overall a waste of time. So the ringers bit their tongues and settled in for a few weeks of stretching wire and hammering pickets.

Wade said I should go with Dustin, his favored brother-in-law, and Ivan. These two were the most carefree and easygoing of both crews. We loaded the "Choice" ute, the truck's name stenciled in blue cursive on the side, and set out. The fences were rusted, torn out, fallen over, or nonexistent. If a station were to have cattle that could be managed by a small crew, it needed paddocks. And paddocks needed fences. A paddock without a fence was just grassland. That made sense to me; I was ready to do my part to impose order. I didn't yet know that some of the crew felt differently. The ones on the lower rungs, I was to find out, the ones used to exercising a limited degree of authority, didn't really care who was boss—a station manager, a head stockman or two, or the place itself. They had learned from the circumstances that wildness was the authority and would continue to be so; they just had to put in the time to get paid at the end. On the other hand, I came from a family that valued work above all else, and I was ready for a hard day of it. The other two were less inclined.

Ivan, with his faded ball cap, loose shirt, tennis shoes, and sunglasses that were actually just black welding glasses, looked ready for whatever the day might throw at him. He was elusive, energetic, and not overly concerned about anything. He didn't say much about having to pound pickets instead of muster. He just grinned, nodded, and said, "Yeah, man, let's go." He threw a few fencing tools into the ute, folded himself in to slouch in the driver's seat, and handed across a small parcel wrapped in newsprint. Dustin tucked it under the seat by his sneakers.

"I know what this is," Dustin said with a wry grin. "We're starting early."

"Yeah, man." The crow's feet crinkled by Ivan's eyes, his darkened face gaunt.

He had wrapped six or seven cold beers in the newsprint and brought along a thermos of hot water, a mix of coffee granules, milk powder, and sugar, and a bag of biscuits. We had added another thermos of hot water, a frozen water bottle, tin cups, and a couple of sandwiches. Dustin and I had loaded a roll of barbed wire, some extra-heavy smooth tie wire, and pickets in the back. Before we left, Dustin pulled up beside a drum of petrol and used the hand pump to fuel the ute. He let his blue dog off the chain below the fig tree, and Ivan set his little black puppy on top of the wire. I had a map that Wade had handed me before we left, a mess of black lines on a sheet of paper that tried to identify roads, rivers, and paddock fences without much accuracy or success. I sat between these two young men in faded jeans and frayed sneakers with scarred, sun-darkened hands clutching the map.

Dustin shifted down into first gear to ease the truck over the places where pigs had rooted the once-wet swamp ground into a site of destruction that had hardened in place. When we passed a broken wire, Dustin stopped the truck and we all unloaded, taking pliers and reaching for the ends of the barbed wire to twist them into loops. One of us threaded smooth wire through, twisted one end, and used the pliers to tighten the fence and twist the other end of the wire to hold the repair. Then all of us piled back into the truck, Ivan and Dustin hollering at their dogs to get back in, and we bounced farther along the fence. We had to stop every hundred feet or so, the wires rusting or gone altogether, barely getting our doors shut before Dustin took off and we had to stop again. The radio blared static. Then Ivan drove and Dustin sat on the bouncing bonnet between repairs. Ivan couldn't really see out the windshield, though, so he just leaned his head out the window, pressed the accelerator, and careened down the road, screeching to a stop at another break and almost throwing Dustin from his precarious seat out front.

"Whoa there. Easy," Dustin called. Ivan just grinned.

We followed the dividing fence between two paddocks, North and South Gum, and found a long stretch of the bottom wire that had rusted in the swamp grass, oxidized by brackish water and sea air. Ivan drained his second beer and tossed the can behind him.

He asked, "How far is the coast?"

Dustin replied, "Just on the other side of that sand ridge."

"You think the ute will make it?"

"No, we'll have to walk."

Dustin shifted to slow the truck across a muddy arm of the swamp. "There's a pig over there," he noted, "other side of them brolgas."

Ivan replied, "Dead pig right there."

"You shoot that one?"

"No. Another one just there."

Dustin pointed to a smaller pig decomposing in the mud. He pulled his sunglasses from the crown of his silver hat and put them on. Ivan rolled a cigarette and drove with it out the window. Brolgas rose from the swamp on elegant caped wings, the late sun catching their red helmets. A few ibis took to the air, and beyond, clouds of white egrets landed along the edges of the water. We parked at the edge of the sand ridge, where the soil changed from hardened clay to soft sand and the trees thickened into a forest tangled with rubber vine. Ivan lifted out the esky with the beer and the one with thermoses and coffee and started walking up the sandy track through the trees. Dustin had his pliers in his pocket.

"How far'd you say the coast was?"

"Not far."

"Like hell." Ivan took off his sunglasses. "Looks like another five."

Green ants made small leaf huts in the tree branches by gluing the broad green leaves together. Ivan showed me how to eat an ant by holding the front feet and head and biting off the abdomen. It left a spurt of tang on my tongue.

"I busted into a nest of these on the motorbike, and had them in my shirt, pants, shoes, on my two-way—and all of it came off, shirt, shoes, pants," Ivan said. He gave his sudden laugh.

The dogs yelped and darted after a group of the feral black pigs. Dustin took off through the deep sand and vines after them. If the dogs managed to catch one of the babies they would sink their teeth into the squealing creature. I grimaced at the prospect, but the tangled figs of the sand ridge proved too thick for the chase, and the puppies came back without any blood smeared on their jaws.

The coast appeared suddenly, glittery across a band of white sand and a crusted shelf of compressed shells. The fence ended some seventy feet from the tide line, the wires rusted through from the salt water. A post stood out in the water, beckoning someone to brave the crocodiles and string new wire. Ivan drank beer and I had a cup of coffee from the hot water in the thermos. Dustin had both. Ivan did a couple of awkward flips off the ledge and landed in a tumble in the sand. He stood up, coated in fine sand, and retrieved his pliers from the bank. "Fencing doesn't get much better than this."

Beyond the shore, shallow water turned blue only at the skyline. Ripples lapped a few crumbling rocks at the shore. The gulf itself was barely deep enough at high tide to cover the sandbars for miles out to sea, but a channel had been dredged at some point to enable the passage of the ships that took the live export cattle and ore from the loading docks at Karumba across to Indonesia and Asia.

Pelicans drifted on sail wings, their heavy beaks tucked back to their lithe necks. Sea eagles landed near a large nest in a dead snag.

At the time I had reservations about sitting in the sun and wind along those thirty miles of private coastline. But when Wade and Miles later bragged quietly about the size of the barramundi they'd caught on their fence run near Spider's Camp on the northwestern coastal edge of the station, I didn't feel so bad. After a few hours, we walked back to the truck on the far side of the sand ridge, leaving the last stretch of fencing for another day, perhaps getting there before the tide would rust through another wire, perhaps arriving at the failing fence to find lines of crocodiles sunning on the white sand.

That was the way it was. Far from the voices of civilization, the world took a shape and a pace of its own. I wondered what would happen if the lines were let loose altogether, and nothing were to connect us to the rest of the world. The cattle would go wild again, the humans too, and perhaps we would all be fairly content. Or perhaps, lacking the structure we all desired on some level, we would go insane.

~~

On another run, Dustin and I went out to check the fence around Talbot Paddock, one of the southernmost on the station, undersupplied with two pairs of pliers and several coils of smooth wire. I drove the station Trooper with one of Claire and Angus' visiting grandsons, Nick, riding out to fix fence with us for a few hours. Dustin, almost eighteen and prone to drive at high speeds, rode the motorbike, flying along at a pace that sent spirals of dust drifting out across the bunchgrass. When we reached the paddock fence, Dustin said he would check the northern stretch by motorbike. We could meet him at the grid on the main road, and then we would drive in one vehicle to the more accessible section of fence between the road and the river. He said he would only be five minutes or so, and took off again down the fence line, disappearing in the forest of bright green tea trees.

"He can't even see the fence going that fast, much less catch a broken wire," I said, mildly skeptical and not impressed.

Nick leaned out the window to watch for the smoke signal of Dustin's path.

Dustin would float down on the motorbike, reaching sixty miles an hour as he bounced across the dusty holes, breakaway gullies, and bunchgrass, and then make a circle to the vehicle. Soon Nick heard the whine of the bike, and we saw the advancing dust cloud. Dustin pulled up alongside the Trooper, took off his helmet, and handed it across to me.

"Nope, no breaks."

"You gave it a thorough check?"

"Yeah, mate." He grinned, plastering his long hair back under a dusty white stockman's hat and placing wraparound sunglasses over his eyes.

He parked the bike and took the wheel of the vehicle from me. Nick climbed over to the back seat. Dustin flicked through a hundred CDs until he found a favorite AC/DC album. He wiped the back of it on his pants, the same pants he'd earlier used to wipe spilled diesel off his hands, and slid the dusty disc into the player. Dustin and another ringer had found an old speaker in the dump, and they'd wired it up in the back of the Trooper. Dustin had used his pocketknife to cut the plastic off the ends of two other electrical wires and rigged up another speaker that sat on the dash, wedged in so it didn't bounce free. He turned the volume up, bass throbbing.

"Music's not too loud for you?" he asked with a half smile.

"No, you're all right." I smiled back, not wanting to dampen his vicarious glory. Music, like velocity, made the monotony tolerable for him.

Dustin spoke up. "We'll drive to the river and follow the east fence back here to the grid. We'll take the shortcut."

I refrained from commenting. I did not know the paddock, nor did I have any idea how far away the Powder River might lie. Dustin shifted into first. Nick gripped the edge of the seat in front of him.

Dustin drove slowly through a mob of cattle at the lick tubs, then hit high gear as the dirt road opened between scrubby tea trees. Cattle tracks, pressed into wet-season mud and baked dry, made for a jolting ride, and the CD stuttered and skipped in its screaming. Dustin drove as if he were still on the motorbike, the vehicle sliding around corners in crusty soil. We reached the fence and turned toward the river, slowing our pace just enough to keep track of the wires. The Powder River appeared suddenly in front of us through the trees, and Dustin asked, "Gun it?" He braked to a sudden stop on the bank just above the river, the still blue water deceptively inviting.

Nick leaned forward after the vehicle had ceased its mad careening and braced his elbows on the backs of both front seats, watching the river. "They reckon there's big crocs in the Powder."

"I don't know," replied Dustin, "a guy I talked to at Spider's Camp said there's a thirty-one-footer in the Solomon."

I said, "I thought the longest one they've ever caught was only twenty-eight-foot something." Beyond, I could see the deep bend, the tranquil tongue of it licking the cut banks.

"Yeah, at Normanton." Nick rested his cheek against the back of the headrest, his dark hair spiky with static, still gazing intently.

"But *this* one hasn't been caught," explained Dustin.

Nick said, "I go swimming in the river near Karumba."

"You'll be crocodile bait," replied Dustin, gently teasing.

"I'm still alive!" Nick responded, defiant.

We had reached the end, the winding blue boundary of the station; we could go no farther. The river rippled and shuddered, like muscle beneath steely skin.

Dustin turned the Trooper around and took off down the east fence line, back toward the grid where he had parked the motorbike. He braked to a stop when I spotted a sagging wire and backed up through the dust until we found the break. The oil in tea tree bark rusted wires quickly, as did termite mounds built up a yard high along the fence and standing salt water in the wet season. Cattle pushed through the fence, and sometimes the grader snagged several wires at once, but this fence was relatively new and didn't require much repair. We should have carried a chainsaw to clear some of the tea tree scrub along the fence, a sledgehammer to break down the termite mounds encasing the wire, and barbed wire to replace the rusted bottom wire. We should have driven slowly. The paddock fence stretched for so many miles that a thorough repair job would have taken several days, while our method consumed only three or four hours.

But "should" didn't mean much to us, as hot, dusty, and hungry as we were. We covered the miles quickly, stopping, starting, and stopping again. Dustin had a remarkable ability to remain cheerful, though we were both tired of broken wires. He sang along with the CDs, slowing for the bumps only when he didn't want the CD to skip during a favorite song.

While Dustin crooned, my mind wandered into the boundless wild around me. We were working at the edge of the known world, an ambiguous line between sensible order and complete, unfathomable emptiness. I sensed laws of a different dimension slipping through the porous border. Life could easily lose all meaning, days lose their positioning, and we could reel off into the endless grassland, never missed. I dragged my focus back to the reality of the fence work: Dustin had a loose grip on the steering wheel and we slid around corners, jolted across the flats.

He hopped out when we reached the motorbike and took off in front of us. He stopped to open the gates at the yards, waited for us to pass through, and shut them behind us. Clouds of pink-breasted galahs lifted from dead snags, filling the air with wings and screeches.

I followed the cloud from the motorbike home. Blue night descended, bounding the day as a river or a gulf might, defining the edges—amorphous, infinite, unfazed by tea tree oil and sea air.

Fishing

THE NEXT SATURDAY MORNING Stephen Craye and another man pulled up in Stephen's ute, towing an aluminum boat. I was putting a final edge on the killing knives when the vehicle arrived. Claire had warned me that they were headed on a fishing trip, and that I was invited. I guessed that Stephen wanted to show me more of the station.

He crossed the lawn beneath the mango trees, eyeing the stack of knives with a grin, and asked, "Are you going with us?" He introduced the second man: "This is my Sicilian sidekick." The other man said his name was Luci; it was a while before I learned that this was short for Luciano.

I slid the knives back into the leather case, put away the stone, and left to get my backpack. Claire unhooked a couple slabs of ribs and a backstrap from the overhead rail in the meatroom and wrapped them in white plastic.

We headed north along the coastal plain, toward the mouth of the Solomon River. Wide grassy clearings gave way to mudflats, salt pans, and stretches of thin, bushy-topped black tea trees. Rubber vine grew in clumps of looping tendrils. Wallabies leaped away from the vehicle, and white pelicans sifted into the sky as we approached.

Stephen pulled up on the bank of the Solomon and parked underneath the spreading branches of a ghost gum. Beyond the sandy bank with its dead bur plants, the river languished, disappearing upstream and downstream at bends lined in mangroves. A few rusty drums filled with beer bottles and weathered trash suggested fishermen had camped here at some point. It was a strange, paradisal moment.

They left me with a fishing pole and took off down the small sandy track to a fisherman's camp, saying they wouldn't be long, they had some business to attend to.

How often do people find themselves alone with a river, especially one like this, with a current so imperceptible it seems entirely still? I was caught in time, stilled. Hardly a breeze shuffled through the ghost gum leaves. I tried not to think about the past or the future, only to sit quietly and find my place in the present moment.

Eventually they returned, explaining that the fisherman living at the camp had invited them in for a cup of coffee; he didn't seem surprised to see them. Stephen had been thinking about the encounter for days, he admitted, running through scenarios in his head before the time came to approach the camp. He told Luci to act aloof and shady, to stand back and not say much. Stephen introduced him as Luciano. Luci wore his black hair short, and his narrow eyes gave him a shady look anyway. When the fisherman asked where he was from, he said simply, "South."

Stephen told the fisherman he needed to remove himself and his camp from the private property within the week, that there was no room for negotiation. Then he and Luci left. He had it all arranged—the timing, the tone, the movements. He was not new to such encounters. He worked mostly alone, and he was still alive. His reputation accompanied him like a weapon he could use to his advantage. His eyes said as much. Stephen leaned against the truck with a beer.

After a while he mused, "We might check out a camp a little farther away from him. He restrained himself, but he might be throwing things now. He could be dangerous."

The mottled chalky trunk and erratic branches of the ghost gum cast a shadow on the salt-crusted flat.

"He'll need at least a fortnight to clean up that spot. He even had chooks!" Luci added, referring to the domestic nature of the camp, complete with chickens.

"He's probably been there twenty-five years," joked Stephen.

We drove up to another camp farther along the river. This one was abandoned, but still featured a tin shelter beneath eucalyptus trees a little ways back from the bank. Peeled tea tree posts held up the roof and sections of poured concrete covered some of the floor. The inside was littered with rusty drums of trash, a few metal buckets, and pieces of fishing net. Black writing on the posts listed the names and dates of those who had been here before. We unloaded the eskies, water jugs, green canvas swags, two folding metal cots, guns, four crab pots, and fishing gear onto the concrete floor.

Stephen walked to the bank to see if he could back the boat trailer down, and though the short drop-off was steep and sandy and the access blocked by a scraggly mangrove tree, he decided to give it a try. Luci directed him back down the cutout and they slid the boat into the water, where it cut a rippled V in the lazy stream. In four-wheel drive the ute was able to climb most of the way up the bank, but then the narrow tires started spinning in deep sand and it bogged down.

"Might need to winch ourselves out," Stephen deadpanned with a grin.

Luci seemed to ignore him. "We'll need to get some bait for the crab pots."

"Shoot a fuckin' wallaby."

"I guess we'll winch it off that tree," replied Luci.

Stephen dug out the electric control switch and the cable for the winch from behind the seat. He pressed the button and the winch whined, releasing cable from the covering attached to the front of the vehicle. I pulled the hook and cable up the deep sand of the bank and wrapped it once around the stout tree and back onto itself. Stephen got back inside the ute and, holding his arm with the switch out the window, pulled the truck out of the deep sand and onto higher ground. Then he wound up the winch cable without expression.

"Let's get that wallaby," Luci said, obviously relieved.

He dug out his rifle and they both climbed into the truck. I sat in the open back against the spare tire, wondering why I had been called along on this journey. Stephen hadn't gone a hundred yards down the sandy track when a little wallaby bounced out of the trees.

Luci leveled his rifle. I saw the wallaby slump to the ground a moment after I heard the shot. Luci took his fillet knife and crossed over the leaf duff to the little animal. Stephen stepped out of the truck and walked off through the dense blue-green woods on the sand ridge, his feet softly crunching eucalyptus leaves, disappearing without explanation. I climbed down to help Luci.

Squatting down next to the wallaby, crouching in his shorts and hiking boots, Luci lifted the animal up by its tail, repositioned it on its side, and slit the skin of the belly. A little pink joey clung to a teat inside the pouch.

He said, "That's one thing I hate about this." Then he killed the joey with his knife.

Slitting the skin of the wallaby's long hind legs, he tugged it away from the lean muscle. With one boot planted on the hindquarters of the wallaby, he pulled the skin back so it came clear off, turning inside out as it separated from the long tail. Then he chopped off the end of the tail and sliced through the small tailbones to part the upper section of the tail from the body.

I held open a black plastic trash bag, into which he dumped the tail and chunks of meat as he removed them from the carcass. They smelled of hot blood and soaked fur. He left the viscera and thin bony front quarters, which wouldn't serve for crab bait.

Luci wiped his knife and I lifted the sack of meat into the back of the ute, thinking that to anyone born in the bush, this would be second nature. Instead, everything felt terribly unnatural. A wave of queasiness overcame me, and I leaned back against the truck, trying to distance myself from the soft bloody patch of the murdered marsupial. I focused on the stillness and the close trees, the streaking light and carpet of fallen leaves.

Stephen emerged from the woods without a word and we returned to the boat. Luci pushed us off and Stephen navigated to the opposite bank, upstream along the mangroves. The wire crab pots were folded up into long metal-framed net boxes in the boat. Luci cut lengths of old wire he had found in the hut to repair the pots and twisted other wires to hang the meat inside each one. I tied plastic water bottles onto lengths of rope to serve as floats. Rolling a cigarette and holding it in his mouth, Luci dropped the crab pots into the water and tossed a plastic bottle and rope in after each one.

Stephen asked Luci if he wanted to shoot the rifle. When we had reached the shore again, I figured that since the show at the fisherman's camp hadn't been much fun, he was offering his sidekick a chance to blast the big gun.

"Aim for the far bank, but hit the water," Stephen advised.

Luci loaded a shell in the rifle and leveled it on the surface of the wide river, aiming toward the mangroves on the far bank. The shot sent a surge of water up from the glassy surface, but the sound disappeared quickly in the carpeting of trees on the sand ridge.

"I remember mowing down trees with a rifle as a kid," Luci said. He lowered the gun, slipped another shell into the chamber, and blasted a thin tree while we waited in the shade.

"Clear through it! Wouldn't want to be shot with that thing." Luci walked over and peeled some of the shredded cambium, the white wood sticky and wet with sap. He returned with the massive rifle. "We should check those crab pots anyway."

Stephen nodded. We climbed back into the boat and he took the handle of the motor. As we neared the first pot, Luci clamped his cigarette between his lips and leaned over with the metal hook to snag the float line. He pulled up the dripping wire cage. Four mud crabs clung to the netting.

"Mud crab for tea."

He stood braced in the middle of the aluminum boat and shook the cage over the bucket. The crabs gripped the net with their monstrous claws, and all that fell out was a jellyfish. Stephen reached over with a wooden bat and smacked at the claws. They dropped the three larger crabs into the bucket and tipped the fourth, smaller one back into the water. Luci wired the cage closed again and leaned over to drop it flat into the water. It disappeared beneath the surface.

The other pots provided two more crabs. We put the lines

in the water until the sun crept down into the green brim of mangroves. Then Stephen turned downstream to catch the sunset over the ocean, and we flew across the water, spray mixing with the cool evening air.

The flat-bottomed boat plunged and bucked as we reached swells coming in from the gulf. Luci sat on the bow initially, then slammed against the metal covering until he slid back and stood braced against the seat. We pulled the boat up to a white sand beach where the gulf opened into a shallow expanse. Thousands of shells stretched in thin tidal bands, and a tangled fishing net reached a line of light-blue plastic mesh along the shore. The setting sun seared a hole into the water and disappeared. We cruised back to camp as the moon burned its own white fire into the still river.

~~

Starlight glistened on the water. Luci and Stephen left to take showers in the bore hose several miles away. The hose had been plumbed long ago to provide a warm stream of water for tourists who had since forgotten the place. In the quiet the men left behind, the darkened outback framed the naked river, an outline of mangroves surrounding the glossy surface. I draped a sarong clear over my head to keep the biting sand flies from my neck, arms, and hands. When the men returned, I was curled up against a post of the shelter, writing.

"A few bloody sand flies," Stephen observed.

"A few," I said.

"I thought you might have caught us some fish," he said.

"I turned them all loose."

"Bloody hell."

Luci called to him, "Want a beer?"

"Naw, I'm feelin' a bit crook."

"Must have been those warm beers you were drinking last night," Luci retorted.

"Coulda used more." Stephen sat on the chain mesh of a cot.

Luci started a fire beneath the tin shelter, opened a beer, rolled another cigarette, and said he'd go get some salt water to cook the crabs. The fire cast an orange glow on his flannel shirt and face, on his cupped hand when he tilted his head to light the cigarette.

When the fire burned down and the salt water rolled in a boil, Luci dumped the clawing mud crabs into it, and they almost came over the top. He set a lid on the bucket to contain their escape and sat down to wait.

Stephen smoked, staring off into the night.

"We should cook up some of those ribs. I like my crab better cold anyway." He often didn't eat dinner at all, but that night he humored us.

"I can't believe anybody likes ribs," objected Luci, "just a bunch of chewy gristle. Especially those."

"We might have some backstrap you can gnaw on," Stephen said.

"Only if you're cooking."

They bantered, Luci sounding as if he was mildly concerned, and Stephen as if this time, too, would pass, one small ripple in the tide of the universe. Somewhere out there a fisherman was seething alone with a smoky fire and the endless night, animals were prowling the darkened scrub, and waters of the silver sea were tearing against the empty coast, but Stephen just hauled a rolled-up canvas swag to make the chain-mesh cot more comfortable and relaxed with the beer he eventually accepted from Luci, along with a can of bug spray. Luci finished cooking dinner about midnight, set the tin of blackened ribs and tough steak on the crumbling concrete, and took a crab from the basket for himself. Using his long hunting knife, he smashed a pink claw and sucked out the sweet meat.

Stephen said he was going back to the bore to camp away from the mosquitoes. The rest of us could camp wherever we bloody well liked. Luci stayed at the camp, but I climbed into the truck for the ride, curled up in the back between swags, stars ducking in and out of the trees on the sand ridge. At the bore, I spread my sleeping bag on the ground beneath tall blood-woods. I had just fallen asleep when I woke up to Stephen calling, "Hey, Rafael!"

"Yes?"

"If you get bit by a taipan, I'll be responsible. You'd better sleep on the back of the ute."

Too exhausted by the absurdity of the day to argue, I dragged myself back to the truck, its hard metal tray not as comfortable as crushed bloodwood leaves. Stephen had his swag rolled out on one half of the back, the canvas, foam pad, and blankets making a comfortable traveling bed.

"Do you have a pillow, Raf?"

"What? No, I'll be all right."

Night folded around me—full of stars, a cool fall wind, and silhouettes of leaves. I slept.

I woke once. The anxiety that had pulsed subtly through my veins since we'd left the station compound had dissolved, and in its place I felt a vague emptiness in my chest that the night seemed to fill completely. Why had they invited me?

Even brave men can be overwhelmed by solitude. Luci, for one, seemed more disconcerted by the outback than by the potential reaction of any angry fisherman. Maybe the nervous energy stemmed from his own expectation that he be courageous, and he didn't know how to play the part other than by conquering uncertainty with a show of death and weaponry. We were an odd crew in any case, and I was at a loss.

Had I been invited because I was young and female? Or as a gesture of generosity, so that I might see more of the landscape they found wild and magnetic? My defense was not one of ammunition and firepower, or reckless action and overt control. While I had wanted to escape earlier, at that moment I felt only a sense of alertness, the presence of the world around touching the edges of my consciousness. The soft night wind brushed my cheek and I let the stars fill my vision until they faded on the edges of sky. Somewhere the sea lapped against my dreams and I slept again.

~~

In the striated gold of early dawn, Stephen and Luci said they would go for a drive and leave me in peace if I wanted to have a shower at the bore. I waited for the dust to settle before taking off my clothes and stepping onto the old piece of tin that served as the shower floor. The bore water felt almost warm. Mud and grass seeds splattered up around my feet from the edges of the tin. Sunlight streaked the tall castles of termite mounds around me, many of them over five feet tall, like an army of chess pieces in the pink glow.

We ate cold mud crab for breakfast back at the shelter. Luci started a fire to boil water for coffee. Stephen said he would show us another fishing hole along a little current called Cattle Creek, some ten miles away. I went out in the boat with him to pull the crab pots out of the water, unhooking the dripping pieces of wallaby meat and stacking the pots in the center of the boat. Two large sea eagles coasted along the rim of mangroves.

The day was a blur, filled with the lazy blue water of the creek. Crocodiles lurked beneath and herons hung above in the branches of tea trees. I caught one small barramundi completely by accident, snagging him on top of the head. When dusk closed in, the water looked more forbidding; shadows concealed every lurking crocodile nostril. The pink and blue shell of dusk floated on the water, and the sky turned upside down until the moon was a swath of silk, shredded by ripples. We took the boat out of its wrapping current and loaded it on the trailer.

We drove back to the station compound. I curled up in the back of the ute again, nestled between a pair of rifle cases and the fishing rods, and laid my head on a swag. I pulled my arms in, away from the fast cool air, and listened to the muffled bass line of music from the cab.

Stephen pulled open the gate to the station compound and drove up to the house where the owners stayed on the rare occasions when they visited. Stephen lodged there often, but he didn't take much trouble keeping up the place. The blue house sat perched on metal stilts, eight feet off the ground and out of flood danger. In front, a huge fig tree drooped twisting branches.

Stephen and Luci climbed the stairs and piled their gun cases and gear in the breezeway. The water in the sink smelled like sulfur. Stephen said it came from an aquifer that stretched all the way to Papua New Guinea, and that it surged out of artesian bores. They filled bottles of it to put in the refrigerator, where the flavor seemed to settle enough to make it tolerable. They didn't drink much water anyway. He and Luci rolled cigarettes, drank beer, and sat on green plastic chairs while mosquitoes attacked, the night pressing black through the branches of the fig. When I retired to my bunkhouse, they were still up, beer cans piling on the low plastic table, cigarette smoke drifting around them, dissipating into the thin veil of stars beyond.

Miles Carver

THE FOLLOWING MORNING, I took the headlamp to cross from my bungalow to the workers' kitchen. Miles arrived on his four-wheeler, and he and Wade planned the day.

Miles had lost a dog the day before. Vic had found her dead, kicked by one of the cows. The skinny little red and white puppy had been worth about $2,000, and Miles was more than a little downcast.

He took me on a drive to check the salt and mineral tubs around some of the paddocks. This was so I might begin to learn the lay of the country, he explained, but it seemed more likely to me that he wanted a little company. Miles had spent his life working stations like this one. A competent ringer and stockman, he was no stranger to the mysteries and vagaries of the outback. And he too wanted to learn the nature of this particular station.

On our way out, Miles stopped by the small junkyard of dead and nearly dead trucks, where he had his working dogs tied on chains.

He called quietly to the unruly pack, "Who wants to go?"

The dogs yapped in a chorus; a few leaped on top of the vehicles, hoping to be released. Miles let several dogs off their chains and tossed them by the scruffs of their necks into the back. They tumbled in, muddy, skinny, brown, red, and black, reaching their heads over the edge with tongues hanging out for the drive to the yards. Miles hooked the bull catcher up to the plastic trailer, which was full of supplement bags for the cattle.

The bull catcher was a late-sixties-model Nissan Patrol with wire mesh for the windshield and roof, roll bars, and tires wired to the front for ramming into feral bulls. The brakes didn't work, so when we passed one of the old drums that held the powdered supplement, Miles downshifted, waited until the vehicle slowed enough to turn around, then approached at a slower gear and coasted to a stop. He lifted one of the bags out of the trailer and emptied it into the drum.

We drove for hours. A few mobs of cattle emerged from the stands as we passed, and one dingo fled, turning back to look at us from a short distance away. Miles wore his narrow-brimmed floppy hat, but the wind plastered it back. He rolled cigarettes as we drove, bracing the bouncing wheel with his knee while he fished in his pocket for the papers and tobacco, lighting them in the slack wind when we stopped for gates or beside the lick tubs.

Out on the coastal plain of South Gum paddock, Miles tried to cross the upper end of a dried swamp, but it wasn't as dry as he'd thought. The bull catcher sank almost to the axles, tires spinning the mud beneath into a black slurry.

He climbed over the roll bars to survey the damage.

"Well, that was stupid," he admitted.

We had a two-way radio, but neither of us wanted to call for help.

Miles unhitched the trailer, but with the weight of the lick sacks he couldn't lift the tongue. He climbed into the back and hefted the big bags toward the rear, and with the help of a lever, the trailer tipped up on its back end. At my suggestion, Miles dug a trough in front of each wheel and poured in some of the powdered lick for traction. After several bags and several tries, the truck lurched out of the swamp. He had enough rope and chain in the back to reach back to the trailer, so we put the bull catcher in low gear and crept forward until the trailer popped free of the muddy ruts with a sucking sound. When it had bounced onto harder mud, we hooked the tongue back to the truck.

"You reckon the main road's not far?" Miles asked.

I didn't really know, but I guessed it wasn't too far, and so we set off jolting across the dead grass of the lowlands. Distance deceived both of us, though, one grassland curving around the shoulders of sand ridges into another, sparse forests of short tea trees blending into thicker stands and opening again. The bull catcher and trailer bounced slowly over the dried mud and through shallow gullies.

Time stretched as we progressed farther from the known world. As Miles picked his way along, I wondered what it would mean to surrender to the spiral of endless time and space in the outback. Would it lead to some core of intimate relation to this place? A threshold, beyond which insights into the depths of humanity and the nonhuman world were attainable?

"If we get stuck here, no one will know where to find us," Miles said.

I smiled. "Have to bring the chopper out."

Miles smiled back, embarrassed at the thought. Mud clung

to the front mesh, to the roll bars, and to the old tires strapped on the front. To this day I am not sure if he ever told the rest of the crew about this episode, but all of them had been stuck before. The muddy swamps and salt arms sucked vehicles in with vehemence. During the wet season the entire country turned into a shallow sea, and living through one of them was enough to give anyone plenty of practice negotiating mud.

We were given all the tools that were necessary for each circumstance here, even if it meant having only two legs to walk several hours. Perhaps, I thought, we needed to be delayed a little in order to give time for other events to unfold. Learning faith in spontaneity, developing sea legs through minor adversity: these were the essential first lessons.

Miles didn't share my sentiments. He was more than happy to reach the dirt road, to leave the teacher behind, and be driving the muddy bull catcher back toward the station with certainty. That evening we saddled up to walk the weaners back to the yards for the night, and I took the tail, singing while the sea wind blew dust away and shadows slanted.

The Killer

WADE MET US AT THE YARDS in the small ute. There were two kids with him: his five-year-old son, Wyatt, and another of Claire's grandsons, Tommy, who was around eight years old.

"Do that killer now?" he asked quietly.

I was tired, but I climbed into the back of Wade's ute anyway and sat down between empty eskies. One of the younger boys climbed into the back with me, and Miles took his place on the passenger seat. We circled completely back to the yards before we found the mob of older cattle, drafted off for the next road train, and Wade stopped the ute. I guessed at the one they'd selected, an old black cow separated from the mob.

Choosing who will live and who will die happens quickly and easily on the station. This cow would be the sacrificial beast to feed the crews for a week or two, and then they would choose another. Wade loaded a bullet into the chamber of a small rifle and got out of the ute to lean on the hood, tilt his hat back, and aim. The boys plugged their ears and squeezed their eyes closed. The old cow dropped simultaneously with the sound of the shot.

Miles took the knife, crossed the grass to the fallen animal, and kneeled next to her warm neck. He grabbed a handful of the loose dewlap skin next to the brisket and sliced it off, leaving a white circle of the inner fat. He then shoved the knife in to the hilt and sliced the aorta to bleed the cow and keep the meat clean. Hot blood poured out across her neck and foreleg. I swung a chain down from the truck, and Miles helped to loop it over the back leg of the cow—still kicking from the random firing of nerves—then wrapped it around the trailer hitch. Wade gunned the ute and dragged the warm beast out from between the trees and termite hills, leaving a trail of crushed and bloody spear grass. He stopped when we reached a small clearing.

The men brought out their knife pouches, Miles standing to one side in his shorts and hiking boots, a hand-rolled cigarette in his mouth. Miles slashed his knife across his steel a few times and tucked the blue-handled steel into his belt. He leaned over the beast's side to make a lengthwise slit along the ribs, through the skin from the flank to the throat and down both legs, and then he and Wade grabbed a corner of the hide to pull the skin back and expose the top side. They made small swipes with their knife blades between the thin fat layer of the body and the tough inner white of the hide. The skin rolled back heavily and sagged in thick folds. They freed the skin completely, exposing the naked meat to the sky. Wind flecked it with dried grass. Miles worked bent over the cow's shoulder, cutting thin connective tissue to free bundles of muscle and tendon, slicing down along the shoulder blade with efficient strokes to pull off the meat in huge chunks of muscle and fascia. He handed smaller pieces to Tommy, who held the meat in front of him, trying to keep it clean as he lifted it over the side of the ute.

Miles grasped the front leg. "Tommy, here, you want to hold this?"

The young boy gripped the bloodstained leg with both hands as Miles set to work along the muscle lines and beneath the shoulder blade to free the leg from the joint.

Wade started on the hind end, deftly running the long blade through the flesh to pull off the rump roast and knuckle meat, then worked down to the bone of the back leg. He hefted the leg and sliced through the hip to separate it from the animal, then set it—a massive piece of meat with bones exposed and hoof attached—on the back of the truck to finish boning out.

They worked toward the center, carrying pieces to the truck and laying them on the bloody tarp. The pungence of blood and warm gut cavity wrapped me in its cloak. Wade took an ax to the top and bottom of the rib cage; he sliced between the ribs a couple at a time and bent them backward until they snapped free.

Wyatt begged, "Dad, Dad, can I have that one? Dad! Can I carry that one?"

Wade handed him the bloody section of white and red rib bones. Wyatt gripped the greasy fat-and-bone rail in both hands and hauled it to the tailgate, reaching up above eye level to set it on the edge of the tarp.

Taking the steel to sharpen his knife again, Wade finished the knuckle and silverside roasts from the hind leg and hip. Miles cut out the heart and liver and told me where to cut into the fat for the sweet meat. We rolled the cow to butcher the other side.

Wade said, "Looks like she's going to have a poddy calf."

Wyatt asked, "Dad, where is the poddy calf?"

"Inside her belly."

"I want to see the poddy calf. Can it come out?"

"It's dead."

"Why is it dead?"

"Because we killed the mom."

"I want to see the poddy calf."

After the cow had been butchered and the large roasts filled the eskies on the back of the ute, Miles said, "Wyatt, look here."

He sliced the placenta and the small calf slipped free. Wyatt scrunched up his nose and stepped back. I watched his expression. He wiped his little hands on his pants and turned away. Miles just rolled a cigarette, globules of fat still clinging to his hands, then collected the knives and slid them back into the case.

Late sun leaned shadows longer and longer, until they blended into darkness. Within an hour, the two men had reduced the old black cow to a pile of bone, gut cavity, and head, and left the carcass in the grass for the throngs of fork-tailed kites that descended above us and the dingoes that would come in the stealth of the night to finish.

The station didn't have a cold room, so the meat would hang overnight in a screened meathouse and be cut up in the morning. Claire came out in a skirt and sandals, carrying a plastic bin of salt to rub into the meat. The roasts would soak in salt and their own brine until she pulled out chunks to boil for cold meat. She hauled the dark jiggling liver into the kitchen in a large flat pan.

Angus ambled over, limping, with a cigarette and beer. With one hand, he reached over the side of the truck to the unfolded tarp, picked up one of the dirty hooks, and jabbed it through a slab of meat. He followed the procession into the meathouse, Wade and Miles carrying hooked pieces to hang on the rail to tenderize until they killed another animal. Miles took half the animal back to the mustering camp and hung it on a chain for the crew to hack off pieces as they needed them.

We would all eat, be nourished by that animal that was made mostly of grass and sky and salty air. She was plentiful enough, despite her age and bony scrub existence, to feed everyone on that station for a fortnight.

The Mail Plane

ONCE A WEEK, ON FRIDAYS, the mail plane came from Cairns. It always made a wide circle to the far end of the airstrip, the whine of its engine fading as it arced and disappeared behind the trees to descend. Hearing the drone of the engines, we would stop and look up to see the small plane circle, then come to a stop near the house. This small vehicle linked Stilwater to the rest of the world with its thin track across the blue, a line to places where the world operated as we all thought it should. Angus and I drove out to meet it.

The pilot climbed down from the seat wearing a uniform of white and black shorts, a short-sleeved shirt, and black leather pull-on boots. He nodded and opened the rear door. The small craft was crammed with bags and parcels for all the stations across the peninsula. The pilot pulled out the boxes marked "Stilwater Station." Machine parts, cattle vaccines and tags, packages for the ringers, and a canvas bag of letters. The plane was always a source of relief and frustration; Angus surveyed what had and hadn't come, trying to keep the operation in sync with the global network of supply and demand.

"I think that's it," the pilot said. "Do you want some papers?" He pulled a few newspapers from a plastic-wrapped stack and handed them to Angus. The *Cairns Post* and *Atherton Tablelander* both featured the local births, deaths, and rodeos, but contained only small paragraphs of national and international news. I always found this disappointing, since the single television was invariably set to horse races and cricket matches, and the computer with Internet access in Claire's office was mostly off-limits to the crew.

"Thanks. See you next week." With a small wave, he climbed back across the wing into the cockpit, started the engine, turned the plane back to the airstrip, and severed our ties once again. The plane picked up speed down the dirt strip, roaring through the quiet morning, and pulled into the air.

Angus and I drove around to the shed where Mike, the mechanic, was servicing one of the Toyotas. He came over to sort through the boxes and pick out any that might contain needed parts. He was expecting parts for the grader, but they had missed the plane and would show up in a week. Then Angus drove back to the house, where we unloaded the rest of the boxes and the mail and hauled them up to the kitchen for Claire to sort—making stacks of letters and boxes—when she had a few minutes free.

Day Off

CORELLAS ROSE INTO THE AIR in a screaming flock and descended on the tea trees, overwhelming the morning with their screeches. Wyatt came out on the porch in shorts and little cow-boy boots. It was Saturday, and we had the day off. The muster-ing crew had gone fishing. Angus sat in his chair by the table on the veranda, snapping peanuts from their shells, his bare feet tucked under him. He had worked at Stilwater thirty years earlier as a contract musterer, he said, and was back again as the manager. The little fox terrier, Frankie, strutted around the kitchen and the veranda and perked up his ears only when Angus whispered, "Wallaby, there's a wallaby." Then Frankie snarled, showing his teeth and sticking his short tail straight up in the air. Angus usually took the dog with him in the truck, and the windshield on the passenger side had a smattering of nose prints from Frankie's wallaby watch. Angus swept his pile of peanut shells back into the plastic grocery sack.

Ross, the bore man, came back from the crab-checking op-eration and brought his tin cup full of coffee out to the veranda. He said of the corellas, "They have a million square kilometers of country, and they have to camp right here."

"They only pick on certain trees—that tea tree by the saddle shed, they don't worry about it."

The two men communicated in a checkers game of com-ments handed out every once in a while, seemingly after long thought.

"Nearly killed those other trees."

"Picked all the insulation off the power lines."

Corellas used the branches to sharpen their beaks, stripping them clean of bark and leaves in the process. Thousands de-scended at a time, loud and unnerving, making it look as if the bare tea trees had burst into sudden copious blossoms. Wyatt cruised through flocks of them on the ground on his minia-ture four-wheeler, disturbing them into agitated flight just to feel the flurry of wings and hear them screech. They lived in those trees because the station existed and they had someone to bother, perhaps, or maybe they had been there long before the station moved in, and stripped clean the trees by way of objection. Occasionally someone would take a shotgun to scare them away from the trees around the house, collecting the dead birds and carrying them out to the bush. Otherwise, they waited in the trees at the edge of the compound, hassling and being hassled and screeching an alarm to the rest of the world, a warning of the way things were.

A new plane made a half-circle and descended onto the runway, engines roaring over the clouds of squawking corellas in the gum trees. A pilot who worked exclusively for Sutherland Corporation, Mitchell, had flown in to give a trucker a ride back to town after he delivered the huge road train that was to stay at Stilwater. Sutherland Corporation had dedicated the monstrous vehicle to us and found someone in Melbourne who wanted a vacation to drive the thing. Alan, the temporary driver who thought he was on vacation, was going to haul cattle from the yards at the north end of the property to the house yards, where they could be loaded onto other road trains for the long transport south. Alan would arrive by the mail plane in the coming weeks.

Clouds dulled the morning light.

"How you going?" Mitchell asked.

Angus grumbled, "Yeah." And then, "Good flight?"

"Yeah," the pilot nodded. "Not so cold this morning."

Angus limped into the kitchen to turn on the teapot.

The three men smoked and talked about the impending operation of baiting dingoes, scattering poisoned meat to kill as many as possible. I watched the peewee birds dive-bombing a new hatch of large butterflies.

Mitchell commented, "Find someone with a strong stomach for that, eh?"

Ross said, "Rotten horsemeat. You feel every bump of the plane sitting in the back there, and you can't see the horizon, tossing that meat out."

Angus waited in the silence that punctuated the conversation, then added, "They reckon they'll use that 1080. You know it come from the sap of coolibah trees?" Sodium fluoroacetate, or 1080, was a poison approved by the government to control the population of wild pigs in the region.

A long quiet spell followed in which more butterflies lost the fight against the birds.

I asked, "What keeps raptors from eating the poison?"

"It don't affect 'em; different nervous system or something. Had a fellow with some chooks right next to where they were fixing the bait, an' he threw a piece of poisoned meat in with the chooks. He said if the chooks died he'd replace the whole lot, but it didn't affect 'em," Angus retorted.

Mitchell said, "Can't wait for the wet season to start. Do a bit more flying then."

Ross said, "Reckon it might come early this year. Already clouding up."

Across the lawn, Wyatt picked up his puppy and placed him on the back of his miniature green four-wheeler, using one hand to steer and one hand to hold the spotted dog. Peewees swooped in front of the veranda, in and out of the drifting conversation about the wet season and flooding.

"My father was here in seventy-four," Angus said. "He said it was a sea of water, all the properties around here. Cattle just bobbed out to sea. Some of 'em survived up on the sand ridges. They had a bunch of heifers on the coast that floated away. Couldn't get in or out for months."

Ross offered a story in return. "Was on a station near Cloncurry. They were grazing sheep in the channels, trying to get the last bit of grass before they moved 'em to the higher paddocks."

He paused in contemplation. "First it rained a nice eight centimeters. We thought it was lovely, creeks flowing a little. Then a neighbor called, and it'd rained twenty-three centimeters on him.

By then it was too wet for us to move the sheep. Floods came and killed a thousand of those sheep; they were all heavy with twelve months of wool. Was a sad muster, sheep all strung up high in the trees, smell of rotten meat. And the live ones wouldn't leave their dead friends. Run about six thousand head of sheep then. Other stations that mostly run cattle didn't suffer so bad."

Ash fell from a cigarette supported on the edge of a stained ceramic ashtray on the table.

"That flood ran twenty-eight kilometers wide. We used to mark the water level on a tree just above the channel. We made three ax marks that summer, top one a good two meters off flat ground." Ross looked off into the blue.

Angus stubbed out his cigarette and said, "Caretaker lived in the house here had a boat to paddle across to the kitchen. It wasn't the depth of the water, only a meter or so, but what was in it, snakes and crocodiles."

He added after a minute, "Used to be a twelve-footer in the swamp right there. See him stretched out on the bank in the sun."

Mitchell lit another cigarette, carefully placing the pack back in the top pocket of his shirt, creases from the ironing still visible. He said, "You see some big ones flying over the rivers here. You have them salties too?"

"Big salties. They caught one on the road the other day, young contractors. Had him by the tail."

Ivan had told me about grabbing a crocodile on a road nowhere near water, and how the croc spun around and almost took some flesh off his rear end.

I leaned back, alone amid their company, and tried to adopt the same laconic air and patience. They were the counterpart to the hectic chase and chaos of the station, holding it in balance with their slow thoughts and periodic conversation.

Claire joined us from the kitchen, her short sandy hair swept back, traces of flour on her skirt where she had brushed her hands during baking. She did not speak much in the company of so many men, but she carried the resolute and thoughtful air of a station matron.

Mike, the mechanic, came up onto the veranda later. He wore a long-sleeved shirt with the sleeves rolled up, torn jeans, and heavy work boots. He still had grease stains from the grader on his pants. The trucker who had brought the road train up the night before came across the veranda and Mitchell walked with him back toward the plane. Soon the engine of the 206 Cessna started, the propellers whined, and it took off down the runway.

Ivan came to knock on my door in the afternoon: did I want to come tail the weaners in, or no? I retrieved my boots and took the four-wheeler out with Miles and Ivan on a bumpy ride behind five hundred slow-walking calves. The ringers spun rooster tails with their motorbikes and rode up on their back tires. The calves set a steady pace and took hours to make it the few miles down the lane to the yards.

Afterward I went with them to the coast, crammed in Miles' orange bull catcher between Miles and Ivan, with Miles' dog on my lap. Our route did not always follow the track because, without brakes, Miles hit the sandy corners too fast and decided to just go straight. Heat blew back from the manifold and sand spun up from the tires.

The rest of the mustering crew was still at the salt arm, some of them fishing, some pulling in the motorboat through knee-deep mud after checking the crab pots. I slipped off down the beach, sand and shells under my toes, and did cartwheels. I didn't see any crocodiles or the tracks where they slid into the water from the sand. Ivan caught up with me to try a few mangled cartwheels. He made Miles stop on the way back, though the catcher didn't have any brakes, and hopped out in the sand to pick me a bunch of tea tree blossoms.

I wondered if it was an offer of romance or friendship or reconciliation, and kept them in a vase in my private refuge overlooking the lagoon. They bloomed for a long while and

then withered, dropping petals onto the lip of the sink and offering something delicate to the grit of the days.

Bull Catching

WE ATTEMPTED TO MAKE AN ORDERED WORLD on that far reach
of land, and each time solitude threatened to overcome us, one
or another of the crew would say that we really should go get
some of those cleanskin bulls, the ones gone feral. It was almost
as if the monotonous work of fencing or truck repair or putting
out lick for the cattle made the wildness of the place less tangible, and so we had to go in pursuit to tame it.

Numerous cleanskin bulls—those not yet branded—ran on
the station, some of them up to ten years old, with massive shoulders and big horns. In Australian stockman tradition, ringers
pulled bulls over by the tail or bumped into them with a vehicle to
tip them off balance. After the animal tumbled, the rider leaped
off his horse or out of the vehicle to wrestle the bull and tie his
hind legs together with a bull strap, or tie him to a tree. The tips of
the horns would be sawed off, the beast castrated if it was deemed
appropriate, and branded. Then he was released back to the mob
or collected with a trailer and hauled back to the yards. Most bulls
suffered the latter. I wondered why none of the saddles we rode
on had horns on them—roping seemed much more effective and
less dangerous—and I wasn't impressed by the ease with which
the ringers dodged the mad beasts.

Most ringers used bull-catching vehicles—old Land Cruisers
or Jeeps with the tops cut off, roll bars welded on, and tires
wired to the front for a little padding. They roared their welded-
up vehicles through the trees until they came close enough to
bump the animal. There was a knack to catching bulls, and it
required a bit of adrenaline and stupidity as well. Many ringers
lived for the few moments of a bull chase.

I helped with the smashing and snaring and tumbling and tying of those massive animals, until I lost count in the madness. I didn't ever tip one myself, but I was close enough to feel my heart throbbing, the sweat of nerves as I wrapped my hands around the leather straps and pulled the legs of the bulls to be tied. I came close enough to get covered in their snot, to feel the daggers of their eyes and dodge their huge horns.

The ringers gave them little room to go peacefully; why go peacefully when you could cover the same distance fueled by a rush? That was the thinking of the younger, male members of the crew. The bosses didn't have much say in it, and they weren't opposed to a little more stirring of the dust and days anyway. After all, the place needed to keep its reputation.

Stilwater had an uncommon number of cleanskin bulls left over from the years of minimal management. One day Wade said he'd seen two of them feeding at the lick tubs in Talbot Paddock, so Dustin and I took the ute and backed it up to a heavy trailer. A sheet of metal on the back functioned as a sliding ramp to haul the bulls in. We drove past the mustering camp, where Tanner and Ivan were trying to start Tanner's bull catcher, and Cole started his monster four-wheeler which was modified with tires wired to the front roll bars and a platform on back.

Dustin called to them, "Wade said we'd just go up ahead of you and see if we find those bulls at the tubs."

"Right-o. What channel you on, mate?"

"Ten?"

Dustin reached up to turn the dial of the two-way radio. He was brave enough to join in any bull venture, but he would have been plowed over altogether had he joined the mustering crew; they were not a gentle lot.

We waited in the ute while the crew fastened bull straps and smashed and tinkered with their temperamental vehicles. Troy, the cook, decided to climb in with us just for the ride. He limped over, his left arm dangling at his side. I stepped out so that he could be the copilot, and he slid into the front seat, opposite Dustin. Young Tommy and I climbed into the back of the ute and sat between the crates of plastic pipe fittings and tool boxes. None of us had much to do but go along for the ride, find a few bulls, help haul them up onto the trailer, and be the audience. Reckless acts of foolish bravery are always better with an audience.

We drove for twenty minutes, the winter sun warm and glaring off the white dust on the road ahead. As we passed a cleanskin bull, a big black and gray beast four or five years old with smooth ears, Dustin gave its position to Cole, Tanner, and Ivan over the two-way. Dustin drove the ute and long trailer around the side of a swamp, circling the muddy hollow, and a mob of red, black, and gray cattle filtered away ahead of us. Dustin pointed through the window. "There's another. That yellow brindle one."

The bull moved through the cattle, threading behind trees.

Dustin picked up the two-way. "You copy there, Tanner?"

We waited in the shade of the trees, watching the cattle.

He repeated, "You copy there, Tanner?"

Finally the answer came back. "Yeah mate."

"Where're you?"

Tanner's voice cracked back. "Just got this other bull tied up here."

"Yeah good. We got another one here."

"Good, yeah, where're you?"

Dustin gave him directions over the radio, and pretty soon we could hear the groan of engines through the trees.

Troy mumbled, "They could put a muffler on that thing."

Tanner's vehicle had a loud roaring engine that prevented a subtle approach. We saw dust through the trees, and then the vehicles emerged.

Dustin said over the two-way, "Come around the back side of the swamp there."

Then, to us he said, "Oh, Cole's spotted him."

Cole had turned across the upper end of the swamp. His

four-wheeler was in high gear, churning up dust as he raced across the flat toward the bull. With his bright purple shirt, black hat, and wraparound sunglasses, he cut a flashy figure in the swamp. Tanner and Ivan, in Tanner's beat-up white bull catcher, turned out onto the flat in a grind of gears and growling cylinders. Riding in the open seat with dogs tied up on the back, they flew past us, splattering dried swamp mud into the mob of agitated cattle. Cole cut the bull out of the mob so he could get at him easier, and chased him in big dusty circles on the flat and around through the trees. Within two laps, Cole closed in enough to bump the bull with the front of the four-wheeler, the wired-on tires cushioning the impact. The beast crumpled in a heap.

Cole leaped off and jumped onto the bull's neck, pulling up one of his forelegs in a lock until Tanner and Ivan roared up and jumped out to help. The bull lay still. Each of the ringers had several leather and nylon belts, a few inches wide and long enough to wrap around the bull's back legs twice and buckle. The four of them tied his back legs and looped a head rope around his horns.

To collect the sweaty beast, Dustin backed the trailer up to the yellow mound of him and Tanner pulled the bull catcher alongside, facing the trailer. Cole tied a long rope to the bull's head rope, passed the other end around the front of the trailer, and looped it to the roll bars on the bull catcher.

This was the moment of glory, when they could be stars in their own movie. They acted out the parts carefully, stuntmen and heroes, having mastered the dangerous sweaty beast that lay bound at their feet. Tanner backed the bull catcher up slowly, the rope tightening and the bull sliding toward the trailer. They tied his head to the side, his eyes bulging, his nose blowing snot, and then folded up the ramps.

Wade drove up in the Trooper. "There's a couple other mickies in this mob, if you want to get them."

Cole just nodded.

Ivan gave his sudden laugh and said, "Yeah!"

Tanner had to yell at his dogs because they'd stepped on the battery in the back of the truck, disconnecting the cables. He untied a fuel can and poured fuel into a plastic tank that straddled the roll bars behind the seat. The vehicle needed several repairs, including new brakes and a fuel lift pump. He offered me a ride, and I climbed in beside Ivan. We drove off through lean-trunked bloodwood, and I kept one foot braced against the metal side panel.

Ivan said, "Watch your hand holding on to the side bar, there." He held up his hand to show me a big scab.

Cole must have seen the bull, because he turned the four-wheeler ahead of us and scattered the mob. Another young brindle bull separated from the rest and took off through the swamp, splashing the ankle-deep water. Tanner turned, and as soon as the bull left the swamp for higher ground, he churned through the gears and put the bumper on his tail. I gripped a metal handlebar and prayed that we wouldn't tip over and be pulverized in the savanna soil.

We roared through the trees, smashing smaller ones and making quick turns to avoid the ones that wouldn't break. The bull cut back and forth and made a dash into thicker timber. Heat from the engine flew back into my face, and branches crashed on top of us, filling the cab with leaves and sticks.

"He's heading for the fence line!" Ivan yelled above the engine noise.

Tanner drove the vehicle to the open graded section along the fence, then paralleled the bull for twenty yards before turning him back into a clearing. He gunned the engine. A quick bump, and the bull toppled in front of us. Ivan jumped out, wrapped a belt twice around his back legs, and buckled it. My heart thudded in my ears and my legs felt shaky, but the ringers showed no signs of stress or worry, just exhilaration from the chase. The dogs, tied to keep from being flung out during the chase, jumped up on the battery again and the truck died. I

pulled a few branches out of my hair and climbed down, thankful that we were all alive, including the bull.

"Good fun, eh?" Ivan's dirty baseball cap was a little skewed.

Tanner looked like Wyatt Earp with his drooping mustache and big hat. He tried to start the bull catcher again, standing beside it and turning the key with one hand while he pressed on the gas pedal with the other. The engine cranked but didn't turn over. Ivan stood up from the bull and walked over to the vehicle to pop the hood. They peered inside.

"I think she's flooded."

"We'll just wait a few minutes."

Ivan took a jug of water from the back and poured it over the radiator. Steam fizzled and popped and coated them both in hot water. The dogs on the back strained against their chains, and Tanner tied one of them to the bars a little farther away from the battery.

Dustin pulled up with the trailer, and when they had the bull catcher started again, they dragged the newest victim onto the back beside the first. They tipped, tied, and loaded another bull, and the three bulls on their bellies filled the flat bed of the trailer. Dustin and Troy took them back to the yards to unload.

Tanner and Ivan climbed back into the bull catcher with me seated between them and drove to where Cole had another bull tied to a tree. He was a black monster, snorting and slashed on the side where he had hit the ground. He had worn a track around the trunk. Tanner pulled up under the thin, scraggly shade of a gutta-percha on the edge of the dry salt pan, and Ivan stepped over the roll bars and sat down in the coarse grass. He leaned back against the wheel, rolled a cigarette.

"Reckon they'll be a while."

Tanner said, "We could rope the back legs and get him stretched out."

I heeled the bull the way I used to catch calves on the ranches in Arizona, just walking up behind him and taking one shot with the rope to catch both back heels. We looped the rope around the roll bars, and Ivan pulled hard on his tail to tip him onto his side. When Dustin and Troy returned, they loaded the last bull and took him back to the yards.

~~

The four mad bulls spent the next few nights in a pen in the yards, eating huge round bales of Flinders-grass hay and charging anyone who taunted them.

Another bull joined them the next day, one who had been hanging around the house and ended up grazing on the airstrip when the owners flew in for a brief visit. The bull gave the pilot a little rush—he weighed almost as much as the plane—and Angus ordered him removed.

Wade and I drove down the airstrip toward the yellow bull. As we cruised the long runway, Wade said, "Just put out your arm, mate." He had his free arm stretched out the open window, fingers spread, and I realized he meant we might lift off in the old ute and take to the sky. I started laughing, but then the bull saw us and started a head-down charge. He was serious. We had put him out of the home paddock twice already, and he wasn't excited about a third round.

Wade backed up so that the bull wouldn't do any serious damage to the hood or tires. Dustin rode behind in the four-wheeler, but neither of them could coax the one-ton bull any closer to the yards without getting pulverized by the full mass of muscle and horn. Wade went back for Randall, the new fence man, and a pack of his dogs.

I drove Wade's wife, Cindy, her infant daughter, and a carload of the station kids so they could watch and video the ordeal. This was their chance to see up close the danger that might be in their future, while staying protected safely behind the sheet metal and thin panes of glass in the truck. Bulls represented the edge of the civilized world here, domesticated animals turned feral by over-exposure to the bush. In the taming, the stockmen saved them-selves from the same fate, proving they were different.

Wade, Dustin, and Randall roped the bull to the little ute, pulled him down, and tied him up. Wade lifted the bull with the hook on the bucket of the huge tractor, the bull's eyes bulging as he hung upside down by his strapped hocks before they lowered him onto the back of Randall's flatbed. Then they deposited him, snorting, into the yards with the other bulls.

I was assigned to feed the bulls, to coo and try to coax them into believing they were now civilized without getting myself plastered to the rails. They weren't to be convinced, those bulls, but judging from their heroic stunts, none of the other members of the crew really felt that being civilized was worth much anyway.

Dusk

I HAD NEVER SEEN THE MOON SO BIG, a dome above the coastal plain glowing pale pink, the color of ice blushing in low sun, a rose quartz ball on a blue robe, and the thin line of bloodwood trees could not hold it down. Brolgas cried, harsh and stuttering, and flew toward other lowlands. The wind died for the night. The sun had left only tatters of cloud, and gray sashes across the moon made a halo and then a wave on which it rode, higher and higher, until it freed itself altogether, and I turned and walked the long dusty track in the growing dusk, toward the distant lights of the house.

Advice

STEPHEN CRAYE WOULD INTERMITTENTLY arrive and then disappear from Stilwater. One evening the stars of the Southern Cross hung over the lagoon when he came over to have a yarn. We sat in the dark while he smoked, his feet propped up on the rail. Gene and his son Sean Sutherland had met him that day at another one of their stations, and he had toured the property with them before driving on alone to Stilwater. There was never any stress with them, he said, good people to be around. Gene just laid down how the decisions would go.

I'd met Gene only once, when he came into the kitchen during a short stay at the station. He was a portly gentleman who wore a well-tailored suit even in the heat and dust of the station. He greeted me with courteous consideration. The peripheries of our worlds had crossed for this brief exchange, both of us respectful and light, though I would never know the operations as they existed in his mind, what it meant to own the largest livestock and beef operation on the continent, and he would never get a glimpse into the dusty world I called my own.

Another time I went out for a run as darkness descended and saw Stephen's truck parked at the compound after one of his absences. I took a cold shower when I returned and then headed over to the blue house beside the fig tree, where he sat in the dusk. He didn't eat dinner with the people at Stilwater, preferring instead to sit on the high porch with a beer, looking out through the woven branches of the old fig tree. A white corella huddled injured at its roots, carrying perhaps a piece of lead shot from a shotgun. Stephen's presence seemed to placate the night, the old fig, and the small white bird into stillness.

He spoke through the dark. "How you going?"

I smiled and pulled up a chair on the high veranda. "Yeah, good."

The night hushed except for a few wallabies out beyond the fence. A fistful of Australian stars slipped through the fig branches.

"I caught a few barra today." Stephen gave a sly smile and held his hands a couple of feet apart, a beer in one of them, to show me the length of the fish.

"Where?" I asked, remembering the fishing trip near Spider's Camp.

"In the salt arm. I took a long walk down along the coast,

and guess what I saw?" He paused. "A sandbar full of crocodiles, all sunning themselves just out of the water."

He would be leaving soon, he said, to live alone at a new property of the Sutherlands called Ibis Downs. He would be the caretaker there until they could call up a mustering crew and try to turn another station into a profitable operation. He was looking forward to the isolation, living on the banks of a wide river for months at a time. Ibis Downs lay farther inland and to the south. He said he would be back intermittently to check on us.

"You'd better be careful running after dark," he said. "I've seen enough tracks across that road in the mornings." He traced a sinuous pattern in the air.

I didn't speak. I was reluctant to give up my twilight runs, when the horizon burned long and red, moon waxing, stars coming out, wallabies' tails thumping as they bounded away. Just the time alone with my blood moving.

I thought I might have to beg the indulgence of the snake gods. Three of the deadliest snake species in the world haunted that corner of the continent: taipans, death adders, and king browns—not dangers to consider lightly. I had seen four brown snakes killed in as many days on the station compound, slender creatures with no obvious markings that slithered across the lawn and up to the porch. Taipans, usually the most aggressive, looked similar to the other species but could be distinguished by their length, a more rounded head, and scale counts. I had seen a taipan only once, decapitated when it tried to strike the radiator of the truck. Stephen let the subject rest and instead told me where to find a sea eagle nest, and not to walk too close to the shore because of the crocodile prints he'd seen in the sand.

After a while, I bid him good night and crossed the dark lawn. Most people carried flashlights just to cross the lawn at night, but I moved deftly and defiantly, feet crunching the fallen mango leaves. Crickets and frogs screeched together, and the generator hummed through the darkness. Inside the kitchen,

Dustin and Angus sat on two of the couches around the television, white feet bare on the floor, beers in hand, watching a cricket game. Frankie commanded the third couch. Claire set a pan of corned beef and another of potatoes on the long table and called that tea was ready.

After Stephen left the station, I shortened my runs in the dusk but did not cease them altogether. I did not walk too close to the shoreline, though, and I never saw the saltwater crocodiles of the coast.

Reflections

A CROWD OF PELICANS DRIFTED on the water, their heavy necks curled back to balance massive fish-stabbing beaks. They flapped black and white wings above the runway of the lagoon, cruised just above its surface until they found another swirling school of fish. Elegance emerged at the rugged and torn edges of this place, and I wondered at my own tenuous place in it all: a strange flower on a briny lagoon, belonging to a continent and culture far away, trying to blend in, become part of, be taken over by the coastal wind and tattered tapestry of work and wilderness.

The station has a pattern that exists in the months beyond the mustering, one I would only glimpse. Ross and sometimes Angus made frequent water runs. These rambles gave them a familiarity with the country and how it changed through the seasons. True intimacy with the cattle and landscape develops only after months of building and repairing fences, grading roads, checking water, watching as the land changes through the year, blushing an intense brilliant green after the monsoon rains and then drying. Water holes fill with rain and flood and remain full well into the winter, until months without rain turn many animals to the man-made troughs filled by the bores.

A life dependent on the land requires a visceral knowledge of place. To live in a place is to witness and discern the details, adjusting management to the variations that occur within the predictable, understanding the land and its cycles more deeply each year. Layers of experience form a lens through which the place slowly reveals itself. The first layer of knowing might be recognition, but a deeper relationship comes with understanding how a place transforms over time. Seasons and weather, the phenology of growth, migration, feeding, and breeding—the environment revises itself over the years. People adapt to the character of the landscape just as flora and fauna have adapted for millennia, becoming both resistant and resilient, living within the geography of its dynamics. Who is to say one doesn't become the place after a while, drinking water from the rain cistern, absorbing color from the sun, living under a thousand sunrises and sunsets and the fierce stars of the southern hemisphere?

Isolation

THE COAST OF THE AUSTRALIAN CONTINENT scribes a meandering line that has been more or less the same for about the last ten thousand years. The supercontinent that it was a part of began its rifting in the distant past. The cracks that appeared initially failed to split the landmass, but eventually succeeded—one ocean closed, others opened, and the Laurasia landmass holding North America in its grip rotated away from the block, followed later by other continents that parted and floated out. Gondwana, a large resistant mass containing the future continents of Africa, South America, India, Australia, and Antarctica, began its disintegration during the Jurassic period, around one hundred and eighty million years ago. Madagascar and India pulled away to the north and then split apart, Madagascar moving over to weld the African plate. New Zealand parted, drifting into the Pacific.

Only then, between thirty-five and forty-five million years ago, did Australia release its cling on Antarctica and angle north, alone, an island continent that still maintains a course to the

northeast, gaining about two inches a year, colliding imperceptibly with eastern Asia.

The Australian continent includes New Guinea, but remains separated by oceanic crust from Indochina. The channel
has threatened to close at times, narrowing at one point to only
sixty miles in width, but never closing entirely, so that species
on the great island continent have remained mostly isolated—
save for those that could fly or found themselves afloat—
evolving undisturbed and bounded by water since the split from
Antarctica.

In its semi-isolation, Australia became a continent populated
with animals unlike others in the world, monotremes and marsupials among them. The monotremes—egg-laying mammals—
include the platypus and two genera of echidnas. The ubiquitous
mammalian marsupial births live young and carries them in a
pouch close to the body. Marsupials first appeared on the Laurasia
landmass, spreading and radiating into what is now North
America, South America, Antarctica, and finally into Australia.
A few hopped islands back toward China, almost reaching their
ancient cousins after a circumnavigation of continents.

A few marsupials inhabit other landmasses, but nowhere
have they found the evolutionary advantage they did in Australia.
They morphed and evolved to fill many of the niches that their
corresponding placental mammals filled in distant parts of the
world: the equivalent of mice, rats, moles, squirrels, wolves, and
lions. Wombats, bandicoots, bilbies, numbats, koalas, kangaroos, wallabies, and sugar gliders live in deserts, tropical forests, high mountains, and coastal savannas across Australia.
They have pouches, and the young cling to their inner skin
until they are old enough to bounce, scramble, climb, or sail
through the air on their own.

The living refugees of all kingdoms followed the same
patterns, settling in to the continent, developing unique adapta-
tions, radiating, migrating, and speciating into strange endem-
ics, many shared closely among Tasmania, Australia, and New

Guinea. A few new species made it in, wayward birds or those in transit on migratory routes. Seeds and spores of faraway lands dropped from the birds' wings. Insects blew in with dust storms. A few made it away, swept with broken-off pieces of bank in the cyclones, or lifted and carried on the winds. Weather shaped fungi, plants, and animals, as it did stone. Different soils formed. Forests changed or stayed the same while their counterparts on other continents transformed in other ways. Over millennia, the thrust of evolutionary desire emerged to fill hollow spaces in the landscape, and Australia became something altogether distinct.

The Crossing

THE FIRST PEOPLE ARRIVED BY CROSSING the narrow channel of sea from the islands of the Asian chain of Sunda to the landmass of Sahul, which included both Australia and Tasmania. No one is sure when, or why, or how the passage occurred, but it was perhaps during the time when the Timor Sea had receded significantly below its current level. The waters dropped around seventy thousand years ago, and did not rise again until the last ice age ended, ten thousand years ago. At some point during this period, humans crossed the channel and set up camp on the shores of the great island. They spread to every reach of the continent over two thousand generations, and, through their use of fire to stimulate grass growth and expose fauna for hunting, plant selection, and settlement patterns, they played a role in shaping the landscape, plants, animals, soil, and maybe even the weather. They survived in every region, with complex cosmologies and over two hundred and fifty language groups shared and divided among some four hundred distinct peoples. They domesticated no animals except for the dingo, the Australian dog that arrived on the continent from Asia around four thousand years ago. They did not practice agriculture, but rather an intricate and sophisticated system of hunting, gathering, and ecological ingenuity that fed the thriving peoples for longer than any other continuous culture on earth.

If you ask, there are many versions of this story—each true. Multiple truths may exist simultaneously, and none compromise the integrity of the others. Some say the people came from across the waters in a canoe, to walk across the country following the rain clouds. Others say that ancestral beings—called, among hundreds of identities, the Rainbow Snake, Lightning Brothers, and Cloud Being—traversed the earth's surface, creating its diverse topography and the first inhabitants, who were themselves part animal, part human, and part supernatural. In this version of the story, the world's formation doesn't necessarily take place in the past. Time moves in a rhythm of repeating patterns, incremental, linear and nonlinear, and the Dreamtime, the sacred era of creation, might not be a time at all, but layers overlapping, making beings from what we might think of as different eras accessible through intense ritual and ceremony. In this communion, the land and seasons and universe renew in each cycle within the rhythm, and each version of the story helps one or another of us maintain our center on this spinning earth.

Colonization

THE STORY GOES THAT EUROPEAN MARINERS first reached the shores in the early 1600s. Between this contact and 1770, when Captain James Cook mapped the eastern coastline in detail, some fifty-four ships from a number of nations touched the continent, many of them merchant ships from the Dutch East India Company. The Dutch explorer Abel Tasman first sailed the Gulf of Carpentaria coastline in 1644. He might have passed right along the shores of Stilwater, in fact, past Spider's Camp and the point where the river meets the sea.

The first Europeans to establish themselves in Australia

arrived in 1788 on the north shore of Botany Bay, near Sydney. Eleven ships containing over a thousand people sailed from Portsmouth, England, and they hoisted the British flag to proclaim a colony.

The colonization process did not transpire peacefully. Marks on the landscape of blood and brutality have stained it, in name and in memory. Captain Cook returned from his 1770 voyage with a contingent of natural historians, astronomers, and draftsmen to report to the British government on the magnificent opportunities in Australia, and to claim the continent for the king. Fifteen years later, the British authorities, in a move to develop a strategic position in the Pacific, and to dispose of a growing number of convicts they couldn't house, decided to establish a colony on the far-flung shores of the continent. They sent warships, storeships, and transports stocked with two years' worth of provisions, as well as all types of livestock, seeds, and seedlings, four companies of marines, and 759 prisoners—men and women, though the former outnumbered the latter three to one.

These early initiatives did not fare well. The country proved inhospitable and the prison colony presented its own challenges, but in the end, by its own terms, the experiment was successful. Fifty-five thousand convicts reached the harbors of New South Wales, the name of the Australian colony, and more reached the British establishments on the island later to be known as Tasmania. This is the story most of us have heard, at least its rumors or tendrils. But in reality, men and women of all classes and ranks and nationalities immigrated to Australia in order to test their skills and ingenuity, to seek refuge or renewal, to establish plots of farmland or push herds into the interior, to find freedom and folly, exploration and adventure, and to generate wealth from gold, opals, pearls, deserts, grasslands, and mountains.

This is the story: a contingent of colonizers reaches an unknown shore and pronounce it wilderness. In the naming, the land becomes wild, uninhabited, open, and the namers are free to claim ownership for a crown across the waters. If people exist there, they are pronounced savages and captured as slaves, slaughtered, or decimated with the deadly fevers of distant shores. In the naming of a wilderness, one denies that humans exist there, and that they shaped the very landscape one stands to gain. And so the Aboriginal culture, forty or sixty thousand years old, with its webs of intricate storylines and detailed environmental histories wrapped up in language and memory and practice, became part of the wilderness that would be colonized.

As a global society, we still make the same mistakes, designating reserves and national parks to preserve the "untouched wilderness," forgetting that the landscape has long been discovered and explored, shaped and reshaped, defined and redefined.

The explorations and conquests cut into a land woven into an ancient cosmology, a network of dreams and social hierarchies and ties, the interlocking knowledge held in the minds and bodies of its inhabitants. The paths of this place were understood and imprinted into the lyrics of a few hundred distinct tongues and dialects, and every living and nonliving and supernatural being traced and tracked through story, paintings, and song. The lure of discovery and exploitation of resources tore apart entire paradigms, ushering in a new vision and with it a struggle to establish it as the single view of the world.

The Aborigines suffered the incursions as the settlements spread and grew, resisting, retreating, and, in the end, enduring the onslaught of the offenders. They weathered the imposition of a different cosmology. They suffered the costs, as the land would suffer the costs, of a way of living devoid of the foresight and wisdom necessary to sustain such a culture for another forty thousand years.

In the mid-1860s, shortly after their government drew the line on a map between the states of Queensland and New South Wales, the Australians decided to create an outpost on the peninsula of Cape York in order to facilitate the Torres Strait pearling operations and the expansion of the settlements and stations associated with it. The magistrate of this outpost initiated an expedition in 1864 to bring cattle from the town of Rockhampton, farther to the south, to populate the peninsula. His sons and a small crew drove 250 cattle through the forests and mud and onslaught of Aboriginal attacks. They lost cattle to the mangrove swamps and crocodiles, and survived brush fires, starvation, and the onset of an early wet season. They also killed three men near the banks of the Powder River.

The same team of brothers had engaged in a bloody battle on a nearby river a few years before, killing several people. This was only one of many massacres and silent murders that haunt the region. Such atrocities included the slaughter of entire villages in a genocide sanctioned by those above, making the frontier a frontline of bloodshed. The brothers eventually arrived at the outpost, parting the waves of the gulf country behind them to open up colonization of the northern swath. Explorers, Torres Strait pearlers, sandalwood cutters, miners, and cattlemen followed, swarming across the farther reaches of the peninsula.

The landscape still holds the conflict in its thick coastal scrub. Tribes shifted away, individuals were abducted, and the harbor and prisons of the newly established stations filled with Aborigines. A mission established at a river's mouth tried its best to further civilize the wildness of the culture so feared by the colonizers. The mission offered food and a few medical services, and eased the genocide by instituting its own form of cultural usurpation. Who were these people, the ones who initially fought back, stalking, spearing the intruders and their large beasts, raiding the settlements, setting fires to the brush? Who were those who dispersed, died, and integrated into a world wholly foreign, transformed in the transition?

The imprinted braille of history held these stories—not obvious, not visual, distinguishable only by those willing to learn its language. Clashes continued even as I was there, the disparate universes of settler and settled colliding still, one changing the other, until lines blurred and new entities and identities emerged.

I wondered what it meant to be an Aborigine in these times. The Aboriginal communities I had seen did not seem to be in the greatest shape. According to the last census, Normanton's population of fourteen hundred includes twelve hundred Aborigines of a few different tribes. Most of the town's inhabitants live several to each house, parents, children, cousins, aunts, uncles, and grandparents in beds, on couches, and on the floor. A typical family has four to eight children. Because their population is small, the Australian government provides a monetary incentive for Aboriginal families to have several children. They also provide Aborigines with enough money that none of them has to work. Most of the kids struggle to make it through tenth grade, and very few leave to go to university. Those who do usually don't return, and, of the people who stay in town, many are alcoholics, and most are unemployed. A dole check comes from the government every Thursday and lasts through a drugged and drunken weekend, during which knife fights and brawls occur more often than not. I heard of husbands beating up wives and wives beating up husbands. I had seen situations all too similar on the Native Nations in Arizona, cultures lost in the confusion of a changing context.

The Aborigines remained a taboo subject among those living in Stilwater; a few of the crew and one of Angus and Claire's grandsons carried the older blood of the continent, but no one spoke of it. Stockmen and ringers bore the long history in their attitudes and sentiments, but it rarely surfaced, and they gave me few insights into the complexity of the narratives.

Mystery

THE PARTICULAR HISTORY OF STILWATER remained a mystery, hinted at only by a few gravestones in one of the far paddocks.

The ambiguous nature of time in that region had allowed the accounts to be diluted in the tide. The gravestones were fenced to keep them from the wild, which had long ago eaten the corpses from below and within anyway. Those buried there could have been a family, or perhaps they were stockmen of some kind, people with no home to return to in the end. They lay out beneath the gum trees. A hundred or two hundred years of European inhabitants had engaged with the cyclone coast and gulf savanna, and order had never prevailed, certainly not during our interval as witnesses. Perhaps at some point order would transgress farther, only to regress as the wild—perpetual, immortal, and alive through all of us—regained its ground and its sea.

After the conquest, history would repeat the pattern of experience on that remote station: the bloodshed and violence, a touch of compassion here and there, the long isolation and thrashing storms of the wet, the endurance through the dry, a series of lessons learned and forgotten. But in the end, order would always succumb to the spirit that was Stilwater.

No visitor would ever know the true stories; not many visitors lingered longer than a season or two, a year or two, a decade or two; they were too unsettled to learn the nature of that distant shoreline. They could leave anytime they wanted. Not many cared enough to learn and make that station the center of a world. Not many roots sought the structure and grain of sandy soil deep enough to keep themselves from flooding in or out. Instead, for most, Stilwater was a stop on their eventual migration to other places.

History gave all of us at Stilwater struggles to carry forward, wounds to assuage. It was unclear whether we were spiraling up or down, but we rode with courage, some our own, fought for and won, and some inherent in our genes from previous generations. We had the angst and desire to escape, daydreams and internal drives, an interplay of experiences and hopes overlaid by moments ahead and behind. We all had both the history of the country to contend with and our own stories, diverse and disparate.

One can't arrive at a place and not take on the history that has shaped it. The challenges at Stilwater were like the Dreamtime: past, present, and future all at once, often drawing in the unsuspecting like a whirlpool. We were all visitors for a short while. We engaged fully and changed the course of the stream, turning it in imperceptible ways, and its currents carried us deeper into ourselves. We wrote our own scripts, day by day, fulfilling the journeys, known and unknown, that lay like the cattle pads between the bloodwood, or following the courses, almost invisible, that rivulets took when it rained.

II

Perspective

LIFE ON THE STATION INCLUDED the houses and lawns, the workers' quarters, the mango trees that cut apart the stars, and the
flock of pelicans that landed on the lagoon. It also included the
people who emerged before dawn to drink coffee on the kitchen
veranda and returned after dark to eat again, along with the fire
lit under the hot water barrel, the wind at night off the coast, wallabies that hopped onto the lawn, the brolgas circling, and corellas that rushed past on their way to haunt the stripped tea trees.

After weeks without leaving that world, having absorbed
even the most minute details, I climbed into the small helicopter
with the pilot, Flynn Cooper, for a trip over to Whetstone Station
and back. It was my second helicopter ride and my first away
from Stilwater, and within a few minutes of lift-off, my vision
expanded and stretched, the houses and lawn and mango trees
turned miniature and disappeared in the expanse. From above,
the architecture of trees and plains and fences made sense in a
new way: fence lines were long threads that held taut across the
flats and through sand ridges, endless even from high above.
The country patterned and opened toward the broad blue abandoned sash of the Powder River.

Flynn nudged my shoulder and pointed out of the helicopter at the shallow blue water.

"Fish," he said over the radio.

He swooped in a quick, low circle over the river and the
barramundi leaped and slashed through the current, heading
upstream, water clouding around them. Wind tugged at my
shoulders and hair through the open side of the small helicopter.

Below, the water glowed like azurite. A crocodile slept on a sand-bar. The fish darted again, long and gray. White pillows of jelly-fish swayed in the current. We banked away from the river and prowled over the reds and golds of the savanna.

The GPS unit in the control panel registered our position, but Flynn knew these thousands of square aerial miles by memory. He told me stories of the wet season, how it rained for weeks on end, and the way you could see the line of fresh water six miles out in the ocean, where it pushed the salt water back.

I could see so far that I began to feel as if I might have another point of view, a vantage from which I could see how Stilwater tied into the net of other places, other people, into the rest of the world. My thoughts drifted to how the crew was beginning to mesh and change, becoming, like the place, unpredictable in both their amiability and their cruelty. The strange and isolated coastal stretch attracted strange and isolated individuals. I wanted to see from this vantage their past and present and future, just as I could see where the rivers came from and where they were bound.

But our errand was finished too soon, and we swept back over the small cluster of buildings and descended into the ruckus and reality of Stilwater, and my own more limited perspective.

After that flight, though, things were cast in greater relief. I began to see the ironies and inner conflicts of the crew, insights that emerged as time cleared the murky waters. Stilwater was like a mudflat with tracks written across it from every direction. Mud at low tide looks like a premeditated painting, with pockets of water and ripple marks, a crab, rivulets and channels, a fan of marsh grass, long-legged birds that might be terns leaving tracks crosswise with those of the white heron, clues to the functioning universe. But then the tide comes in and washes over the painting, and only the long-legged birds and the heron remain.

Ross Porter

ROSS PORTER, THE BORE MAN, drove his bore runs barefoot. He was a big man in his sixties, with short gray hair that stood up a little on the top of his head. He usually wore a long-sleeved green shirt; in the mornings the shirt was often streaked with a few creases left from a hasty hanging, while at dusk it was smeared with road-grader grease or rust. His work was defined; he was to trace every pipeline and set of waters on the whole place, repeating the pattern once he had finished, to make sure everything functioned and cattle didn't die of thirst. If metal pipes rusted or clogged, or dingoes chewed through water lines to make their own personal fountains, he fixed them. He drove his own ute, the back full of metal and plastic pipe fittings of all sizes, a shovel, pipe wrenches, a spare tire, fishing line, and more tools. He worked in the muck of leaking pipes barefoot, walked the hot sand barefoot, and used brute strength to push the shovel into the sucking mud.

He came once when Dustin and I got the little ute stuck.

Ross brought a chain, but ended up just pushing the ute out himself. He was bigger than Dustin and I put together, and even with the weighted load, he pushed the truck out of the sand without too much effort. He said he'd been bogged in exactly the same place, a small rise with spreading chinaberry trees.

Ross often brought me pawpaws from another abandoned fishing camp called Beck's Camp, simply because he knew I liked them. I could only guess where he was getting them, because he kept it a secret. He liked bearing gifts, bringing the small pile of soft green fruit to the table. I saw Beck's Camp a few times on lick runs, a mess of fuel barrels, old vehicles, refrigerators, and the remnants of structures on a blue bend in the Powder, just before it reached the Gulf. Mosquitoes clung to my arms every time I went there, and with the piles of abandoned appliances, the hot sand and dead weeds, I did not care to stay long. I did eventually see a pawpaw tree there, fallen. About that time the gifts of green fruit ceased.

Corrosion

WADE, DUSTIN, AND I SET TO WORK cleaning one of the sheds while the mustering crew was on vacation. Inside was a tangled rat's nest of old wire, spools of cable, sheets of punctured tin, metal bars, machine parts, wooden posts rotted and splintered, pickets, barbed wire tangled like fishing line, irreversibly caught and knotted. We sorted out what we thought might be useable— fencing equipment, angle iron, corrugated tin. We pulled pieces and hunks free, stacking and piling them onto pallets, where they could be lifted with the long tines of the tractor bucket. Dustin drove the tractor, transporting heaping pallets and piling the old dump truck high with waste.

I wasn't sure what they would do with it, or if the old dump truck would even start. They would likely dig a pit and bury the metal galaxy in sand. Floods would seek the rusted treasure and give the soil its fair share of heavy metals and a toxic plume from old batteries, leaking acid, motor oil, radiator fluid, tick poison, fertilizers, and who knew what else from the oxidized metal barrels and cracked plastic jugs. White metallic mold grew on the sand from corrosion and precipitation of salts. In other places, the concrete floor of the shed was stained with dark oil and a fine fur of rust and metal dust.

I found an old foam fishing float and played a game of keep-away soccer with little Wyatt between the pallets and the shed while we waited for Dustin to return with the tractor. Wyatt laughed when he pounced on the ball, his brown hair tousled, and then gave a mighty kick that sent the foam float flying into the wire pile, where it snagged high in the tangled mesh, which made him screech and giggle more. He ran in his little cowboy boots, the kid who loved being around his father and his soft-spoken, gently teasing uncle, Dustin, even if it was in the middle of a mound of junk. The kid for whom the station would be the place of his childhood memories. I pondered what the station meant to children—its chaos and brokenness, the wilderness, rough ringers, and soft sea wind.

We continued with the work at hand, but the presence of the child gave it an underlying sense of danger, of wanting to create a safe place where none existed. We piled rusted sharp metal and stacked containers of spilling chemicals. We cleared an entire bay and made it into the fencing supply center, with spools of new barbed wire stacked in rows. Beyond the shed, rows of dead vehicles and old tires along with broken machinery and abandoned, unidentifiable pieces of metal sank into the ground.

Dustin

I RODE OUT WITH DUSTIN TO EMPTY BAGS of lick into tubs for the cattle. He had said to meet him in a half-hour when we parted ways at breakfast, but by the time I reached the lick shed he had already loaded into the truck twenty-five bags, his puppy, and Claire's two grandsons. We drove the rutted tracks, bouncing to different lick tubs and past Beck's Camp along the Powder, backtracking to a hidden bore surrounded by tangled fig trees, and coming out through the rubber vine, where Dustin spotted a bunch of wild pigs running toward the road. He immediately leaped out with his blue puppy and the kids, Tommy and Nick, to ambush them.

When the near-blind pigs came close enough, Dustin sprinted forward and caught one of the babies. He handed the piglet to Tommy to hold and took off running after another. The second little piglet outdistanced him in the hardened uneven mud of the old swamp, and Dustin returned, breathing hard. He took the squirming piglet back from Tommy and held it above his blue dog. The puppy whined and jumped, finally latching on to the throat of the piglet and shaking until blood plastered his gums. Dustin pried the pig back and started using the tiny creature in a dog-training lesson. Catch and release, catch and release, until I couldn't stand it any longer—the squealing, bloody baby pig, and the bloodthirsty dog. Dustin finally let the pig go altogether, and it ran away, perhaps mortally wounded.

By nature, we are still animals on some level, harboring a desire for that primordial stalk and prowl and ambush and chase. At Stilwater, this desire often rose to rule the ego and the personality, revealing one of many that might surface from the subconscious to escape, untethered, in the actions and reactions of the crew.

That evening we went to shoot a calf with a bum leg, to put it out of its misery and cut it up for the dogs. Dustin stopped by the house for a .22 rifle and a couple of dull knives, and we drove out to the yards with Nick and Tommy again. Dustin raised his rifle through the window of the ute and dropped the calf. I climbed out of the back to carry the chain over and laid a hand on the calf's forehead, rubbing the soft hide above the bullet hole.

"Thanks, little guy," I said.

Dustin slashed the calf's throat, and the boys stood back. I couldn't do much with the dull knives, but we skinned it and cut the small muscles off the bones for dog meat. The boys threw pieces of meat at each other, and then Dustin joined the chase and smeared one of them with a snowball of fat and fascia. They taunted and teased, eight-year-old Tommy testing my patience with his racist and sexist jokes. I gathered up our chain to leave, and Tommy rushed up to slobber me with the calf's loose green tongue.

Tenderness

OUT IN THE PADDOCK we had a red heifer calf who was so sick she couldn't eat. I picked her up one day when I was hauling feed out to the calves and carried the little knobby-kneed baby to the water trough so she could drink. She needed a bottle still perhaps, young and pot-bellied, weaned too early and the abandonment too harsh, but no one on the station needed another poddy calf to care for, and so I just held her by the water trough and rubbed the small curls on her forehead. Angus, teasing in a gravelly voice, had said that it was my job to name all 138 poddy calves, if I hadn't already. They needed a mother, and if I was so bent on loving things, go right ahead.

In this expanse, the gift of compassion dissolved in a flood of need. A hundred calves needed more to eat, needed their mothers, and only the tough would survive. I stayed, holding the wobbly calf for a long while as she slobbered and labored to breathe. Finally I let her collapse gently in the grass, and when I returned she was gone.

Little Did the Sea Wind Care

MILES HAD GIVEN DUSTIN A PUPPY who fell sick and lay for days in his cage beneath the trees. Dustin was supposed to shoot him, but he kept forgetting, perhaps avoiding the chore. Finally one morning he borrowed the station .22 and unceremoniously shot him on our way to fix fence or put out lick, I don't remember which. I do remember that he hauled on the chain and the weak little dog couldn't even lift his head. I gave him a hard time later about not feeling anything for the puppy he'd just put a bullet in. For weeks after, when we passed the spot, he made a comment about the dog, something gentle, like saying hello to him. The small carcass was out beyond the burned trunks of trees, picked apart by kites that landed in the charred grass, a few feathers mixing with the dog hair and ash.

I recalled feeling a similar sense of immense sadness when I worked on a salmon boat, with the massive cascade of death typical in fishing. But the glinting red and silver fish would have died in a few weeks anyway, after spawning in the northern Alaskan rivers. On Stilwater, I did not have enough energy to love all that needed love, I could only give what compassion I could summon and observe the rest. I was a distinct outsider in this sense, quick to exclaim at beauty— wedge-tailed eagles flying, a low sun on bronze grass. But brutality was never far behind, and my gaze would shift from the light to two of the ringers chasing a mob of pigs in the ute. When they caught up with a baby, one of them bashed it with a metal picket.

I hoped, at times, for a touch more gentleness, but it was not a gentle life. The days evoked not gentleness, but a fight to protect our own selves from the nature of the work. We slipped sometimes, the exhaustion and inner fatigue rendering us vulnerable to injury. And we were all a shade mean-spirited at times, our behavior expressive of the storm that brewed within.

Little did the sea wind care. Nor did the brolgas that carried poetry written into the feathers of their wings. As a strange morph of wildness and civility, we had established our niche which any living being would do. We had engaged with our own process of adaptation, and we even conquered, at least for a time.

I rose each morning with more questions than insights into

the world of Stilwater. I had been initiated into the station crew by hard work and happenstance—I happened to be there, and after a long while, they knotted me into the net like a repair in a long seine. We rode upon the landscape and it rode upon us, leaving its mark. I still have a scar on my hand from a tea tree branch that tore away a piece of hide and left its harsh oils burned into my raw flesh. The scar has faded a little with the years, but the memories haven't receded. I can still ride through forests of tea trees, feel the scratch and brush of them against the skin of my throat, neck, and shoulder when I duck to the side to avoid the branches.

Landscape subtly and acutely changes the very paths of neurons in the brain, opening up ideas with the savannas, closing them in the darkness of inner forests. But we would all forget this sacredness and ride across the shaded grasslands with thoughts of other things, distant places or shallow yearnings. Who would be there to guide us in? Who would tell the stories—long, vital, looping—that were necessary to the knowing? Most of us were new to the place, and no one cared much anyway. There were bulls to chase, rodeos to attend.

Botany

THE MUSTERING CREW LEFT for a ten-day vacation; they packed up their gear and fifty dogs and a big beast Tanner bought off the Sutherlands to use as a bucking bull. They left with trucks piled high, gear roped and strapped and held on with big tarps, and packs of crated dogs yelping. A semi-quiet eased in and the station crew tried to catch some of the loose ends, so we could continue the muster more effectively when they returned. Others on the station crew left to drive who knew how many hours to a rodeo in a town called Laura, and Claire left to see her family in Karumba. Only Wade and his family, Ross, Angus, and I remained.

I could tell by the heaviness with which he climbed the stairs before he sat down at the table and lit a cigarette that the chaos of the station and the pressure of its management still weighed on Angus, even during a pause. A huge load of cattle sent south had tested positive for ticks when they arrived at the line, which meant our chemical vat wasn't strong enough. A couple of tally books containing numbers requested multiple times by the head office had disappeared, and we spent the morning searching the office, the boxes of branding supplies, the vehicles, and the shipping container. Wade and I ran a mob of wild heifers through the dip vat to stir it up, and then fixed a wire to a plastic container and lowered it into the murky liquid to get a sample. Wade took the plastic bottle full of foamy tick poison, put it in a box, signed a mail slip saying nothing toxic was being transported in the package—it wasn't toxic enough to kill the ticks, anyway—and sent the sample away on the mail plane. Wyatt brought the incoming bag of mail back on his little four-wheeler and hauled it up to the empty kitchen, where no one sorted it because Claire was away. Then Angus fell asleep on the couch, the horse races blaring on the television.

We had almost seven hundred head of weaners to load onto the road trains and ship to a station near Cloncurry for fattening in more fertile pastures. We were a little shorthanded, but Miles had the weaners trained well—he had been working them with the dogs, teaching them to move down the race and through the pens—and with Wade and me working the race, making tally marks, and urging them onto the trucks, we had them loaded in a little under two hours.

Afterward Wade drove me out to make a wide circle of the station. He lifted Wyatt's puppy into the back of the ute and his little son in rubber boots onto the front seat between us. Wade was approaching the feral station differently than Miles; he had to think of the long-term. The roughhousing and wrestling of cattle into shape was the concern of the mustering crew. Instead, he thought quietly about the overwhelming mess, spoke softly and kindly, and tried not to do too much damage. He wasn't very effective at changing the way things were, but he had more time and less pressure. He just had to try to keep up his end, keep the owners pacified, and not stir up trouble or generate animosity. Years would make the difference, not one winter season of reckless mustering, if he could keep quiet and virtually unnoticed for that long.

Wade had given me a lesson on the motorbike earlier, explaining how the engine worked—the gears, the suspension, the buttons—and demonstrating how to check the fluids, start the bike, and change gears. Then we took it for a spin. He drove it first with me sitting behind, calling back that I should lean into the turns. Then we switched places. He started it first and handed me the handlebars. I cruised down the road, practiced changing gears, and then made wide turns on the flat near the yards. Galahs fled from the snags on the fence line.

The bike felt heavy and dangerous, but Wade coaxed me through the moves. I said I would still rather be on a horse; at least they watched where they were going. Riding the motorbike, I felt like one lapse in attention or focus, one turn of thought, and the tire would hit a melon hole or downed log and send us flying over the handlebars or skidding across hard mud. Wade just smiled and said, "Plenty of horses, mate, and sometimes they'll send you flying too."

We drove in the ute out across the station, a joyride through thousands of hectares, past hidden water holes, mysterious swamps, thick forests, and oxbow lakes, which Wade called billabongs. A dingo froze, tawny gold against the grass. We saw piles of manure the brumby stallions had left, one pile on either side of the fence. Wade said quite a few of them ran in North and South Gum Paddocks, and they might try and bring some of them in with the chopper. Landscape stretched past, the sameness confusing me, directions blending together in forests of slender weeping trees below an incessant blue sky.

I asked Wade, "Which paddock are we in now?"

"I don't know, mate."

I made a guess. "Talbot Paddock?"

"You'd bet on it?" He made me think forward and backward, trying to picture from above the fences on that few thousand square miles of country, until I came up with the right answer.

I knew some of the trees, but none of their botanical names, none of their intimate characteristics of leaf or pistil, and nothing about the grasses with long inflorescences. I recognized a few genera from another continent, their morphology different here, but their names sounding familiar on my tongue. *Acacia, Ficus.*

I worked for years with a professional botanist, a family friend who received contracts through public and private entities to document the plant species of places, to study genetics and distribution, habit, habitat, condition, and characters. Years in a certain terrain provide opportunities to learn, but only elders with their wisdom and science and stories, only intimate hours and days and years, can open the mind to knowledge of both names *and* uses, the many languages spoken by the autotrophic community.

The names of Stilwater's plants are as distinctive as the place: black wattle, ironbark, paperbark, quinine, nonda plum, carbeen gum, and kurrajong. When I did eventually find their Latin names, I was far from the trees themselves, and the language overlaid memories in a disparate poetry. There were the crushed leaves of the broad-leaf tea tree, family Myrtaceae, *Melaleuca viridiflora*; the dappled shade of the weeping coolibah across the shoulders of my horse, *Eucalyptus microtheca*; and others in a lyrical litany: *Cochlospermum gillivraei, Allocasuarina littoralis, Parinari nonda, Petalostigma banksii, Acacia auriculiformis.*

I might have learned the plants if I'd had years in that northern outback. Stephen Craye taught me some of them—the poisonous neon leaves of the Cooktown ironwood, the blue-green of coastal she-oak, and the staining sap of bloodwood. I might have gathered stories to accompany each of them; I might have learned the edible roots and berries, the Aboriginal uses and stories. As it was I would have to leave and return or seek other sources of knowledge to add the scientific, the global bio-geography. That day, though, we cruised the paddocks, and I just tried, hopelessly, to memorize the layout of the station. The ute bounced over broken sticks. Wade, Wyatt, and I were crammed in the cab, laughing a little with the windows down. The puppy had her feet up on the side and her nose to the tea tree-scented wind.

We returned under the evening star, which we thought might be Venus, and found that Ross had the fire going. I walked up to the donga alone to feed Snake, whom Miles had left in my charge, and then took the shortcut back, along the edge of the lagoon. I slipped my boots off at the door of my small house and waited, barefoot, on the veranda.

In the stillness, beans dangled from the acacia trees, crows perched in the branches, and as night plummeted, mango leaves turned pale maroon on the branch tips. A blue-winged kooka-burra ate a snake in silhouette against the sundown. Flocks of bright green budgerigars etched the teal sky, the little parrots sweeping through the gum trees long-leaved and faintly blue. They came to the stock tanks by the hundreds, by the thousands, taking turns in their groups and never mixing, Angus said. You could watch one get stranded from a group, and instead of joining another flock of identical birds, the lost parrot waited, screeching in its loneliness. Currents of bright green parrots surrounded the lost individual, and it found itself isolated on the banks of the dam, where water held sky and a thousand strange birds.

Garret

WE WERE STILL WAITING for the mustering crew to return, and so we picked off little tasks here and there. Angus hired another ringer to join us on the station crew. His name was Garret, and he showed up one day with a truck and a couple of his own horses, which he turned out with the mustering crew's mob. He had light brown hair cut shorter on the neck and left a little longer on top where it curled, and his dark eyes tended to narrow in what looked like a glare. He was not tall, but I soon saw that he made up for it with cynicism and, in that way, carved out a place among the ringers.

Angus thought he had asked for the road train on Monday, but really he had arranged it for Tuesday, so we shuffled cattle, waited, and then reshuffled them so they could be on water another day. When the road trains did finally make the drive, Wade, Garret, Angus, and I loaded a mess of cleanskin bulls that jumped through the rails and broke welds clean off. We didn't lose any of them, though, and by ten o'clock the trucks had pulled out with the snorting bulls packed together for a long ride from freedom. Garret and I took the welder around to fix the rails, but it would start only if we shorted across the terminals of the starter motor with a screwdriver. Garret held the screwdriver, leaning away from the blasting shower of sparks before the motor kicked into its upset shuffle.

We fixed fence the following day. Dustin had dislocated his shoulder riding bulls in the Laura Rodeo, so he drove using his right hand to reach across and shift gears. He insisted on pounding pickets with one hand. Garret had to sit on a water esky in the back, grumbling for Dustin to slow down or speed up along the many miles of bouncy road. He had also left his smoko biscuits in Wade's truck. And so when Wade did eventually catch up, Garret said it was high time for smoko.

Wade gathered a few sticks from under the tea trees and, holding the small bundle between his hands, scraped a clearing in the fallen leaves with his boot. Garret had a lighter and lit the crushed tea tree leaves until they sent up a flurry of smoke and caught fire.

"Did you bring the quart pots?" Garret asked.

"Yeah, mate."

"I doubted you, Wade."

Wade didn't doubt that Garret doubted him, but still just replied with a nonchalant smile. Wade and Garret did not get along well, but Wade kept the humor light.

Garret: "Wade, did you get my tobacco in town?"

Wade: "Nope, they were sold out."

Garret: "You lying bastard."

Wade brought the two tin water containers from the truck. The blackened quart pots fit into leather holders strapped to the saddles most ringers used in the bush. Wade slipped the lids, which doubled as cups, off both of them and filled them with water from the esky. He slid the quart pots up against the flaming sticks, where the water would heat quickly, then went back to the truck for two plastic bags, one with sugar and the other with tea bags. Dustin took off his hat, leaned back against the papery trunk of a large tea tree, and fell asleep. Garret crouched near the fire, waiting until the water boiled, and then he reached in with a pair of pliers and gripped the little handles of the quart pot. We pulled out biscuits wrapped that morning and stirred sugar into the tin cups of tea.

Wade pulled the truck up next to the fire and left the door open so we could hear the radio. Dustin shifted in his sleep, and Wade said something about staying up all night at the rodeo.

"Must have been thinking about those bulls, and what was it they'd heard happened under the mango trees?" Dustin had fallen in love with the daughter of Mike, the mechanic. She lived in Mareeba, where another rodeo would be held in three weeks' time. Dustin couldn't stop making comments about his girlfriend, the bulls—which he said were the best stock around—and how he was going to work every weekend so he could ride a bull in the rodeo. Garret glowered at the mud, flat-brimmed hat set low over his face. He was mad because he was stuck with a crew he thought of as inferior, on a property where equipment was lacking and chaos prevailed. He eventually closed his eyes, and his expression almost relaxed. I leaned back against my own paper-bark tea tree with a hot pannikin of black tea, dusty from the dried mud on which I sat and covered in charcoal from fixing fence through the burned thickets.

Lying there in the outback shade of tea trees, we listened to the radio commentator speak of nuclear fission technology, the state of affairs in Zimbabwe, and a decision by the Japanese paper industry not to purchase old-growth timber. I listened intently, ready for perspective and stimulation, while Garret, Wade, and Dustin talked about football and hunting pigs. On Stilwater, the outside world was little more than a backdrop. The world consisted of pigs and tea trees and dead brown grass. Beyond that, nothing much mattered. News came in as entertainment, less important than football or rugby. The radio provided the company of human voices, to the degree that the three of them left the radio in the truck on all day, even when only static made it through. One or another of them would lean out the window and adjust the piece of wire that functioned as a makeshift antenna. The radio suggested that we were not alone in the bush.

We split up then, Wade taking Garret ahead so that the four of us could leapfrog the fence and broken wires. I didn't mind; Dustin and I joked and jostled over who would pound the pickets. Endless sun, swamps, and forests of tea trees filled the rest of the morning.

Dustin had a way of saying, "I couldn't tell you, mate" in answer to every question I asked and then later turning my questions into a lighthearted joke.

"There's your black tea trees." He pointed toward a stand of charred trunks. I had asked about a species name.

"Don't you think they've just been burned?"

"I'd say so." He grinned and shifted into high gear for the long stretch across a flat, not even slowing for some of the snapped wires. Sometimes I had to ask him twice if he was serious or not. If he was, he often said, "Fair dinkum," meaning true, or for real.

Wade and Garret came back to see what was taking so long. Dustin said, "We're actually fixing the fence, mate."

Wade said we could head home, Garret and I, because he wanted to take Dustin on a wider run to see more country, and Garret wouldn't work a minute past five if there wasn't a good reason. And so Garret drove us home with his foot pressed to the accelerator, miles rushing by, cattle running into the scrub. Open expanses and long distances in the outback begged for either ridiculous speed or aimless wandering that bordered on stillness. Garret just wanted to get back so he could watch football.

A small herd of brumbies raised their heads from the tall grass of the swamp: a chestnut mare with a little bay colt, another bay, and a chestnut mare and colt. They started running as we drew near, a couple of them old station horses perhaps. They disappeared into the comb of bloodwood trunks.

I wanted suddenly to stay out there in perpetuity, to feel the storms of the wet season and catch a couple of brumby colts to train. I likely would have gone insane, but I felt the addiction of the wildness, the speed, and the forests pouring onto the metallic sheen of the plains.

Solitude

SOLITUDE HAS ITS OWN WINGS, and I had felt them before, many times, alone in the mountains, riding across rugged slopes of granite and oak brush. And yet still I wanted more, just to see if ever I would be able to sit quietly, to listen and wait and learn the pace of places unhindered. But even in the far cries of the outback the work and people kept away the inner voices of Stilwater. I could hear them sometimes, just whispers, and I wondered if anyone else feared what they might say if the solitude soaked in completely.

I felt fear, but also the desire to know. I wanted the rains that would flood everything and wash it clean, smearing the charcoal into black runoff as if my hands and face and the trees could be free of smudges and scarring. I wanted to be carried out to sea and feel the saltiness within and without, to become the rivers and turning tides and the dreaming. If the stories and songs were audible enough, and if I knew the words and repeated them again and again, weaving the tattered battlefield back into the folds of history, I might emerge with a more tangible feeling of my place in the universe. I might have enough meaning to fill the emptiness when the work settled for a moment and left the hollow into which the wild seeped. But I had no song lines; my own strings were tenuous, and I had to weave them again and again in order to keep moving forward.

The station itself provided work and hierarchy, and the world beyond the station provided its reason for existence. We were part of a grander scheme of capital. We were the pawns and the consumers, of its products and ideology. We all knew the architecture and its scaffolding—a simple profit-oriented operation: work, efficiency, markets; money in, money out, paychecks to those of us who labored and money skimmed off the top by those who owned the means of production, the land and the cattle, and access to markets. Every place on earth had to listen to the same story, again and again in different manifestations: timber for Japan, land reforms and the ensuing lack of food in Zimbabwe, wars on distant continents. We all took part; we were none of us innocent. We all needed to eat and participate in our own society and so we played the game, even at the farthest shores of the outback.

The world beyond also provided escape and allure—rodeos or bulls or a girlfriend, or the horse races and cricket games. Dreams filled the days and made the work tolerable. That was how we survived, and that was also how we died. We spent hours of the day not living within the day, in the sacred offering of the moment; instead we lived in a thousand places and times, past and future, real and imagined. Was this why we didn't care? Because escape came so easily? Few would embark on this journey of initiation, knowing the toll that it exacted. And even fewer would ever come to know this place intimately.

Island

RED SUNDOWN BURNED ABOVE THE TREES of the sand ridge between the house and the coast, as if the edge of the world were on fire. I had walked out alone through the gathering twilight. The opaque color reminded me of blood. The price of pregnant cows for slaughter had risen. Fetal blood of unborn calves—called fetal bovine serum—was used in culturing cells, tissues, and organs. These would be used to save the sick and the wounded, to prolong life for some by slaughtering pregnant cows for the blood of their unborn. I lay on my back in the scratchy grass. I wondered if I, as an American, was partly to blame, whether wars in Iraq and Afghanistan had generated the need for more medical supplies, with repercussions that filtered down to the Australian outback. A swarm of screeching corellas approached and flew overhead in a white winged storm. Sun caught the faint green and yellow under their wings. I could feel the wind from their flight, the parrots close enough that I could reach up and catch one if I stood up. But I lay still. The storm passed and the screeching faded in the distance. The sky seemed more immense as it darkened. Fires at the burning edge died and the long horizon turned to charcoal.

Global politics may have ruled Stilwater, even from far away. But I surrendered to the wild. The world there made more sense to me, or at least what I knew of it did. Crocodiles ate when they were hungry; corellas returned to the same trees in a pattern stitched through time. I would lie in the grass and wait out the wet. I would let the pulse take me in completely and not struggle anymore. I would ride out just to feel the wind and know the pads that ran through the forests. I would memorize bogs and swamps as if my survival depended on it. Maybe this was the reason for rituals and rites, to prepare one to surrender to the precision of the universe, to give, to move, to endure and release. To be grateful and humble. To survive cold and heat and wet. These qualities were not often cultivated anymore, putting us in peril, leaving us vulnerable when we encountered the rawness forgotten in our civility.

Cycles

A CONTINENTAL SHELF REACHES OUT from the northern tip of Australia. Some of the water on its thousand-year cycle from Greenland to Greenland surfaces from the depths here, warmed by the accumulated heat of the water's surface. In the North Atlantic, the same current dives just off the Greenland ice sheet, plunging deep and heavy and then meandering, circulating, and circumnavigating the depths of the globe. The current drives the complete mixing of the ocean and modulates the world's temperature on long timescales.

Many currents move through the oceans of the world, driven by wind, temperature, salinity, and the spinning earth. They circulate heat accumulated at the equator, influencing temperature and precipitation around the globe. The oceans are an interconnected body of water with gradients—hot to cold, shallow to deep, salty to almost sweet—and eternally dynamic. They have small currents, and larger currents moving through small currents, swirling in vertical to horizontal three-dimensional rotations, with a cycle of about a thousand years.

The atmosphere has its own cycles, related directly to the oceans', but they are quicker to respond and to forget. The atmosphere has a memory of roughly one month. Every summer, the wet season hits Stilwater: storms are predicted, awaited, and weathered year after year. The earth tips back and forth, its fattest middle gathering most of the sun's strength. Water evaporates up and rains down, shifting in its intensity north to Asia or south to Australia depending on the season. The storms come in one way or another. They define the wet and, in their absence, the dry.

Another lower-frequency cycle is animated by the trade winds, blowing west around the equator. The winds are driven across the Pacific by rising air off the northern tip of Australia and sinking air over the Pacific coast of South America. They pull surface waters off the coast of Chile, and colder waters rise to the surface in their place. Warm equatorial water is pushed, piled, and held in the eastern Pacific, against the islands of Indonesia and the northern corner of Australia. When the low pressure weakens, warm water sloshes back across the ocean. When the water relaxes back toward South America, the phase is called El Niño, and when the wind presses wet, hot, heavy rains against Asia, it is called La Niña. The rhythms in the flux between Asia and North America provide some sense of predictability, moving in three- to eight-year cycles, though the rains that come from those rocking waters often escape foresight.

Cycles themselves are changing. As temperatures rise, glaciers pour their cold liquid of millennia into the sea. As more fresh water melts off Greenland, the current mixes salt and sweet and will not dive as deep, or might not sink at all, disrupting the circulation patterns that mix the seas, move heat around the globe, and keep it in dynamic balance. Some places will not receive the warmth of the tropics, some will not feel the cooling breath of the poles, and the storms will shift in range and intensity, as will their counterparts, the droughts. Every continent, ocean, and sky will be changed, subtly or acutely, and we don't know exactly how it will all play out.

In our remote outback patch of scrub and tea tree, not many of us cared. No one knew what the currents did around that northern tip of the continent; where they were going or from where they came; which pressure differences drove them; how the water heated and moved; how the currents pushed across the shelf, through the basins, around the volcanic island chains, over subduction zones, into the Gulf of Carpentaria or through the Timor and Arafura Seas. No one knew whether the currents had come most recently from the Pacific or the Indian Oceans, or where they headed after touching the white sand coast. No one knew the atmospheric spirals and movements, the warp and weft of weather. No one knew the paths winds took across the sky, their speed or intensity, the shifting pressure gradients, and the way they magnetized the storms. No one had an inkling of how sensitive and how complex the processes were, how small shifts in one region had tsunami effects in another. We did not have the memory of the atmosphere or the ocean, and so we did not know when the wet season was coming.

Miscreants

ABORIGINAL CULTURES EVOLVED TO PERSIST beyond the arrogance of the individual. Strict laws and practices kept the net whole and stretched across the environment that harbored them. Over millennia, the practices that most closely matched the dynamic earth or formed the strongest cohesive webs within tribes were the ones to become engrained, through myth, taboo, or tradition. Such sticky, interlocking fibers resist dramatic change. When new concepts emerge in the collective human psyche, an individual can move much more quickly than a crowd, but the freethinking, self-centered individual threatens the tribe's long-term viability. Tribal structures are imposed to maintain cohesion and save the reckless from themselves. Tribal structures, morals, and practices can also facilitate the long-term productivity and health of the landscape and its life.

On Stilwater, most of us thought that the old tribal laws

wouldn't apply anymore. We didn't recognize that we were simply spinning new tribes, colonized with modern individualist sentiments. We were out for money and profit, out to take control of the wild and use the landscape and all it had to offer for our personal benefit. We knew we had the freedom to do so, and we didn't understand the way that acting on such freedom would accelerate the speed with which we altered the landscapes and living webs on every continent, the cycling in the atmosphere and oceans.

Given that we have such influence and the potential for such insight, I thought we could try to redirect the process rationally. I thought we could all choose vision over intentional blindness, and begin to develop a new perspective.

Out in the scrub, some might have picked up a few lessons, the unavoidable ones. But I soon learned that most of us would never live in accordance with the wisdom of the place. Given an ounce of humility, we might have listened to a throbbing pulse within, the buzzing vocal hum of the didgeridoos. Instead, the hunger to be free and independent, the illusion of power, was the driving force. The chaos at the edges was more compelling. Most of us miscreants preferred to swim against the current of the place.

The Screamin' Demon

WE HAD A MUSTER TO DO, and who knew how many cattle to work, and we had to get the crew mounted—either on horseback or on motorbikes, or vehicles of some kind—in order to get the work done. Not all of the crew had returned from vacation when we set to work, but we were determined. The fences were more or less in order, we were well rested, and time was slipping away toward the wet. We would shift out to Carter Yards and begin mustering the middle swath of paddocks on that immense station.

We salvaged an old vehicle from the wreckage pile. As the station horses had gone wild, the vehicle had gone rusty, but we thought we might put it into action again. On a spare afternoon we replaced the drive shaft, cut the doors off halfway, welded on a few roll bars, and wired old tires to the front bull bars. Garret, Wade, and Dustin pieced it together in an afternoon, Garret growling throughout that we should be doing it right if we were going to do it at all. We certainly weren't taking the time to do it right.

He and I had had a talk the night before. He said I asked too many questions and I said he might consider a more positive attitude. I said that if he were nice to others, they might be nice in return. He retorted, "Maybe in a perfect world."

"Seems to work that way in my world," I said, realizing as I did that not only did we hail from different continents, we lived our days on different planets. And yet there we were, together, covered in axle grease. He said he would try a positive approach, and though I didn't believe it, his attitude turned around completely, for the day anyway. He asked if I could I hand him a shifter, which I called a wrench, and the world and words of the shop absorbed both of us.

As part of the hasty renovation, I painted a name, the Screamin' Demon, on the side of the bull catcher. But I didn't feel at all comfortable when we took it for a test run to catch a bull. Wade and I had piled in along with little Wyatt, but the truck only started, it wouldn't move. Wade assessed the underside and said it must be stuck in neutral from when Dustin had replaced the drive shaft. He found an arm in need of a pin, and we were on our way. But when we did find the bull, he was too far away from a road to drag a trailer to retrieve him, so we aborted the mission.

Instead we made a loop to check the crab pots in a long blue arm of the Powder. The tide had dropped the waterline low, exposing muddy cut banks at the bends. Mangroves sketched a green band with spiderweb roots and stems reaching toward the sea. After Wade stopped, the truck refused to start again. We stood in the haze of biting mosquitoes, stranded out by a middle-of-nowhere loop of the river. Wade leaned in over the engine, beneath the yawning bonnet, and tried to figure out which wire had bounced free. They found a dangling copper end, tried attaching it in a few different places, and finally relieved us of having to walk. We flew back with crab pots bouncing and a lone crab clinging inside a rusty cage.

~~

We soon had the vehicle running more consistently, and more of the crew returned. The Sutherlands were pushing Angus to increase the outflow of cattle; it was essential in order for them to keep financing the operation. So far we had been largely unsuccessful. We needed to work faster or we would all be replaced. Angus summoned the mishmash of us for a good lecture on efficiency. The helicopters were on the way, and we would begin in earnest the next morning.

I drove the Screamin' Demon in the muster. I would rather be on a horse, I said, but they said no, the vehicles were more efficient over long distances. But as soon as we reached the middle of the paddock, the rattling starter on the truck decided not to work.

Our crew consisted of the station hands—Garret, Dustin, and me—and those of Miles' crew who had returned: Ivan, Tanner, Max—the youngest of the crew—and Jenna, Max's girlfriend, whose job was unclear. With Jenna as copilot, Ivan drove Miles' orange bull catcher, having repaired the brake line with a piece of aluminum foil. The foil popped out after the first bump, leaving him brakeless again. The orange vehicle wouldn't start by itself either, so Garret pushed one or the other of us with the four-wheeler.

He started the four-wheeler with a half-finished cigarette in his mouth and crept behind the orange bull catcher, spinning his tires until it started moving. Then Ivan popped the clutch and the rig roared into action. Garret swung the four-wheeler around behind my bull catcher for another round of the push-start routine.

Static and voices over the radio located Flynn working above a sand ridge and Max and Dustin on motorbikes beneath him. They had an old bull that wouldn't move and other cattle running. We circled around a few heading for the gate, and then retreated back to the shade of coolibahs and turned the engines off again. Ivan rolled a cigarette and opened one of Jenna's fashion magazines. She was afraid of spiders, she said, and the bush was full of spiders. When she looked at me I just gave her a reassuring smile.

~~

The next morning Wade and I drove out early. The sun was hitting the dirty pocked windshield of the Screamin' Demon at an angle that completely obscured our vision. I tore part of the seat cover off and handed it to Wade to clean the glass. He leaned out the open side to reach the windshield, one foot still on the accelerator. I reached across to take the wheel, steering off the road in one direction and then the other, unable to see. He wiped some of the dirt off the glass and folded back into the cab, his foot never leaving the accelerator. Wind swept through the torched-off sides, chilling us as we sped down the dusty road toward the middle of the station. Within minutes, the clutch gave way completely and we coasted to a stop.

"Well, that looks like the end of her," Wade said mildly.

The motorbikes and Ivan's bull catcher would be coming along at some point, so we leaned against the dusty truck and waited, the morning suddenly serene.

Ivan arrived not much later, dusty from the ride, and asked, "How's yous goin'?"

Wade just nodded. "Yeah mate."

"What, you need a push-start?"

"No mate, she's finished."

We piled our bull ropes and water eskies in the back of the orange bull catcher, tied up Max's pig dogs to wait by the dead rig for the day, and climbed in with Ivan and Jenna. Wade, the head stockman, was reduced to depending on a lift in a bull catcher that wouldn't start of its own accord.

We made it to the paddock and pulled off the track to wait for the helicopters to start bringing cattle down. Flynn called on the radio that he had a couple of bulls beneath him in the next paddock. Garret and Tanner left on motorbikes to give chase. Max zoomed away to chase another bull when he jumped the fence. Wade, Ivan, Jenna, and I remained in the shade and listened to the drama over the two-way radio.

We could hear the chuckle in Flynn's voice as he viewed the action from above. Max attacked the bull who had leaped the fence, slipped a head rope on when the bull charged him, and then tried to pull him down alone. The bull just galloped along, dragging Max with him until he swung back around to charge and Max got enough slack to wrap the rope around a tree.

Garret and Tanner came back, the four-wheeler missing its plastic front cover and the bars covered in manure. They had tied the bulls to trees and then rocked them upright so their shoulder muscles wouldn't go numb from the weight of lying on their sides.

I headed back with them after lunch to retrieve the bulls, one of whom died of stress and dehydration before we could get to him. After driving the narrow dirt tracks for almost an hour and then crashing through the scrub, thin tea trees snapping as the truck hit them, we reached the farthest bull.

Garret walked around the trailer with an armful of ropes and groaned. "We got a flat."

Tanner went into a tirade about the lack of management, the trucks, dogs, fences, trailers, and anyone whose name found his tongue. "Fuckin' equipment on this place," he swore. "Can't depend on anything!"

Garret and I jacked up the truck and removed the tire, but the spare didn't fit. We had a flat tire, a useless spare, several thousand miles of bush, a screaming ringer, and a mad bull.

Tanner swung a loop of his rope in front of one big hoof, and when the bull stepped into the loop, Garret helped him tip the bull on his side. They used the second vehicle to drag the bull up onto the trailer, one horn leaving a trench in the earth. Then the rope snapped and Tanner started swearing again. We replaced the rope with chains. The bull lay heaving, his eyes rolled back.

Tanner got into the driver's seat and started back through the scrub, flat tire notwithstanding. The other tire on the trailer was flat by the time we reached the pens at Carter Yards. We untied the infuriated beast, and he wasted no time trying to pulverize us. But he was shaken from the ride and didn't get far before he stumbled and stood—trembling, snorting, pawing the dust. Garret shut the gate on the pens, and we took off the other flat. The spare fit the hub, but that still left us with one flat tire

and two bulls roped to trees out in the scrub. The sun sank as we headed back to the station compound for another spare. We ended the day after smashing and prying the ruined tire off the rim, and trying unsuccessfully to get another fitted.

The bull saga continued most of the following morning. Tanner and Garret tried to get Tanner's bull catcher running because Claire had taken the Trooper to Normanton. They found another spare for the trailer, and the three of us set out to find the bulls. Tanner's bull catcher died on the road, but he got it running again. Every time he started it after that, he had to lift the bonnet and pour petrol into a hole in the carburetor, or get a push start. He swore in an endless litany at the vehicle or the situation. Garret gave him a hard time for messing around with the mechanic work instead of just getting the bulls. Then we realized that the other front tire on the trailer was almost flat, and we didn't have two spares. We finally made it to Max's big black bull after smashing carefully through the trees.

The bull had worn a track around the tree, moving in circles all night. Dust covered his belly, his bulging eyes looking out wildly even as the rope kept his head stretched to the tree. The bull wrestled Garret and Tanner even with all four of his feet tied together—all fight and scrub and salt, he wasn't going to surrender easily. Tanner backed the trailer up between trees and Garret sat on the bull until he stilled, sunglasses hiding his expression and his black hat pulled low.

We took down the fence to cross into the next paddock for the last bull, and then drove the fence line back to Carter Yards. The bull released the night before charged the truck, and I nearly landed on Garret's lap in my effort to get away from the side of the vehicle he was ready to gore. He pulled up short, a few inches from smashing the glass and puncturing the vehicle with his horns. The massive beast stood trembling, mucus hanging in a string from his flared nostril, pawing the ground and readying for an attack.

We untied the other two bulls with the first one stirring dust and snorting behind us. Tanner sawed off their horn tips with a hacksaw, but the blade broke and he had to bash the last tip off with a hammer. The bulls on the trailer were tied down, but even after we undid the ropes, they wouldn't get up. Tanner zapped one with the electric jigger, and even then, Garret and Tanner had to run in front of them, waving their hats to get the bulls to charge off the trailer. We left them in that remote set of yards to blow off some steam.

That Sunday afternoon, Tanner left to work on his vehicle, I left to sit on the veranda in the company of mosquitoes, and Garret watched a football game. From my perch I could see that the tips of the mango branches hung in maroon bud, anticipating an end to that gulf winter. The breeze wrote and erased tracks across the dusty earth, murmuring through the trees and hushing the grasses. A hatching of black butterflies with white-ringed wings laced the air. The world was moving forward while our work remained stalled.

Victoria

VICTORIA CAME BACK from the races with a broken foot; her horse had rammed her against a rail during a warm-up. She'd won one of the races, though, and had more scheduled for her big thoroughbreds. Vic said she used to run four miles a day, plus race riding, to keep in shape for being a jockey, but she didn't get to do much prep out on the mustering crew. She'd once been skinny and lean, but her short shorts were now a little tight. After muscling huge bulls and her horses and several thousand yearlings, she was not quite as petite as jockeys had to be. She limped around, but not for long—a broken foot wasn't to be taken too seriously. When Vic returned to camp, things at least began to look clean again, and the crew had real food.

Cole

COLE TACTFULLY TOOK CHARGE of the crew, since Miles hadn't yet returned. He sorted the gear, unloaded bags of horse feed and groceries and barrels of fuel, and organized the random machinery that floated around the camp. He unloaded new bull straps and tie ropes, new parts for dead and dying vehicles, saddles and blankets, salt blocks, horseshoes, horseshoe nails, vet supplies, the crew's duffel bags of clothes, and a few extra things for the kitchen. He tied the two curly-haired lap dogs next to the donga, and parked his beefy four-wheeler with tires strapped to the roll bars out front. He stacked the firewood and piled up chains in a mass. He had cut his dark curly hair short again, and gave an easy smile, his brown eyes keeping their quiet shine even under the dusty matte coating of the camp. He never said much, but he contemplated efficiency and casually set about making it happen. And because he didn't order anyone around, no one could contradict him; because he didn't lose his temper or berate anyone, no one had a reason to speak badly of him.

Dasher Paddock

THE CREW WENT TO LOAD UP a small mob of cattle the choppers had cleaned out of Dasher Paddock, just east of the house yards. It took six of them the better part of two days to get a mere thirty cattle into the trucks. Jenna rode in the huge yellow stock truck with her purple-painted fingernails. I assumed she would get a rougher coat on her eventually from life in the bush, but she basked in the world of tough young men, and took every opportunity to dress skimpily and sit squished between them. The boys put on a show, of course, and Vic ignored them all completely.

Cole ran the operation—all fight, dogs, dust, and hollering. Wade, Garret, and I had stretched a hundred yards of hemp fabric they called hessian in a big wing by the trap yards, wiring the rough cloth to thin white trunks of coolibahs. The wires held the top neck-high, and the bottom hemmed edge brushed the ground. The virtual fence, used frequently on stations to gather micky bulls or remnant cows, would fool the beasts, funneling them into the pen. The helicopters had flown in the night before and made an early clean-up sweep of the paddock. The choppers had yarded the cattle easily enough, but the wobbly race and dilapidated fences hindered the loading. The roughed-up ringers, most of them still charged with renewed vigor from their vacation, roped cattle, jiggered cattle, bashed cattle, and dragged a few of them up the race with a truck. They had several thousand head of cattle to entertain, and they weren't about to let a paltry thirty head delay them for long.

Wade sent Garret and me to put bags of lick in the tubs while the rest of the crew smashed the adrenaline-strung, resistant cattle and carted a couple of loads of them home. Garret drove, bouncing along the roads too fast. He had been excused from the action by Wade to put out supplement, essentially rendered worthless. He said he didn't want to be associated with the mustering crew anyway. Or the station crew—and the whole lot would be more effective without both Wade and Miles in any case. Evidently he was there to make $160 a day and tell me how everything should be done differently. We put out lick in several of the station's paddocks—North and South Gum before smoko, and then Powder and Talbot Paddocks.

I was exhausted just trying to keep a positive attitude around him, his negativity a black hole drawing in sharp splinters of meanness from wherever they flew, airborne fibers around us. But eventually I couldn't pacify my emotions and so I confronted him. He was nice afterward, at least for a while, but I was close to tears anyway. He was a bitter tonic, astringent. Such medicine could be more effective out there than anything sweet, I suppose. He preferred darkness and the way it limited his responsibility, made his job easier.

Garret didn't have a high standing with the mustering crew, particularly Vic. Vic and Cole fed his horses for a while, but quit when Garret never returned the favor. He worked and fed his own colts and a buckskin mare he used for camp drafting, but only when he felt like it. Wade once sent me out to the yards to check on Garret, who was supposed to check on the horses. I found him riding one of his colts, unconcerned about anything else. I slipped in with the rest of the herd and found that they had almost covered themselves in the molasses we set out in tubs as a supplement. They pawed at the gooey liquid, smeared it against each other's shoulders, flanks, and manes. When they tried to rub the dried molasses off, the caked sugar pulled hair and skin with it. The herd ran around in a mangy mess, skin between the molasses smears rubbed raw and bleeding. Fortunately, the horses belonging to the mustering crew were kept in a separate paddock, and they weren't quite as barbaric. They managed to lick the molasses without getting too much of it on themselves.

I caught one of my geldings, Crow, and washed the sticky sweetness off of his coat, his face scraped raw where the bridle hit and his shoulders raw where the saddle rubbed. I felt frustrated with Garret because he couldn't care less, frustrated with Wade who didn't care much either, and frustrated at myself because I didn't have the energy to catch and wash the entire herd. Although even if I had done so, they just would have gone swimming in the goo again anyway.

Eventually we washed all of them and put them in another paddock, away from the molasses tubs. We caught each horse, scrubbed off the matted molasses, water from the bore hose making a sweet muddy mess, and we rubbed cream on their sores. Such kindness seemed a luxury in the bush. And even then, the horses didn't look much better than the cattle returned from Dasher Paddock, all scrapes and bloody patches.

The following day, I stayed to help the fence man, Randall, pour concrete on the renovated loading ramp at the yards—a job Angus had given him before we had to load cattle again. Randall was a lean man with dark skin and curly dark hair. He had a young bloke working with him, and I offered the kid my place in the crew for a day, which Angus said was fine, to let him play rodeo in Dasher Paddock. I said I would rather wrestle wet cement than scared cattle. To my surprise, Garret said he would stay to help with the cement too.

The cement truck had a layer of hard concrete caked inside it. It barely rotated and offered only a thin stream of its gray contents when we tried a practice load. We enlisted the help of Mike, the mechanic, coaxing him from his axle grease. He was usually full of good ideas, but he couldn't seem to think of anything other than an acid wash that would make the cement mixer work better. Aside from that issue, the metal paneling used to form the ramp wasn't level across both sides, or consistent in its slope. The dirt packed between the forms, over which the concrete was supposed to be poured, bucked a good foot in the middle, and there was no rebar or mesh for the concrete to bond to. I overstepped my bounds a bit by pulling a string top to bottom and asking for a shovel to level the dirt. I asked if we had any mesh, and Randall said he knew of some. Both he and

Garret had raised their eyebrows a little when I started giving orders instead of taking them, and Garret even smiled. I said the forms needed to have the same slope at least, and I took a shovel to the dirt and packed it down below the forms, grading it more or less evenly. Randall raised the wooden forms a few inches and wired in a gridded layer of mesh and bars, and by the time the cement crew—Garret and Mike—had a load mixed after lunch, we had the ramp ready for the pour.

Angus came to give meaningless advice for which none of us had patience, but we got most of the cement down before the cement truck coughed, sputtered, and died. The cement inside set before we could get to it, adding to the layers of hard feelings in the future. But Randall, Garret, and I shoveled heavy wet cement onto the ramp for an hour. Half of it dried before we could get it completely leveled, but Garret rose to the occasion more than I would have expected, and Randall worked hard, motivated and enthusiastic, even if he knew little about cement. Then the crew returned in the stock trucks, rallying at the yards in a roar of engines and cloud of dust. They pulled right up alongside the renovated ramp and emptied a load of mangy, half-mad cattle down the half-set concrete slope, pocking it with hoof marks and adding some texture it needed anyway. They stayed to help us scrape and clean up the mess.

The crew headed back to the donga, all sweat and blood and testosterone. Jenna climbed down from the monstrous truck used to haul the flailing cattle with her tentative smile and painted nails, blond hair pulled back, clean when the rest of us were covered in manure and cement. The mustering crew retired to drink beer and work on their motorbikes and broken-down vehicles. Watching them leave, it was impossible to understand how Vic managed her regal alternative reality amid the rabble, participating yet somehow above it.

I didn't know what to do with my own sensitivities and emotions; I was sinking in swamp mud when I needed to be swimming, caught in the sticky molasses of human interactions when I needed to get some work done. I asked Wade if they had retrieved all the cattle from Dasher Paddock. He said, "No, six we couldn't load. We'll have to shoot them." Then he smiled. "Yeah, mate, all of them."

Later I found myself alone at the yards, having stayed to tend to the horses again after we rolled bales for the cattle. The crew had left without me. There was a motorbike still parked there, one belonging to Max, but I wasn't confident enough either to borrow it or to ride the distance to the house. I contemplated the walk home, a good four miles, but I was worn out and just sat down on the concrete ramp until I could summon more energy. It was Garret who realized I was missing and came back for me on the four-wheeler. "Thought you'd have run home by now." I rose up with a weak smile. "C'mon," he said gently. "I'll take the bike." He took the motorbike, and I rode the four-wheeler down the long stretch, tears squeezing out of my eyes to be whipped away in the wind.

Slatter Paddock

IN BACK OF SLATTER PADDOCK, on the road near Running Bore, with four horses, four dogs, the little ute with two avgas fuel drums, and another welded and renovated bull catcher, seven of us waited for directions from the chopper. Flynn radioed to ask if a couple motorbikes wanted a job. Cole took off on his beefed-up four-wheeler toward the fence line and Tanner followed on his bike, bull straps on the handlebars and a catching rope looped over his shoulder and under one arm.

Garret leaned back against the bonnet of the truck and asked if I'd remembered a pack of cards. Dustin sat on top of the bull catcher in tennis shoes, the sleeves of his plaid shirt rolled up to his elbows, his white hat pushed back a little, and his two-way strapped to his chest. His dad had come for a couple of weeks, visiting from a station farther south. Together they had welded up the new version of the bull catcher. Vic sat in the scraggly shade of a coolibah.

Miles had taken the long road out to the middle of the paddock in the back of the horse truck, his big strong body wedged among the tied and saddled horses. He was shaken up from the bumps, and his sweat-stained white hat was coated in dust. He had returned the night before, newly shaved, almost unrecognizable, but with an ache to make a difference, to build up again a reputation that was on the verge of breaking, to be the boss, to be respected, and, though he wouldn't ever admit it, to be loved by his makeshift temporary family. His beard would grow back to hide his sensitivities, but today he was trying for a fresh start.

Miles seemed not to know where he fit in with Angus and Wade, not to mention the helicopter pilots and the physically absent but still influential Stephen Craye, Vic, and the rest of his crew. He maintained a little distance at first, to preserve his tried-on new authority and in deference to the ragtag crew that had kept things moving in his absence. He had spent the entire holiday replacing the engine in his old truck in order to be better outfitted for the job, but then he suffered a pair of flat tires on the drive back. He startled me when he pulled in after midnight and came to the kitchen in the dark a few hours later, before the choppers left. I wasn't expecting to see him, and he seemed bigger, more imposing, clean-cut. Now he just waited, like the rest of us, in the shade.

Horses banged about in the truck, metal shoes against the metal grate. Tanner had commented on the shoes on my horses that morning as they had clanged on the loading ramp. He asked if I had shod them myself, and if I was looking for more such work.

Flynn called on the radio, the propeller sounding along with his voice. "Where're you, Dustin?"

Lying on his back on the roll bars, Dustin pressed the push-to-talk button and tipped his chin to his chest to reply. "Yeah mate, just along this middle road here in the back corner."

"You'll just have to get bored for a while."

The night before, Wade and Flynn had stood in front of

the big map on the kitchen wall and tried to figure out how to muster the paddock. They had traced lines across the map with their fingers, considering options. Where were the corners, the bores, the fence lines, the roads? Which sweep would funnel the cattle most effectively to the yards? Which way could they send the horses and bikes to gather the traveling cattle and keep them pointed in one direction? They had worked it out, the two of them, but Ivan and Max had left without direction in the morning, stoned and free-thinking, or perhaps not thinking at all, and the rest of the crew had idled along some road in the middle of the paddock.

Vic and Garret commented sardonically on the chaos. I propped my feet on the dash of the big truck. Garret took out a rope to practice. About the time we had given up on being useful, Flynn called on the two-way and directed a few of us riders to head toward the back fence. We lowered the ramp on the truck, a few boards broken clear through, and carefully stepped the horses down.

As we rode out across coarse dead grass, the horses left four trails of crushed bronze that caught the sun differently. We threaded through hours and burned sticks of tea trees, ducking under green needles, our legs smeared with charcoal and the white of the bark. We angled north, toward a fence line several miles distant. We rode across the far paddock. Distance was deceptive; we could have been riding through the same grove several times, or several groves one time. I wouldn't have known how to find my way anywhere if I had been stranded there, or if I had found myself alone without the radio in my chest harness, which worked only if it had charged batteries, a pilot flying above watching. We simply rode more or less straight, trying to keep our bearings by the line of the trails behind and points ahead in the timber. Flynn eventually called over the two-way that he had four mickies ahead of us. The day broke then, from a quiet morning to fast hard mustering beneath a helicopter.

Vic galloped her tall thoroughbred gelding into a thicket

of tea trees, blocking the bulls. She put her dogs on to one of them until the bull pulled up to fend off the pack that hung onto his ears and hocks and mouth, biting and barking. Garret and Miles leaped off their horses to grab the bull's tail and pull him down. They tied him to a tree while Vic and I tried to keep up with another of the bulls. As long as the bull traveled in the right direction, we let him go, riding a short distance behind him through tea trees.

Flynn drove another small mob of cattle toward us with the helicopter. We turned one cow we had come across toward the mob, but a small yearling bull refused to go, so Garret pulled him down and tied him up. Eventually the crew loaded the yearling onto the back of the fuel truck for a ride to the yards. I turned back once to see Garret kneeling on the neck of the bull. His black hat obscured his face as his body bent to pull the strap tight around the hocks.

I put my heels to Darcy's black sweaty sides and followed Vic along a narrow cow pad through the scrub. Vic hollered back to me to keep a tighter rein on my horse as we galloped, so that if he went down in a melon hole or tripped on a hidden log, I could use the brute force of my arms to haul him up instead of being pitched over his head. At that speed I didn't think I had much of a chance to correct any blunders. Tea tree branches took slashes at my head, and I ducked forward as we leaped the downed timber that threatened to send us both tumbling. I kept a close grip on the reins, holding them crossed in both hands near the lathered horse's neck. Sweaty leather. No time to take a breath. Hat crunched against my forehead, seat glued to the saddle, shoulders and arms and stomach working with and against the force of the horse beneath me. Our two bodies moved in a mad gallop, in sync, taut muscles flexing and pouring through spaces in the trees.

The helicopter roared above us. Flynn said over the two-way radio, "Vic, I've got two bulls on the edge of the swamp ahead of you." He said something else about being careful, they had big horns, and it made Vic laugh for the rest of the day. She had seen plenty of bulls with big horns and knew how to handle them. She put spurs to her big white horse, and with her blond hair flying back she disappeared into the scrub.

I galloped close behind, leaning forward in the saddle to guide my horse through the trees, riding through split-second decisions with the rhythm of hooves and the slam of trunks against my knees. I relied on reins and saddle leather to be my translators, as if I could interpret through salt and white-flecked lather the torn and rugged script of this fast world. My horse flew through thickets of gum and leaped fallen ones, careening after animals who had the advantage of knowing the twisting pads they followed. We pulled up short when Flynn said the bulls stood fifty meters to our left, and then twenty meters to our right. Vic pointed, and I saw them, a red-horned head and a white-horned head among dense green foliage. We had entered a still life. No one moved. Vic reined her horse back, glaring at each bull, and gave everyone a few seconds to breathe.

"Look out for them," she warned. "They'll charge and hook your horse."

Then she called her dogs, pointing to the bulls until the dogs ducked into the thickets and barked at the large beasts. The bulls exploded and burst out of the trees toward us. I spun after the red one, following him at a gallop through the trees until he ducked back toward his brother. Wade and Flynn must have been watching from the chopper overhead, because they both commented later on how close the white bull had come to spearing his long horns into the flank of my horse. I had turned in time to see the mad charge and spur my horse out of the way, but only just fast enough to miss being skewered. I kept my horse's head reined in and galloped after the white bull, out to the clearing of the swamp, where he joined the other cattle in a flood toward the fence line. Vic had more trouble with the red one, fighting the scrub and the roaring chopper to get him out in the opening. She said to Flynn later, "You almost beheaded me there."

"True?"

"You ducked down near that swamp. My horse was on the beast, and he wouldn't pull up. I could feel that rush of air off the tail prop and was waiting for blood to start spurting."

When I returned to the swamp the red bull had pulled up in the water, where the dogs couldn't get to him as easily. He stood tossing his horns, hooking lily pads and swamp weed. Flynn tried to chase him out by lowering one skid of the roaring chopper onto his back, but he only retreated farther into the muck and lay down. Vic's horse stood fetlock-deep in the mud, still breathing hard. Sweat caked the animals' necks and flanks. The bull jammed one horn in the muck so his head twisted up at a strange angle. Miles arrived, and he and Vic both roped the bull, but their horses couldn't pull him out. They had to wait until Ivan gunned the bull catcher into the opening of the swamp and dragged him out. Vic's white horse had red smears of blood on his ribs from her spurs.

The day was hard on us. Max smashed into a stump on his motorbike and broke the gearshift. Vic and I were both covered in charcoal from the burned tea trees, sweat streaking through it on our faces. Dustin and his father, Dave, had bogged their bull catcher within the first couple hours. Tanner bashed his ankle against a tree so hard he couldn't walk, and no one had anything resembling a first aid kit.

We stopped for lunch at the small swamp near the yards, the helicopter landing a short distance away. Garret handed me the reins of his buckskin mare to take her down to water, and Vic took Miles' horse along with her own. We led the sweaty mounts to drink, stood with our reflections wavering in the murky pond. Wade gathered a few sticks and started a fire to boil the quart pots. Acrid smoke twisted, undecided, and caught for a moment in my nostrils. Garret was uncharacteristically nice to Tanner, bringing him lunch so Tanner didn't have to hobble to the ute. We sat on the dried mud for half an hour or so in the heat and tea tree smoke, eating our smashed beef sandwiches and crumbly biscuits and drinking hot tea. Afterward, a few of the ringers went back to tie up another bull, Garret went for the horse truck, and the rest of us headed home.

~~

Miles came to knock on my door, saying we would start at the regular time the next morning, though he'd originally planned it for earlier. The helicopters were over at Whetstone and couldn't take off until it was light enough to see, about six thirty. When they did come, the helicopters brought almost five hundred cattle from a holding paddock clear to the house yards instead of taking them the shorter distance to Carter Yards. We had to walk them nine miles back, which took five of us a day and a half. The cattle were rank. They broke a few fences, and some were so weak they didn't make it.

Vic got bucked off a little colt she was riding and took a hoof to her head. Even bleeding, she got the cow she was chasing pulled down to a kicking heap on the ground. She kneeled into the cow's neck with one leg pulled up tight so the animal couldn't move, blood pouring down her face all the while. I went to retrieve her horse. She said she was fine, don't bother with her, and she was. Troy, not far behind, had some water for the dogs in an esky in the ute, and more in the old tick-poison container. She washed out her wound and rode back to take her place with the mob without missing much of the action.

Miles put me in the lead for a while. Riding up front, I didn't have to breathe the smog of dust trailing us for several miles. I sat straight in the saddle, writing poetry in my head, turning back to see the mob spread behind me until it disappeared into the haze. In the rear, Troy drove the yellow ute with crates welded on the back for the dogs. I had a two-way in a holster strapped to my chest and across my shoulder blades. The voice of the region-wide radio repeater sounded when we had clear reception through the trees.

Midwinter, the temperature was perfect, sun slowly burning my arms and the hours turning one into another. Garret shifted to point, his mare the color of burned buckskin, the stiff grass through which he rode almost the same color. He cut a classic outline in the clearing, his flat-brimmed black hat shielding his face from the low sun, his rope coiled over one shoulder and under one arm.

~~

The poetry couldn't hold. Later, riding across the plain of dead grass, Miles swore at the helicopters, saying he couldn't see why they didn't block up the cattle on the flats, where we could get around them with the horses. As it was, the cattle ran in scattered mobs toward the old yards on the sand ridge, where thick bloodwood and tea tree stands would make an effective block

impossible. Vic rode the choppy trot of her white gelding, dogs loping behind her. She was as adamant as Miles as we followed the trailing dust and runaway cattle. Tanner came after us on a motorbike, and we held up the sweaty horses at a set of lick tubs.

Flynn called over the two-way that he'd tried to block the cattle on the sand ridge, but, well. . . . Miles swore at him because we'd probably lost those cattle altogether. We were having enough trouble as it was stopping the ones the helicopters brought back to us. Tanner took off after another mob, though he couldn't do much to turn them alone, and by the time Vic arrived on her horse as backup, all that was left were a couple cows and a bull they tied to a tree. We set up a virtual blockade for the stirred-up beasts, horses galloping, turning, and heading the cows into a circle, until they stopped for a few minutes. The dogs attacked the single deviants, following them out until they could get each to stop and turn back into the mob.

After hours of gathering hot running cattle to a set of troughs, the thousand we had managed to block up at the troughs exploded, and flung several directions at once in a galloping stampede. They poured through the charging horses and scattered into the bush from which they had come. The helicopter made a roaring slice to turn the lead and push the cattle back together, and the hard ground pounded beneath me.

In those bristling moments all that mattered was the cattle, dissipating in a hurricane of hooves and madness. I held the reins close to my horse's neck and high to keep him from tumbling if he lost his footing in the race, a dash with no direction and split-second turnings to block some beasts and avoid the gashing horns of others who wouldn't turn. The leather felt smooth and hot beneath my clenched legs, my boots braced in the stirrups, my body supple in the center, hips following the movement of the horse, torso dodging the branches and trees and reining one way or the other, to direct and redirect a mob flying like splintered shards of glass.

We were all hyperalert with adrenaline, but weakening as

the day flew past. That muster felt like a chess game with all the pieces gone insane and thinking with minds of their own. The horses glistened with dirty sweat. Vic's horse had bashed his head inside the truck and was bleeding from the mouth. The roar of the helicopters faded in and out of the trees. Short blips of message came over the two-way radio. On the flat, one big bull charged away, followed by the pack of dogs.

Max called over the two-way that a bull had just died—went down and in a few minutes was just dead. Miles said he'd had a heart attack, maybe, from the stress. They seemed to give up easily, those bulls. We blocked the cattle until Miles said maybe we should try to walk them, but as soon as the leaders headed off through the tea trees, the mob exploded in every direction. Max flipped his motorbike over a fallen branch, and Miles' stallion was so close behind him that the horse went over the top and put a hoof into the seat of the bike. Between the galloping horses, the motorbikes, and the helicopters, the cattle came together again, though we were quite a few head short.

Miles and Vic rode together in the lead. Miles called to her, "If they didn't brumby-run 'em with the helicopters, and we held 'em up on the flat, these cattle would block up and walk."

Vic replied, "The pilots have too much say. They just want to run 'em the whole way to the yards."

Miles preferred to use the horses and dogs to keep the cattle together and calm. His methods of stock management harkened back a century or two, when the stockmen worked intimately with the beasts and knew the ways of handling. He was a good stockman.

In the yards, he would work a small mob of cattle for an hour, sending his dogs around them with a trailing whistle. "Push 'em up. Jack, here."

The six or seven dogs ran like a wolf pack back and forth around the mob of horns, legs, and hooves, leaping on any cow who dodged away, until they had them in a tight bunch gathered along the fence.

"Come, Sally. Sit, Killer. Good puppies. Here. Push 'em up."
And then, "Get the fucking cunt!"

Wade told me later that we could have had the paddock mustered in half the time if Miles hadn't wanted to hold up the cattle. He said they were used to running to the watering place, Blue Hole, and then running clear to the yards. They might lose some calves, and the cattle might be sweated out when they got there, but most of them would get there in the end. We wasted helicopter hours, and at over $500 an hour, it was an expensive muster.

Cattle scattered. Too many minds tried to pull the operation in different directions, too many things were said and unsaid. We did make it to Carter Yards just before dark, the night deep blue against storm clouds, though not before Miles' stallion was peeing blood and Vic's horse colicked, tied up in the guts from the hard fast miles. I stepped from the saddle, the insides of my jean legs polished from the leather and sweat, girth caked as I loosened it and pulled my saddle free, then slipped the frothy bit from the horse's mouth. The day's mounts moved away into the dark, heads low, necks and chests and flanks streaked with dried mud.

I was a visitor to these parts, but a stranger not so strange anymore, caked in the dust deep within, the sweat and occasional tears and grit slowly building into a thicker skin. In other situations, past and future, I was much more judgmental of right and wrong. But Stilwater made the only path forward obvious with each blow it delivered to our order of things.

Who Shared the Night?

ONE NIGHT WE RODE back through clouds and the dim light of the full moon. Bulldust along the road glowed white and the rest of the grassland a darkened flax, wind stilled and tea trees thin silhouettes. Their dogs trailed behind Miles and Vic, shock collars blipping tiny lights as they trotted. The cattle had taken a few hours to move west through the holding paddock into the larger paddock, and sunset had flared and gone. Clouds did not come often in winter, but that night they were swollen with the moon and fluctuating tides, and a few storms brewed off in the gulf. Miles called out, "Snake!" or something of the sort, and the riders jabbed spurs in horses and cried out the harsh, sudden names of dogs. I saw only the slithering black outline, and then we passed and the snake disappeared. It must have measured nearly ten feet long, and could have been anything—a python or taipan—but night swallowed it and left only the sounds of hooves in the dust and stirrup leather rubbing back and forth.

Who shared the night? Slip of silent venom, stealth of dingoes, and sterling moon. Who shared thoughts of the wild, the shiver up the spine, and the way the darkness beckoned as a companion, luring, dangerous by nature but no more so than the day? The moon gave the landscape a different dimension, shadowed, elongated, wide, and naked. The horses cut an erratic path through the stillness, and the night seeped in behind them.

How many nights had I ridden in the dark, seen the country cloaked in strange sepia? I felt as if I were riding in memories, one laid over the other until they blended and I could feel only the haunting familiarity of different moments in the past, or in the future. Time was moving in a spiral, I was sure. The feeling was the same, the saddle leather, the rhythm of the horse's hooves, his tossing head, the lines of black trees and wide plain. Yet the continent was different, and with it the people, the horses, the dusty road along the fence line.

In baked moonlight at Carter Yards the horses pulled away with sweaty backs, and we loaded the dogs into the crate on the ute, packed up the gear, and drove home. Vic and I sat in back, cool wind rushing past with dust and a few stars. I thought only of the night and the piles of dogs next to me, the moon behind the white bellies of clouds, the rattling truck and the filter of dust that lingered long after we passed. The deep sky and black landscape seemed to reach forever in all directions and cancel each other at the flat, circular line of the horizon.

Carter Yards

WE HAD SPENT TWO DAYS drafting almost a thousand head of cattle through Carter Yards. Ivan, Cole, and Tanner had hauled the welder up before the onslaught of cattle, to weld the rails and gates back together. They cut new pickets for the fences and wired them in tight, and so far the yards had held.

Three of us on the crush caught each cow, and after a botulism vaccine needle in the neck, a new ear tag, a squirt of tick and lice poison, a tail-cropping, and a horn-trimming if needed, one of us opened the head gate, and the cow jumped forward into another pen.

Troy limped along between the crew of people drafting and the crew of us on the crush, using one of the last remaining electric jiggers to poke the line of cattle up the race. He wore his drooping, once-white hat, held his limp arm in a sling, and dangled a hand-rolled cigarette from his lips. When one cigarette burned to a stub, he would come over to the back of the ute, fish out his tobacco tin, set it in my way between the ear tags and the tally book, and slowly roll another one-handed cigarette.

"You want one?" he asked.

"No thanks." I reached around him to mark the cow in the book and grab another ear tag. Max slammed the gate on a cow. She wrestled against the head gate, thrashing inside the metal panels and bars, and almost turned upside down in the crush.

"I used to have races with people. They used two hands, and I just used my one. I won too," Troy drawled.

"You were fast, I'm sure," I said.

Cole ducked around the head gate handle for the large de-horners. His face and arms were streaked with dirt and sweat. He closed the jaws down over the horns, one and then the other, and they fell to the dirt. Blood spurted from the empty holes in the cow's head.

"Troy beat me at pool once in the pub, playing with one hand," Tanner said.

"Yeah, lots of practice."

Troy finished the cigarette as I jammed the botulism needle in the cow's neck. I wanted to ask him why he had to roll his cigarette right in my way when we had several thousand square miles of country around us, and I wanted to suggest that he put his cigarette-rolling-speed claims into practice, but the cow slammed against my hand, and I jumped back.

Tick liquid coated the crush bars with an oily glisten that smeared up my arms. I gave Troy a smile as he left slowly, un-knowingly forgiven, and another cow jumped forward.

We stopped midafternoon for lunch. I washed my hands

in the trough, the water turning pink from the blood. Cole let the cattle out into the larger cooling pen, dust from the herd clouding up through the ghost gums and mixing with the winter heat.

Ivan asked me once if I had ever seen snow. We had taken a break beneath gum trees, and he leaned against a post next to the same water trough while white dust precipitated back down onto us.

"I heard it can be soft and hard," he said, quizzical.

I nodded. "And wet and dry." I paused. "And cold."

Should I have told him how snow has as many qualities as rain and dust and eternal winter sun? He might never leave the embrace of two seasons in that southern hemisphere, and I was in no mood for reflection. I left him to ponder, dust obscuring the sky between gum leaves, coating my nostrils, tearing my eyes, fine and gritty in my teeth.

Exactly a year before I had been close enough to the North

Star to watch the Big Dipper swinging almost a full circle, and that was only when the sky darkened enough at night to see stars at all. The waters of the Bering Sea circulated with gray glacial sludge, and the fishing boat had rocked night after night on the slate surface. Small details strung one experience to another, a trick for tying a bowline I learned on the fishing boat automatically finding its way through my hands as I tied a rope around the neck of a sweaty cow. Now, in the darkness before dawn, I could see Cassiopeia as she rotated around the point where I knew the North Star to be, too far below the horizon to be visible.

I joined the crew outside the pens, where they lit a fire and propped the grill over smoldering tea tree sticks. Cole opened the esky and pulled out a couple plastic bags of red dripping meat from a huge bullock they had tied to a tree during the muster and then slaughtered a day later. Alan, the temporary driver, had pulled the long red and white road train up to the loading ramp. We sat in its shade.

Alan had his work cut out for him, making the long slow trip in the metal beast across thirty miles of the station on the two-track roads. He must have been in his sixties, tall, and thin enough that even doubled he wouldn't have thrown a shadow. He climbed around on the huge truck with surprising agility, swearing at the cattle and slamming gates shut behind them. He was at Stilwater on a working holiday for a month, during which time he fixed the huge tires on the old road graders so often that he resorted to filling the leaky tires with air every few days, until a truck came to haul them away. Alan drove the road train through the deep white powder of the bulldust, all the way to the house yards and back, hauling the cattle that would eventually be sold.

The owners wanted the place clean, new cattle released to see if they could turn a profit. The only reason we were out here was to provide the labor that would add value to the raw material, which was in this case a swath of gulf country plain and a herd of motley cattle. We had to be cheap and we had to be efficient. With the right ingredients—good stock, good fences, and fast and thorough musters—they could sell the calves each year, or take them to the meatworks as older animals, and more than cover all the expenses associated with running the station and getting things to and from it across the endless flat reaches between Stilwater and anywhere else. The Sutherlands were experts at managing large-scale operations and generating profits from them.

Stilwater was a risk, however, a place at the end of the line in a state of disrepair, where who knew how many animals could be wrestled from the scrub. The station was thus far a money sink, with costs soaring and returns small. The place seemed to be disintegrating faster than we could pull it together—the wild had too much lead on us.

The ten or eleven thousand old cows and bulls we pulled off the place weren't in great shape: skinny and mangy. In that drawn-down condition, many would not survive the trip to the meatworks, hours to the south. Some wouldn't even make it to the house yards alive, but all of them would give us a fight until the end.

The cattle might not look good, but they had the temperament and instinct to survive in that desolate, desiccated mess of coastal scrub, sand ridges, and salt flats. Many even had calves, which meant they might fatten up a little when the calves were weaned.

The Sutherlands had recently arranged for a load of young blond heifers to be delivered from another station, and I wondered if the new heifers would know how to find the waters, or even be able to drink the brackish liquid, and subsist on the unpalatable gulf-country grass and salt plain.

The crew, too, needed to have the temperament and experience to survive out there. At times I wondered at the fierce way we threw ourselves into the effort. We would be paid the same regardless of how hard we worked, after all. It wasn't a matter of pay, but rather a question of keeping one's job and reputation. And simple ringer's pride. This was a hard job and everyone knew it.

We sat in the dust, in the road-train shade. Cole grilled steaks on the makeshift grill and Vic cut tomatoes and onions. They spread out bread and butter on the back of the four-wheeler, and lunch consisted of a piece of leathery overcooked meat stuck between two pieces of bread.

Alan leaned back again with his steak sandwich and gave a contented sigh. "I wonder what the rich people are doing today."

After lunch we loaded the road train, climbing onto the top deck of the truck, dragging cattle up the race, breaking the last good electric jigger—Ivan was jigging a mad cow that Cole was bashing with a pipe, and Cole smashed the jigger in half—and finally sending Alan down the road through the foot-deep bull-dust for the forty-minute drive to the house yards.

In the back, Wade moved through the remaining cattle. He said in a quiet voice, "Watch out, the puppies will get you." His voice had an edge of tenderness that made me smile, the cattle ready to smash both of us against the wooden rails, and the puppies ready to latch on to a cow ear until flung free, gums smeared with cow blood or their own. Jenna sat on one of the gates watching the drafting, her clothes small and tight, her hand delicately holding a cigarette. We finished drafting and running cattle through the crush, and then caught horses for a ride back beneath storm clouds in the glowing dark.

Mother's Love

MY MOM CALLED FROM THE STATES one weekend morning to see how I was doing. Claire had to come find me, wasting precious minutes of long-distance phone time, and when I finally heard the familiar voice on the other end, I almost broke down in tears. "Remember that it is all about love, all of life," she said.

I visualized our farm in winter's husk, thinking of home, but in fact life was not all about love. What about the white corellas and how everyone wanted to blast them with the shotgun, even me at times, because of the incessant cyclone of wings and noise? Or the way Miles and Angus and Claire sat on the veranda with cups of coffee and tea and biscuits, talking about how to get yellow ear-tag buttons when we had a thousand cattle waiting, the closest source was eight hours away, and the mail plane didn't come for another week? Or how Tanner drove up in the rusty yellow ute just then, saying that Vic's old horse had broken down the gate and was gone, while the ringers just sat on the porch drinking stubbies?

It was nine o'clock in the morning, and Tanner had been out to the yards to feed the horses, gotten a load of firewood, and made a run to the rubbish dump already, while the others had barely crawled out of bed and opened a few beers. Miles said he'd better go see if he could find the horse, and they had forty liters of home-brewed rum at the camp if anyone wanted to come down after.

They found Vic's favorite old racehorse later, dead, and that wasn't about love either, just the world turning on its axis and the spinning currents crossing and recrossing. Every choice in every day generated another set of circumstances and changed the river, from the headwaters to every ripping current and miniature rivulet downstream.

Baiting

THEY BAITED WILD PIGS and dingoes with sodium fluoroacetate, called 1080. One small squirt injected into a piece of kangaroo meat was enough to kill a wild pig or several dogs. Pete Jensen, the one man in the shire licensed to inject the lethal poison, stood out on the airstrip at an aluminum table. He had a gray beard and close-shaved head and wore rubber boots, an apron, rubber gloves, and a face shield. He had come the previous night, driving the rough dusty road from Normanton. When I met him on the kitchen veranda, I thought he might be the pilot for the baiting operation, but couldn't remember having seen a plane on the airstrip. At Stilwater, new people showed up almost daily at the kitchen veranda—plumbers, electricians, carpenters, road train drivers, and backhoe operators—and I only vaguely remembered that they were baiting on July 24. I didn't realize that I was to be involved until Wade informed me that we would spend Sunday up to our elbows in rotten kangaroo meat. Wade wasn't any happier than I was about spending our one day off this way, but the decision had been made by Angus. I wanted to tell Angus that his timing wasn't very considerate, but the Sunday morning quickly turned comical.

Alan started the tractor to push a flatbed truck until Garret, grumbling too, could get it to start, and we drove out to the airstrip. Two big plastic containers on the flatbed held around a half-ton of kangaroo meat, cut and bagged originally for pet food. Pete set up his table on the crushed weeds of the airstrip, and beside it a stand with a hanging bladder of liquid 1080 poison. A cylinder of liquid petroleum gas provided pressure for the injection gun. He showed us a hypodermic needle-resistant glove he wore underneath his rubber gloves.

"You can poke these with a needle and it won't go through."

Wade brought a box of shoulder-length preg-testing gloves, but the orange see-through plastic wasn't very convincing after Pete's lecture. Alan bent his wiry frame over the blue crate of kangaroo meat and hefted up a bloody bag.

"Save a bit of this for Tucker," he said.

"Don't think I'll be staying," Pete commented.

"We could use it to bait a few crab pots anyway."

Wade fished out his pocketknife and sliced the bag open, and Alan emptied a pile of ripe meat onto the table. Pete pulled the trigger on the poison gun with one hand and, with the other, swept chunks of meat into a half drum set by the table.

"That green dye looks appealing."

"They do that to designate it as pet food."

"A few pet pigs will have a good feed tonight."

"But not tomorrow night."

Alan contemplated the dyed green meat and then spoke up. "Knew a bloke who ate 'roo meat. One time I was over there, and he had this 'roo leg on the table—he'd gotten it out of the freezer to thaw for the day. He had this old cattle dog used to hang around the house. Well, the dog got ahold of the leg and drug it out to the yard and had quite a feeding. When this guy came back, he saw that the leg wasn't on the table anymore, then he found it in the backyard. He picked up the leg, shook it off, and said that'll do. It'd been out all day in the heat and everything."

He continued with the rest of us barely listening. The sentences rose to a high pitch at the end, as if they were a series of questions.

"They reckon 'roo shooters work at night. Add a bit to their pocketbook hunting wild pigs—get a high price for them on the export market. They trap 'em in cages with one opening. Pig gets in and can't find its way out again. They bait 'em with dead cows or kangaroos. Might try to get myself a pig one of these days."

Pete nodded. He had the drum filled, and Wade and I heaved it up and carried it away from the trucks where the airplane would stop. Garret sat on a bucket and kept a tally of how many bags Alan set on the table. Wind swept through the broken stems of wild sage on the airstrip, mixing a mint fragrance into the hot smell of rotten meat. I pulled on the thin preg-testing gloves and leaned against the Land Cruiser while we waited for the plane. Meat ants crawled en masse into the drums of meat.

The small craft circled and lowered into a swirling cloud of dead grass on the underused runway. The pilot brought the plane to a stop alongside the drums of meat. He stepped out, a man in his early thirties from Mareeba, and shook hands all

around, even those bloody from the green kangaroo meat. He
pulled out his small duffel bag and swag and set them in the
dead weeds next to the vehicles. Then he took out a couple plastic buckets to transport the meat into a trough inside the plane.
Wade and I bent over the drums and used our hands to shovel
the slippery meat into the buckets. When meat filled the trough
inside the small cabin, Wade climbed across it and into the
back seat. The pilot stepped on the wing to get into his seat,
and Angus, who had arrived with his cigarette to oversee the
operation, limped over to climb into the seat beside the pilot.
The engines started, and the plane turned. Wind from the takeoff knocked over the plastic buckets on the ground and kicked
up a flurry of grass that stuck to the drying meat in the drums
and coated us in dust. We sat in the sun to wait for the plane
to return.

Later, I took a turn distributing the poisoned kangaroo meat.
I feared that some of the meat would slide out of the metal
trough and into my lap as we lifted in a rattling takeoff, so I
extended a bloody, orange-gloved hand to hold it back. Ross
Porter had told me one morning that he reckoned baiting was
the worst job he'd done: kneeling in the back of the plane where
turbulence had the most effect, looking down the chute, and
smelling rotten meat was enough to turn one's stomach. I sat
beside the trough, a thin stream of air coming from the small
vent overhead, and watched the mosaic of segmented landscape
ribbon past the small windows. The wings obscured most of the
view, but I saw the winding salt arm and long brown stretches
of the coastal plain.

Wade eventually turned in his seat and said over the internal
roar, "You can start, mate."

I fished down through the meat in the trough to slide the
old paint-tin lid from over the chute opening. The pilot recommended one piece of meat every two seconds, but the suction
through the small opening pulled out several pieces at once, until

I could sweep them in with more deliberation. I kneeled in the cramped space between the metal trough and the rear seat, and used one hand to slip pieces out.

Red muscle tissue, white fascia, and green dye made a slurry in the trough. During the second between pieces of meat, I could see a small changing portion of the landscape through the tube of the chute. I felt as if I were looking down the drainpipe of a sink, and the view through the hole was a staccato rhythm of meat, dead grassland, meat, blue water, meat, forest, meat. The sudden pitches and drops of the plane made me brace for balance as I tried to imagine and piece together the landscape beneath. We were following a sand ridge perhaps, or a waterway, crossing a swamp, and then I had to focus on the pile for a moment to steady my concentration, the rancid kangaroo meat not hindering my enjoyment of the flight. Wade called back to quit for a moment, and I looked out the windows again.

The Solomon River wound like a long blue snake in perfect oscillations to the coast. Duck Creek joined it just before the mouth, and I caught a glimpse of trash where Spider's Camp had been.

I had been to Spider's Camp once after the fishing trip with Stephen, on a break from fencing with the mustering contractors. Dead bur plants grew up through old fishing nets and crab pots. The sandy bank dropped down to the lapping blue channel of the river. Cole had lit a fire for a barbecue, folding out the black greasy grill to cook ribs, steak, and sausage. We sat on flipped-over buckets, eating chewy meat with greasy fingers. The guys picked over some of the junk at the camp, so much that it would take a landfill to swallow it. Young Tommy chased around a few of the chooks. Tanner made a bet with him that he couldn't catch one, but Tommy sprinted through the junk and landed on a squawking rooster, which he stuffed into a dog crate.

The camp had its own graded airstrip for the drug-running operation that had once thrived there. All that remained now were a few hectares of trash, perhaps a hundred empty fuel drums, crab pots, fishing nets, empty buckets, a shower with a raised water tank, foam floats, books, batteries, shredded tarps, and thirty chickens left by Spider, the fisherman who had been evicted by Steven Craye.

The chickens ran around the camp, somehow surviving though no fresh water existed there. Angus claimed he knew of a bull who had survived off salt water for years up in that corner of the paddock, drinking right from the Solomon, which was as salty as the sea that swept up it each tide. I wondered if perhaps the animals there did not evolve some mechanism of desalination, perhaps a gland below the eyes of those feral bulls. The crocodiles and barramundi made the transition easily, surviving in all bodies of water along the salt gradient. I filled some water buckets again for the chickens, and the ringers caught a few more to take back to Claire at the station.

In the plane, we followed the coast, a line of white sand beach separating the silver water from the green forest of the sand ridge. Inland, the salt arms branched in tree patterns, white salt pans between them, and then the mane of grassland. Wade nodded back for me to start, and I finished the trough as we headed back toward the airstrip. Two horses grazed far below, framed by an expanse of the brown, fawn, and black of burned grassland.

The gods seemed decidedly detached in making rulings on life and death, I thought. Earlier in the morning we had joked with the pilot about being a meat distributor for the gulf land, and then I, with a prayer of compassion, had shoveled enough poisoned meat down the chute to kill several thousand pigs. The pigs and dingoes were the only carnivorous mammalian predators in that country, aside from a few wild cats. A human would have to eat twenty doses of the poison for a lethal effect, a hawk one hundred doses, and the reptilian carnivores, like goannas, five hundred and fifty doses. It was as species-specific a poison as the Queensland Government Department of Natural Resources and Mines could make.

The poisoning effort was part of a national initiative to limit invasive plants and animals on the island; the introduced species wreaked havoc on the sensitive riparian areas, damaging habitat and fragile ecosystems and threatening the existence of several native species. While offering commercial pig hunters the opportunity to trap, shoot, transport, and export the porcine pests had proved effective in many regions, Stilwater lay at the fringes of civilization, and the distances were too great to ensure commercial hunting would be a successful endeavor. And so they resorted to poison.

Miles said he didn't know why they had to bait before the mustering was finished. He and his crew would have to leave their dogs chained up for the next month, or have them killed by even one bite of poisoned kangaroo meat. The crew would seem naked without the wolf pack of dogs running around and attacking feral bulls, circling the mobs of cattle to keep them together, piled in the crates on top of each other for the ride to the yards, and trailing the horses in a panting black, tan, and red furry fleet.

I knew as well as Miles did that not much at Stilwater made sense, but in that flight above the wide forests I could see only simple patterns of rivers and swamps and salt arms, and the gulf. The water looked pleated and tucked along the shore by the wind. Patterns ran together into two horizons, the flat blue of the water and the flat green of the land. The plane cut a course toward the old airstrip and brought us back to the twisting grass, the parked vehicles, and drums of darkening bloody meat.

Wilderness

THAT FAR SECTION AT THE BASE of the Cape York Peninsula, along the drainages of the Powder and Solomon Rivers, is one of the last great wilderness areas in Australia. Looping rivers form wetland systems that draw thousands of migrating birds during the wet season and serve as a breeding ground for a huge range of wildlife. Twisting mangrove swamps open to the gulf, the salt and fresh water, swamp and open sea, offering in their transition thousands of niches to encourage biotic diversity beyond imagination. The habitats and transition zones offer the possibility for adaptation and evolution in all species, even humans.

The peninsula itself, ancient and undisturbed by tectonic grumblings or restlessness, lies flat and eroded by the passing millennia. Its Mesozoic soils are almost devoid of nutrients, unresponsive to fertilization, and so old they do not easily support agriculture, holding at bay all but the cattle barons. Eroding sediments wash seaward. River systems in the remote horn of the continent catch and surge with more water than the entire landmass south of the Tropic of Capricorn, integral water systems that replenish the Great Artesian Basin. The peninsula holds tropical savanna, wetland, river, mangrove swamp, mountain forest, and, on the far eastern edge, tropical rainforest ecosystems. The intact mosaic provides refuge and habitat for over three thousand species of flowering plants and seven hundred vertebrate land animals, a highly diverse mixture of relic species from ancient continental conglomerates, species endemic to the island continent, and more recent invaders.

This place does not receive many human visitors, though a national park covering almost five hundred thousand hectares embraces some of it and a wild river area reaches fifteen thousand miles along the base of the peninsula. The Queensland government defines a "wild river" as a river system with all, or almost all, of its "natural values" intact; the designation does not affect most station operations, nor fishing, camping, hunting, ecotourism, or indigenous activities, and allows mining, aquaculture, and animal husbandry, with only a few qualifications.

I thought the wilderness thrived in its exile, though I knew that peoples who had lived and still live along the lengths—the Koknar, Kunjen, Kokoberrin, and Agwamin, among others—are its traditional caretakers, or the ones taken care of. In their minds the rivers are not isolated on the margins, but cut through the center of their world.

They had developed over millennia knowledge and a set of practices that enabled them to thrive on the Australian continent. Called "traditional ecological knowledge" today, this was the secret to their persistence and continuity. They might have set fire to the savannas as indigenous people did in many regions around the globe, to further the mosaic, to burn the tall grasses and expose the long goannas for bush tucker, to lure the larger prey out to the young shoots that would emerge from the fertilization of ash, nutrients, and minerals, and to cultivate the edges. Ecological transitions always make life more interesting and, in the long term, more flexible, adaptable, and enduring. The Aborigines would know which bird species landed and stayed and which flew through, which made their nests and which harvested the seeds of certain grasses and reeds along the shores. They are, or would have been, an intimate part of the wilderness itself. We could try to know the same, to put in the time and surrender comfort and arrogance. We could not, though, successfully hold or be held in the net of thousands of species over thousands of years. A few hundred years had resulted in waves of mass extinction, and a different planet entirely.

The winding rivers did not seem to be bothered much by the occasional cow or mad dash of ringers, but colonization had completely changed the place. The invasion of exotic species such as pigs, wild goats, wild horses, bovines, rabbits, cane toads, carp, trout, tilapia, pigeons, starlings, acacia, mesquite, mimosa, parkinsonia, tamarisk, gorse, buffel grass, and rubber vine, among countless others—all adapted to different ecosystems on different continents—transformed the systems the cultures before had worked so hard to maintain. The forces of erosion, invasion, selection, and pollution pressured the wetlands, the dynamic floral and faunal communities succumbing or adapting to a system that had never been completely static.

But perhaps the lack of Aboriginal management—of fire and ritual and acute observation and action, all entirely place-specific—had reconfigured the landscape as much as the invasive species had. A few cattle and stockmen and fishermen wouldn't do the same damage as a fleet of incoming tourists or widespread urban or mining development, but neither would the newcomers know by feel, by cellular memory and footprint, the mapping of the waterways and crossings of migratory species; neither could they name the half-million species of plant, animal, fungus, and algae, or trace the weather systems as the sky moved over mangroves and clouds touched the water. We were not creatures of patience and observation.

Knowledge

THE GUIDING FRAMEWORK NOW is a way of knowing called science, a regime of supposedly objective perspectives with little competition. Technology is the way forward. European colonists had arrived in Australia with their own system of knowledge—ideas and implements traded, bought, borrowed, or stolen from other advanced civilizations on continents across the globe. A way of knowing in which we question, test, develop, and adapt hypotheses to match the reality we perceive, science has gained remarkable credibility, even as we have come to understand that the act of measuring changes the measured and observing influences the observed. The human mind understands things when they are controlled, contained, and categorized. But our system of knowledge has provided little understanding of the ways interactions and relations, matter in motion, manifest as something greater.

The colonizers traversed the immense distances of Australia. They combatted and negotiated the brutal aridity and extremes of the continent. They built thriving settlements, mines, and livestock operations, empowered by a few thousand years of science. Now highways, railways, flight paths, electric lines, and radio, cell phone, and satellite communication systems form a net across the outback. The School of the Air, Royal Flying Doctor Service, and postal service systems reach far and wide. Road trains and rail trains cart supplies in and out to the farthest reaches of the continent. And ships, jets, fiber optics, satellites, and airwaves connect the continent to the rest of the world. One can access information almost anytime and anywhere on the Australian continent. But in the information overload, wisdom is nowhere to be found.

Even in the outback, technology abounds. Stockmen and station owners and managers use bull-catching vehicles, motorbikes, and helicopters, and employ solar and wind energy, advanced telemetry water-monitoring systems, computer-chip livestock identification buttons, GPS and GIS digital mapping software, and computer-aided inventories of livestock, stud bulls, stock horses, and station operations. Gathered electronically at a particular site or outstation, data is transmitted via radio signals to a station or headquarters far from the measurement site.

I was up helping Claire in the kitchen once, making short

work of a pile of potatoes, when the son of the owner, Sean Sutherland, came in through the back door. I was surprised when he invited me to come over for a beer later. At dusk, I sat out on the veranda writing until Claire told me that he had returned. I crossed the lawn beneath the fig tree and climbed the steps to the house Stephen Craye had often occupied. Sean was trying to set up a new GPS unit. He showed me a new GPS wristwatch he had as well. He introduced me to two men, a pilot and a hydrologist, who were drinking beer on the elevated veranda. They had a stack of maps piled on the table, corners curling from the memory of rolling, and I gravitated toward them. They were developing a set of satellite maps for the station to use in a database: topography, water courses, bores, fence lines, salt arms.

Mapping technologies are used to delineate pasture boundaries, to pinpoint bore and outstation locations, and to identify vegetation types and ground cover. A team of surveyors will use four-wheel-drive vehicles and helicopters to follow and track on the GPS unit a fence line or road, and to create waypoints at bores, yards, and outstations. The GPS units triangulate off satellites to mark positions on the ground. This data is then uploaded into a digital mapping system and integrated with satellite images, aerial photographs, or topographic maps to develop a multilayered station map. Land cover and vegetation type are assessed and labeled on the maps, as are animal ranges, soil types, precipitation, temperature, and subsurface aquifers.

This data is then verified with monitoring and ground-truthing, a method of gathering information in the field. A team of range scientists collects information on land use or vegetation type and cover, to be used in conjunction with the computer-generated maps. These maps are then used to develop grazing strategies, create forage budgets, redesign paddocks to improve grazing sustainability, and plan new fence or water developments around existing infrastructure.

And yet these days the new systems often revert to ancient knowledge. Rotational grazing and prescribed burning have found their way back into some management schemes as ideas of sustainability gain currency. Some livestock operations fill out environmental reports to post on their websites. They advertise efforts to recognize and protect ecologically vulnerable areas. They try to minimize soil, water, and air pollution, and work with interested parties on land and water management. They monitor grazing lands for vegetation, water, and soil conditions, and prevent weed encroachment and pest invasion through collaboration with research and development groups. These methods are expensive, and they often yield positive results.

I still am not a convert of science, however, though I use it, study it, abide by its methods, and claim it as my own. Science has saved millions of lives, but it has cost as many or more if you consider those other than human. Science has made life easier, or at least allowed us to adopt different realities. Science has facilitated the use of natural resources faster than any other way of thinking, at any time in human history. And yet the greatest insights lie beyond the reach of science, or at least beyond where it has advanced so far. Science provides the illusion of knowing and the fantasy of control, but any scientist knows its shortcomings.

Stilwater reminded me of the fallacy in such beliefs, and the vulnerability they fostered. We clipped in mandatory ear tags that were meant to track meat from hoof to shelf. We smashed up vehicles with work they were never designed to handle, and scattered cattle across the plains with helicopters. We fed lick that contained a concentration of various nutrients missing from the gulf-country forage. But when it rained the various chemicals reacted with water, and the lick made a deadly soup that killed more cattle than it saved. The solar panels would be covered in eucalyptus leaves or coated with corella droppings, and we'd have to revert to the generator, or kerosene lamps or candles. And the ear tags would be torn out in the scrub.

Technology had its limits on Stilwater, and after a while our confidence in it inevitably eroded. If the entire gulf wanted to come inland, let the tide flow. Don't try to hold the sea at bay. Wait for the wet season, when the rivers would swell and push the saltwater several miles out to sea. Then you might have control of the land again, or at least the rivers would, for a while, until another tide pushed them upstream again.

Bulls

IN THE YARDS, TWO BULLS CIRCLED in a pen, resisting the drafting, moaning, and smashing against the rails. They were part of the mob of feral bulls that had been bumped or roped or thrown and tied to trees, left for a few hours or a few days, and eventually hauled back to the yards. They convinced us they did not possess amiable temperaments by charging anyone who crawled through the pipe railing to undo the twine off hay bales, or by smashing the rails from their welds and leaping through the openings into other pens.

On that day, the mob of bulls had to be drafted again, but two of them refused to move into the next pen. Ivan threw a blue tarp onto one bull, and the shredding plastic landed high on his horns and draped in front of his eyes for a few mad moments before falling to the ground, where the snotty beast trampled it. The bulls didn't move forward, or even move at all other than to stamp on the old tarp. Ivan smacked the bulls a few more times with the poly pipe and then leaped into the branding pen to shoulder an old tire used to cushion the calf cradle. He heaved the tire onto one of the bull's horns in an attempt to try to scare the bull into moving, but the bull easily dumped the tire onto the trampled tarp. Max, beside Ivan, grabbed a fallen rail and shoved it into the pen against a bull's head. I sat on top of the rails and thought of bulls and the age-old mind games between man and beast. For a moment Max looked as if he might prove his prowess by strapping his lanky legs around the ribs of one of these beasts, saying, "Look out, look out now." But the simple truth was that the bulls had the better of all of us. So instead Max said, "Look out, we'll have the whole yards in the pen soon," and Ivan reached in, eyeing the bulls eyeing him, to retrieve the old tire and the shredded tarp.

Fighting

MOST OF THOSE OUTBACK CHARACTERS had a fighting sense still in them, born of wide spaces and the struggle for existence, a certain hardness built up in layers over time. Vic loved to tell me about a mentor of hers, an old stockman who had crushed his body a thousand times in various configurations of broken bones, and how even he still mustered and rode buck-jumping horses and didn't let any of it slow him down.

The closer to the end of the dry season we drew, the more fight seemed to swell up in everyone, as if the threat of the wet season meant that all work had to be finished, and we weren't going to let a few lost battles beat us. More ferocity, determination, and steadfastness emerged and dwelled within each of us. This often resulted in standoffs, and in the holding, everyone kept a little dignity, enough to last through another round.

Consciousness

I TOOK INSTINCT TO BE THE MOST TANGIBLE LINK between existence and the divine. Instinct—not necessarily the deepest primal urges, though they were at work too, but rather a moment-to-moment sense of discomfort or inspiration—guided me forward. Instinct and a somewhat malleable code of ethics.

I had sensed Australia, and actually written of my desire to reach a station in the outback in my earliest journals, only to forget and then have the opportunity surface unexpectedly, with just the opening needed to reach the farthest depths. I followed, though I knew not where I traveled, or where the path would end. And yet there was no end, only this pattern: the archetypal battles between form and chaos.

What good were more than two thousand years of Buddhist contemplation on responsibility for one's actions, karmic processes, and the transformation of negativity to light if we all degenerated and devolved so quickly? If, say, one of the ringers were to be hauled—fighting and snarling—to some monastery high in the Himalayas, would he ponder the grief and joy and suffering of others? Perhaps such consideration could be taught. Such sympathy might exist in a place where another layer of order and simplicity had been imposed on the landscape. But this was no such place, and so we were left with our instincts.

I smiled, despite my nausea, at the savageness taking shape in all of us. What a muster it would be if all arrived with a vow to harm no living thing. A thousand monks would have to hold us in their meditations to smooth the ripples in these rivers, for even small semblances of consciousness to surface in that shaking river's skin. Ultimately, I felt, we did not need higher consciousness, but coats of crocodile leather.

Jenna

AT THE MUSTERING CAMP, the crew had a chain hooked between two of the metal porch posts. They hung dripping, hacked-off chunks of silverside roast on it, after rubbing them with curing salt. Miles was sawing a dull knife through hunks of beef from a bullock and setting the bloody pieces on the folding table—next to jars of Vegemite, peanut butter, jam, and cane syrup—to be rubbed with salt. Tanner stood at a tub filled with water and dirty dish suds. Vic sat with the little green and yellow books, tallying cattle numbers for Wade and Miles to consider. Max said, "Plug your ears," before sweet young Jenna blasted a shotgun at the crows in a nearby tree, deafening those of us under the shade tarp for a moment. She lifted the gun and shot again, and a rascal bird landed in a heap of ruffled black feathers before us, one wing pointing out toward the lagoon.

Max had brought Jenna sobbing up to the kitchen one night after she'd bent to light the campfire. Someone had splashed petrol on the wood, and the sudden flames seared her face. Claire called the Royal Flying Doctor Service, and I got Jenna comfortable, sent Max for a cold wet towel and some dry clothes, and took her vital signs. She didn't have any burning inside her nose or mouth, only a few blisters on her nose, bright red cheeks, seared eyelashes, and a small burn on her arm. I kept dipping towels in ice water, wringing and replacing them on her face and arm, and talking with her to calm her down. The Royal Flying Doctor Service recommended a painkiller over the radio. After her pulse had slowed and her burns cooled, we sent her home to bed.

The day before the campfire incident, Jenna had been slammed into the front of the bull catcher when Max hit a ditch. The next mail plane brought an esky full of chocolate and Pringles for her, and we hoped she'd be all right then. Sure enough, she came into the pens the next day in a cute tank top and tight pants, bulls pummeling the fences around her, more of a liability than Miles needed to deal with. I thought she seemed sweet enough, but Troy said she wasn't that sweet, that he'd known plenty of her kind, and he wouldn't say any more.

Vic thought Jenna was there only because Max needed someone to make him feel set apart and validated, a man among men. Vic wouldn't let him get away with any unnecessary arrogance, and always put him in his place. "The little runt," she called him. She was confident enough that no one contradicted her, and she was a beauty. Jenna, in contrast, was doe-eyed and meek, not quite belonging in the mustering camp.

The scene was a little surreal to me. I didn't want to get caught up in the catfights or purrings, so I stayed clear and ignored her and Max for the most part. But I couldn't ignore them completely. Max flaunted her, Dustin fell in love with her at one point, and Ivan had been her boyfriend before, and maybe still was when Max wasn't around. I watched it unfold warily as I would a mob of cattle—waiting and wondering what would set them off.

Alan

IVAN INVITED ALAN DOWN to the camp for a drink the night before he caught the mail plane back to Melbourne. I wasn't sure if Alan was happy to be leaving the wild North, which was as engaging and addictive as it was frustrating. During a lunch break in the yards, he mused that he would be pruning rose bushes again that weekend, and back to fabricating doors in the factory on Monday. He leaned against the truck while we sat near the crush, covered in manure, dust, sweat, and oily tick poison.

He will miss this, I thought. I knew I would miss him—his gentle humor and the integrity that held him stable in the chaos, like a sapling holds in a flood. But he wasn't untouched; he had caught all sorts of driftwood during his short stay at Stilwater.

The most infamous story of Alan involved a day when he went on a bore run with Ross and they spotted a pig sleeping in the mud. Alan leaped out with a gun. Finally, a chance for him to go pig hunting! He stole forward—cautiously, quietly—finally raising the rifle to shoot the still black monster. A perfect shot! But when he went to view his handiwork, Alan discovered the pig's legs tied together with rope. The culprit was Max, of course, the kid with too much testosterone and a penchant for feral pigs. Max would have chased the savage animal down and rolled it with a motorbike. Then, lacking a weapon, he would have tied the pig up so he could come back later. Alan mercifully ended the pig's life, but he was downhearted after the failure of his one killing expedition and naturally he was the butt of several jokes afterward.

Another time, while they were loading one of the feral bulls, Garret had called to Alan that he should "get his attention." Trusting too much, Alan had walked courageously toward the bull, waving his hat. The bull jerked to life suddenly and charged. The massive beast hit the end of the rope just a few inches from Alan's drained white face.

He maintained his humor more than many on the station, though at the yards that last day he was properly swearing at the race full of cattle, ready to shoot them all, he said. Ivan raised his eyebrows at Alan's animosity, grinned, and, when Alan turned around next, Ivan made a face to stir Alan into a smile. Alan only muttered, "Youuuu bastard."

At lunch Garret thought we should sneak Alan's bag of biscuits away from him, and when I glanced over, Ivan was on his belly squirming underneath the truck. I saw one arm reach slowly toward Alan's blue esky, pinch the Ziploc of jam-filled bickies, and retreat. Garret asked Alan if he wanted a biscuit. Alan replied that he had his own, adamant until Garret held out the snitched bag to him. Alan took it back, shaking his head. Yes, he would miss us too.

Alan sent me letters and updates about the continent and afterward he would call me, unfailingly, two or three times a year. Sometimes he caught me at home on the farm; other times he had to try for a few consecutive months, but eventually he would reach me and fill my ears with news of the North and the South, floods or drought. One time he reported that the road train he had driven, not a small beast by any means, sank entirely under ten feet of water in a flood. The station lost a helicopter and a truck too, he said. He wasn't sure what happened to all of the folks there, who was left and who wasn't, but one day he would take a trip back and let me know.

His voice always made me smile, the thick Australian accent hard to follow at times, always ending in a question mark. While the North was flooding, the South would be scorching in a drought, "all the fish boiled in the river and the potaters baked in the ground." Amazingly, he wasn't joking.

He told me of the cyclones, the floods, the droughts, and the fires. He wouldn't let me forget that the wild smoldered, plenty alive, and that it had once ridden with us, throbbing just beneath the skin, at times overwhelming us completely.

That day, beneath the ghost gums in Carter Yards, the tension hung thick despite the necessary humor. The five hundred or so cattle had taken longer to draft than anticipated and keeping them watered proved difficult because only two of the pens had troughs, and the cattle kept those sucked dry. We rotated the mobs so that each could have part of a day on water, but they had also been penned three days without food. The truck that was supposed to haul hay from the station had broken down and Mike had the week off. The situation provided yet another reason for Vic and Miles to criticize both Wade and Angus.

During the tumult, Ivan slashed his finger with the bangtail knife. I had just treated his thumb that morning, dislocated by a cow a day or two before. Cole brought some of their horse medical supplies over, and I wrapped up Ivan's finger with horse tape, adding a layer of duct tape for good measure. He had duct tape on both hands then, and with another gob of it holding one of his shoes together, he looked pretty patched up. Ivan just grinned.

Alan left driving the road train, cattle falling down and getting trampled in the back on the long track back to the house yards. We finally closed the last of the gates and piled into a couple trucks. I sat on the broken seat of the ute, squished between two other ringers, the dogs in crates in the back. As we drove, I allowed myself to feel the exhaustion of nightfall.

That night Angus offered to drive us over to the camp. He had been singing at the table during tea, his deep voice faltering: "Twinkle, twinkle, little star, Grandma in her motorcar, push the pedal down too far, now we don't," lowering into the wavering final notes, "know where she are," and then repeating the refrain again. I preferred to walk the hundred yards to the camp, crossing beneath the sea of stars in a sultry black sky. I entered the light in front of the donga, the fire still burning and a few of the crew washing plates and finishing tea. Miles offered Ivan's beers around—because Ivan had suggested the party and had been providing the camp with beer for a while—and brought out the bottle of tequila and the home-brewed rum. He set Alan up with drinks in both hands. Alan didn't have many before he started laughing at one of Ivan's jokes and couldn't stop. Ivan had all of us laughing, but Alan leaned back, melting in mirth at his end of the table, red in the face and holding his ribs he was laughing so hard. He carried on for several minutes, until we were laughing at him. Vic sat at the table across from me, her long blond hair wet from the shower. Cole retired after a beer or two, but not before pouring me a drink of cider on ice.

The tequila bottle on the table in front of me read *Hecho en México, Tequila, Jalisco,* and in my mind I returned to hills covered in rows of blue agave that inhabited my memory from times past—still vivid, sharp, and so close I could reach out to touch the leathery blue skin, and the hard dark claws along the margins. I looked up at the table of ringers and after two drinks, Mexico swirled into images of the fire and donga, and I quit drinking then. I could barely keep my reality in place, continents and time swirling together.

Jenna walked around in short shorts and a fleece coat so white I wondered how she could manage it in that camp, where grease and smoke and mud or dust stuck to everything. Ivan was in fine form, quite a few drinks along, but he handled them better than the rest of us, acting his usual carefree self. Miles remained a little subdued, and I would look up to find him watching me. Angus staggered away eventually, bidding all a good night. Alan and I walked home in the dark later, but Ivan said he and Miles and Vic stayed up until three in the morning.

Vic's father had died on that night a few years before, and

she wouldn't let Ivan go to bed. He stayed up drinking with her, dancing and perhaps crying, all in the safe company of the night. The crew slept in an hour later than usual, but Miles was up before the stars disappeared, dragging the camp out of bed for another day of dust and cattle. Alan took his small duffel and left on the mail plane that morning. He lifted one hand in farewell before climbing into the copilot's seat and disappearing into the wide sky above the outback.

~~

With Alan gone, the weekend felt a little subdued. Wade went to check crab pots he'd set in the river. He sent Garret and me on a fence run, telling us to be back in time to bring our horses home from Carter Yards. Garret left to pack smoko, leaving me to load the ute with fencing gear, pickets, and the heavy rolls of barbed wire, and to refuel it with the hand pump on the fuel drum. I spilled petrol on my pants when changing drums with the pump, upset at Garret, who had slipped away to do nothing more than pack a few biscuits in a Ziploc.

We fixed wires Ross had broken with the road grader and pounded steel pickets. At smoko and lunch both, Garret gathered small tea tree sticks and lit a wisping fire to boil the water in his quart pot. We sat in the shade of the tea trees, just the two of us, a flame flickering and sending up a twining ribbon of smoke. The conversation was almost sweet, Garret telling me of horses he'd ridden, stations and feedlots and other places he'd worked across Australia. I saw then a glimpse of the wanderer, arrogant by nature, and wondered which track had pulled him to these remote reaches. He had a college education and, in a subtle shift, could carry on a serious conversation; I just never knew when it was coming.

Finally he grinned and said we should get on with the fencing; we were missing a good cricket match. We drove home late in the day with the big stock truck full of horses from Carter

Yards and two young poddy calves we'd stuck in as well. The little calves had to fend for themselves among the horses' legs on the jolting ride back. Miles' crew had a late day too, finishing after dark. I couldn't imagine how they maintained their energy, working from dark to dark without a day off. They subsisted on corned beef, cigarettes, coffee, and their bloodstream ran mostly salty tide.

Rite of Passage

WHEN DUSTIN TURNED EIGHTEEN, Ivan tackled him and wrapped duct tape around his arms and legs. Ivan had had quite a bit to drink, and smoke too, perhaps. Then Ivan tried to tackle Miles, but Miles had quit drinking, at least for a little while, and his body mass was at least double Ivan's. That tackle didn't go far.

Garret thought they should shave Dustin with the horse clippers as long as he was taped up. His ideas always held more malice than Ivan's, and this one sent us into hysterics.

Ivan teased Garret. "I feel good; wanna feel?"

Claire fried barramundi dipped in beer batter and cooked mud crab in chile sauce and coconut milk, and we celebrated Dustin's passage to adulthood.

~~

The next morning, the Royal Flying Doctor Service came out to Stilwater for a field day. They gave us a short lecture when we came in from the yards for lunch. They outlined the protocols if someone were to get hurt and Claire pulled out the big medicine box that they kept supplied. They provided landing flares for the runway in case the pilots had to come in at night. The doctor and nurses offered a clinic afterward for the ringers and families of the station and mustering crews, and saw a few of us in private. For most, it would be a long stint between doctor visits.

From my perspective people in the outback chose to live so

far away because they had an armor of some kind already, a psychological imprinting of independence, and wouldn't be that prone to damage. When people did get hurt, they didn't think much of it, unless they wanted to leave.

The body adapted to this place if it could, it was shaped and reshaped, defined and redefined. If the place wasn't right, then the body knew it and left. We were drawn here, imperceptibly yet undeniably, perhaps not to the place itself, but to a dynamic interaction between the land and our bodies. We were the vessel molded, into which the world poured its offerings, day after day. We could hold the sweet or the salty.

Ivan

THAT NIGHT, IVAN CAME UP to use the telephone. Tanner usually came up for a cup of Milo, the Australian equivalent of hot chocolate, which I never thought was strong enough. He didn't stay long this time, and Ivan joined Garret and me on the couches around the television. Garret and I each had a couch. Instead of taking the third couch, Ivan sat next to me. Joking or not—I could never tell—he said I should marry him. I humored him.

"What would I do then?"

"I've got a property, you could come muster cattle with me."

"You've got a property?"

Ivan, twenty-six and seemingly the least responsible member of the crew except for Max, was not a likely candidate to own anything more than his broken-down truck and his two mongrel dogs. Describing it as a property meant that it would be large enough to run cattle. Ivan leaned back on the couch, beer in hand and a dirty baseball cap over his shaved brown hair. His eyes lacked the irresponsible light they usually carried. The station crew rarely took Ivan seriously. He looked at me steadily.

"How did you get a property?" I asked, still not sure whether to believe him.

"I have two of them." They were each about a thousand hectares, he said.

Garret and I couldn't have been more incredulous.

"I walked into the bank and asked for a loan of $545,000."

"And they gave it to you?"

Ivan nodded.

I was in disbelief, wondering if I could have been wrong in all of my assessments of everyone on that crew.

"I've got one leased for $60,000 a year, and it's paying itself off."

Garret asked, "How did you get enough money to get a loan in the first place?"

"Do you see me driving a new motorcar?"

Most young ringers saved up enough cash to buy new utes— Toyota Land Cruisers with four-wheel drive, and often winches and a second pair of headlights, to spot kangaroos on the long stretches of outback roads. The cheapest of those new utes, or similar models, cost around $50,000. Garret drove one, as did Max and Dustin. Miles just had his old yellow ute, but he also had a large stock truck to haul horses and cattle. Ivan said he hadn't paid more than a couple thousand for any vehicle he'd ever owned. He had a motorbike and two dogs, and the full extent of his wardrobe barely filled one duffel. He worked one job after the next, and then worked on his properties in his free time.

Garret left for bed. Ivan and I stayed up talking until late, of how his mother kicked him out at the age of twelve, and how at thirteen he was working full-time at a mine, and then on cattle properties. He harbored no resentment or animosity.

"I reckon the sooner you have to face things, the better off you are. I learned there are two types of people, followers and leaders. And two types of leaders, those who lead you up, and those who lead you down. I don't want to be working for someone else my whole life. Now? I reckon at least I'm having fun. And if I'm having fun, my dogs are happy. They might be in the way, but they're happy. And if we're all happy, the cows are happy."

Ivan—earrings and torn jeans and sudden laugh and careless, carefree personality—had perhaps the best approach of any of us. He had a perspective born of higher dreams and harsher experiences. He never seemed to get tired or mad, only kept his offhand humor.

I remember when Ivan and I backed up Miles' truck to the old pile of manure we used as a ramp to jump the horses out onto, and a crow hopped off the pile, stumbled, and flew a short distance. Ivan grinned and said, "There's Tanner's crow," because Tanner hated crows and blasted every one he saw with his shotgun. Ivan reckoned, "We should catch it," and he slid out the truck door with a dirty shirt that had been on the seat and ran after the crow. Miles commented that it must have been crook, hopping around like that. Across the road, Ivan caught it. He carried the crow under his arm and would later release

the ruffled bird in Tanner's room in the donga, where it proceeded to leave droppings over the bed and piles of clothes, which Tanner wouldn't be able to see because the generator had blown a fan belt. Miles said he would take the blame, because Ivan had also put a four-foot-long goanna in Tanner's room earlier. Miles also said that he felt sorry for the crow, who was sure to die a painful death. Then we jumped the rest of the horses off onto the old manure pile, unsaddled them, hosed them off, and fed them. Angus and Dustin came back from town with two fuel drums, one for the choppers and one for the vehicles, and eight cases of beer. The crow would eventually escape through a partially open window.

Ivan rolled cigarettes. He hadn't eaten dinner yet and he sank his lean frame deeper into the couch, clothes still smeared with dust and vehicle grease. He took his motorbike back to camp beneath an outback sky netted in stars. I never answered his proposal.

Rain

AND THEN THERE WAS RAIN, suddenly. I had been told that the months from March to November were strangers to rain in the gulf country. Never did the clouds off the water build up enough to precipitate, and rarely did clouds swirl in at all. Yet there we were in August, watching the sky as we branded calves, five hundred of them so large I had difficulty pulling them into the branding cradle.

We alternated jobs, three of us on each calf. Dustin worked with one arm because the other was crushed by a bull at the Mareeba Rodeo, only a couple of pins holding the bones together now that he had thrown his cast away. The swelling had started to go down; dirt and cow blood obscured the line of stitches. Max was dragging, barely able to keep pace at the head, so Ivan switched places with him and we worked together, fast and focused.

And then the rain was on us, pouring, running in red rivers of blood and manure and dust, the yards sodden, our clothes drenched. We made it back to the kitchen and watched the torrents of water. Angus limped over to the window. "Reckon you're stuck here for the wet season," he teased in a gravelly voice. The rivers would swell and several cattle die before we could change out the toxic lick in all of the tubs, but the rain was a purgative, cleansing the turmoil.

A Slow Fall from Grace

THE CLEANSE DID NOT LAST, not even until the rains ceased. Word came down from Gene and Stephen Craye that we would have to finish the mustering in two weeks. Angus told Garret he had only a month left as well; Sutherland Corporation was cutting employees to save money. The muster hadn't returned as many cattle as expected when they purchased Stilwater, and the majority of shipped stock had been feral bulls and wild cows, whose market value was low.

The news left Miles with several thousand head of cattle left to muster, draft, brand, and ship in two weeks, or he would lose his credibility and reputation as a head stockman. Angus would be left with a station half mustered, a minimal crew, too much work to handle, and his own position tenuous. I did not have any reputation to make or save, but I threw bull calves in the branding cradle all the next morning. They fell with a loud crash on the old tire that was supposed to cushion them. A couple leaped clear out of the race before they reached me, almost knocking over the roaring furnace before the ringers tackled them.

Bad news begat more bad news. Word came that Wade's father had passed away. The family had left suddenly, after keeping the father's ailing condition secret for weeks. Angus and Claire got word from Stephen that their grandchildren were not to come to Stilwater anymore. I guess Stephen had issues with the extended stays of extended families. Stephen fired Randall too, and found another mustering contractor to do the work on Ibis Downs, work he had promised to Miles.

A few days before, Ivan had said he might give little Wyatt his catching rope. Underneath the toughness a note of compassion sounded for a child whose grandfather was dying and would be dead by the time Wyatt returned to the station to chase peewees with his puppies in the yard.

Dustin fixed more water troughs and hauled lick despite his broken arm. He was quiet the day we learned about Wade's father. We loaded his blue puppy in the back of the ute and cruised across the paddocks of Stilwater, playing Garth Brooks CDs.

We had a couple sections of fence and a broken water line to fix in one of the paddocks. Dustin couldn't shovel the thick muck with one arm, so I dug up the muddy poly pipe, the muck sucking onto the shovel and making a mess. Dustin told me how to fix it, but not before I snapped a shovel and got thoroughly soaked. He dropped me off at a swampy section of the South Gum fence to run a new bottom wire and went back for another shovel. I was dragging, but after pounding metal pickets and wrestling the hundred-pound roll of barbed wire, I woke up a little. Weariness was a nearly permanant companion by then, subtle in the muscle and in the mind, but it had to be overcome, fought until the muscles became more stringy, tense, hardened. Exhaustion ached like hunger, driving the body through the days on small doses of adrenaline and determination, and because there was no other choice.

Dustin came back in his own truck, a fancy ute, because it had a DVD player attached to the dash, and he blasted an AC/DC video of a woman riding a mechanical bull, driving recklessly with his one good hand. I sagged against the seat, covered in drying mud and watching the electric madness on the dash while the country unraveled past us. I finished the water line repair, and then I finished the fence line alone, clouds billowing and sun angling across the buckskin grassland and the lines of green tea trees.

~~

The helicopters mustered another distant paddock, almost as a side note. They left eighty head of cattle without water, trapped in the old set of pens called Coburn Yards. Angus and Miles had enough work already, with thousands of cattle scattered in paddocks and holding paddocks, or caught in yards and ready to be drafted, branded, and shipped, needing food and needing water. Angus had meatworks trucks scheduled for the morning, but those eighty cattle in Coburn Yards would die if left another day. Miles had sent the boys to pick up ten or fifteen bulls still tied to trees all over the place from who knew when, so we were shorthanded. That night, I saw a set of headlights pull in; it must have been the ringers coming back with a load of bulls, long after dark.

The yards at Coburn consisted of two pens and a race, and a

bull smashed a welded rail clear off first thing. "Don't stand behind the rails," Vic drolly reminded us. We whooped and hollered to push the angry anarchist cattle forward. We had loaded the trucks enough times to know the process. The cattle were mad—"proper serious," Miles called them, before smashing one bull on the head with a metal rail.

I felt the drip of adrenaline and wild animality coursing from the land into my bloodstream. I climbed up and over and through the rails, up onto the trucks, running across the top with cattle trying to hook me and slamming their horns against the wood. Angus sat on top of the race, swinging the truck gates open and closed when the bulls weren't trying to bash through them.

Miles finally got a huge cleanskin bull up into the yellow beast of a truck, and tied the bull in the corner of the top deck by lying on his belly on the planks above the bull. He was able to get a quick wrap around the side railing and take up slack in the rope before the bull could catch him with his long horns and plaster the flesh of his hand against the metal paneling. Miles was a big man, but he could move fast, especially when bulls were after him.

Vic wondered aloud why she wasn't a doctor or a lawyer or something. "I'd be good at it," she said.

I asked her about her daughter, if she missed her.

"She's happier in town with her grandma while we're out on a crew. She can go to school there too." She didn't say that the mustering crew was no place for a seven-year-old, or a concerned mother. Vic showed me a photo of the thin girl taken after she had won a school contest for a relay or hurdles.

She turned and smashed at the cattle that held up against the fence and hollered at those she couldn't reach with her piece of pipe. For the next couple cuts she let her rip-and-grip dogs, Bone and Slasher, off their chains. The loading went easier then.

We had one orphan—probably when the helicopters had chased the cattle into the yards they hadn't gotten the mother—and after four or five days without water the little calf was stumbling and could barely walk. I carried him out and hefted him into the front of the stock truck. When Miles pulled the truck up to the race to be loaded, he said the calf already smelled dead, that his weak stomach was trying to come out his mouth. Vic switched places with him to drive the truck, but even with two feet pressing on the clutch, she couldn't get it pressed in far enough to shift gears. I put the little calf in the other truck, the one Vic and I drove, to ride along with her two curly-haired lap dogs. I didn't think he would be alive in the morning.

Bone and Slasher came back wet, black, and sticky from the swamp. They had jumped into a tub of old molasses, the putrid swamp mud mixing with the sweet syrup, which also contained rotten fish added to the molasses as a protein supplement. The afternoon hung dripping hot, filled with a lot of sweat and Vic coaxing the cows to move into the race: "Rubbish cow, have a look," and all of us climbing all over those trucks, chaining and unchaining gates, loading and unloading the cattle as we made trips between Coburn and the house yards. The weaker ones had collapsed, so we had to drag them out, and one we left in the trailer because all of us together couldn't move her. Even weak, she was trying to slash us with her horns.

Angus drove the road train, looking for the switch for the headlights to drive home in the growing dark, the spacious inside like a cockpit with all its switches and buttons. He limped around Coburn Yards with the yellow jigger, perhaps remembering times he could have crawled all over that double-decker truck, but he climbed heavily up above the race, and bulls smashed through beneath him. On the trips to the house yards, several cows went down in the truck. We grabbed hold of their horns and rocked them upright, their hides rough and rubbed raw, their hipbones jutting and eyes wild, but they couldn't move. The weight of lying on their shoulders had damaged their nerves so they couldn't stand up properly. Dustin shot three of them and the calf the next morning and dragged them out for the wild pigs, fork-tailed kites, and eagles.

Dark pervaded the kitchen veranda, yellow lights barely glowing, Angus' cigarette smoking in the ashtray, the generator humming in the shed, a sliver of a silver moon, the evening star barely visible behind the quarters. Claire had gone to Karumba to visit her grandchildren and daughters for the weekend, so Angus was cooking again. Usually this meant cold leftovers, but that night he had made rice and sausages. His beer can sat, sides glistening, next to his cigarette. Garret had returned from his week off with a haircut, and immediately got smashed by a huge white bull who plowed through the gate, sent Garret flying into a heap, and kept going. The gate hit Garret squarely across his forehead and leg. Claire had given him a couple painkillers before she left, and they knocked him out for several hours. He had been limping around and being quite nice, actually.

The mustering crew came for breakfast the next day, and joined us for a lively time at the yards, drafting the meatworks cattle. I sat on top of the pound gate, riding it open and closed while cattle mashed through below me, trying to keep tally at the same time. Cole and Miles took turns at the draft opening, calling nine different splits—branded bulls, cleanskin bulls, cleanskin micks, cleanskin cows, feedlot branded steers, feedlot branded cows, meatworks cows, meatworks bullocks, and bush cows. Ivan, Vic, and Dustin tried to get the cattle forward, and we dodged cows and bulls and slamming gates and loaded the cattle in about four hours. The process took so long that the cattle would miss the train in Cloncurry.

Garret came across the lawn toward the kitchen. I could hear his smoker's cough through the dark. He put a couple beers in the freezer and then sat down opposite me at the outside table, a beer in one hand, a cigarette in the other. We sat in quiet alliance, free of animosity. Even Angus had been nicer, offering a few words of gratitude after a few rums. He said I might pack my things and shift with the mustering crew to Soda Camp for the last stage of the muster.

III

Metamorphosis

THE MUSTER TOOK PLACE in three parts, like phases of a metamorphosis. The first phase consisted of working the cattle close to the house and driving the mobs back to the set of yards called the house yards, which was so close to home that no one was willing to give any ground on his or her opinions. It was easier to keep up a facade where many things could be asserted, pretended, and gotten away with simply because of our proximity to the civilized world.

When we moved farther, during the second act, to Carter Yards in the middle of the station, more than one hundred miles from any boundary, we suddenly all shifted, becoming almost imperceptibly more open or vulnerable, more willing to reconsider the hard lines of our characters. I learned the most about the crew while we worked those intermediate yards, and felt myself shift into place among them like a link in a chain. Though tangled at times, we did find a certain harmony, or at least a predictable discord.

The third and final phase took place at Soda Camp, so far away that no one could pretend we had anything to cling to but the thin lines that ran between each of us. We were close to a coast that received no visitors, lying isolated and alone, rocking against an ocean that reached to another continent. We could not pretend we were the same individuals we had been any longer. At Soda Camp, the work and our relationships underwent a process of transformation, each of us becoming more like the others, evolution inescapable.

It was only on reflection that I found this three-part harmony;

as in most experiences, the larger order appeared only afterward, form emerging from the knotted lines that obscured all clarity in the swimming school of madness. We tangled ourselves up in that holy mess of lawlessness, not knowing that laws of another order did apply. And then here, in this final place, I experienced a rite of passage.

We broke new trails on Stilwater, but we also followed paths laid down long before. Dynamic webs of energy, emerging from this land, guided our tribe deeper into maturation. Once we had experienced and learned the lessons, simple and straightforward as they might have been, we released, reeling, alone, changed—toughened or more tender, wiser or at least more humble—to find our feet again wherever the globe next magnetized the iron in our minds. The ringers would pull apart; they knew that from the beginning. This wasn't a brotherhood for life, though each shared in the blood of this muster in a far-off corner of the outback. But the ringers were also more than themselves. They were age-old stories of action and reaction, operating under lyrics older than the conquering of land and sea. Maybe we were all influenced by a deeper force, accented by the earliest Europeans to arrive here—the penal colonies and the soldiers or authorities who struggled to impose order on a continent that was not so easily convinced.

Soda Camp

Ross Porter shifted up to Soda Camp before the mustering crew to grade the tracks and fence lines at the far end of the station. He had a new road grader trucked up from somewhere, and he was going to clear the way, or at least redefine some of the lines. He would plow the same tracks every year, and by the time he finished, the wet would come, and he would have to begin again. I wondered if he put shoes on to drive this big rig.

But he probably just sat inside the air-conditioned cab, with his callused heels against the black rubber floor.

The camp itself was not much, a dusty flat with a few scrawny tea trees, plumbed with a thick poly pipe and a faucet from the nearby bore. A short distance away, the yards still functioned, portable paneling bolted together and a race with the boards rotting out where the cattle ran up. An ancient silver caravan still waited there, rusty, left by other mustering contractors from other years.

Miles' crew moved their camp to that farthest set of yards for the last act of the drama. They stretched a couple tarps from the trailer out to metal posts. Beneath it, they arranged their cots, a folding table, a small refrigerator that ran off the portable generator, eskies, a tiny freezer for the botulism vaccine, crates of canned food, and five-gallon plastic buckets of biscuits that Miles' mom had baked and sent out with him, along with fruitcakes wrapped in aluminum foil.

They set up a sink to the side of the donga, with a water pipe draining straight to the front, so when the stopper was pulled one had to step aside or get washed with dirty water. They stretched a laundry line between the silver caravan and a gum tree, on which Vic hung her singlets and lacy bras among the Wrangler jeans and button-down work shirts. They set up the washing machine by itself in the flat, a little ways from the sink, its black rubber hoses attached to one of the poly pipes leading from the bore. They tied their dogs up under the short tea trees, and the puppies dug little nests into the dust between them. They all barked in a nerve-wracking racket when anyone drove toward the dilapidated yards.

Tanner had his own camp set up a little ways farther out on the flat, his saddle on an old post rail, his swag spread out on the dried manure in the high bed of his stock truck, and his dogs tied nearby. Vic and Cole stretched a tarp over their ute and set up a bed in the back. They lined up saddles on the horizontal metal rail to which they had tied the tarp, and their

towels flapped from the taut cords. Ivan slept in the back of his truck, except when it rained, and then he climbed in the front, lying lengthwise on a seat cluttered with his clothes and extra truck parts, and slept with his head hanging out. Miles set his metal cot next to the folding table under the main tarp. Ivan and Tanner later hauled the molasses truck up for the horses in the dark, dust seeping in thick through the floor and doors on that stretch of bulldust road leading to Soda Camp.

Airborne

ANGUS DELIVERED ME OUT THERE the following morning, driving the small ute up from the house with a few barrels of avgas for the helicopter. I sat on one of the folding chairs underneath the tarp while the crew finished breakfast. By one of the posts, a drum overflowed with beer cans. Soot from the fire blackened the outside of the billycan and smeared black on my hands when I poured a cup of tea. The crew unplugged two-way radios from the chargers and fueled up motorbikes using the hand pumps on the drums. The drone of the helicopters cut through the morning air. I didn't have my horses up there, and Miles didn't need me in the vehicles, so I caught a ride in one of the choppers.

We made an arc along the paddock's edge. I could see the Solomon River to the north. Crocodiles darted suddenly from sandbars and disappeared in muddy swirls into blue tidal reaches of salt arms.

We spotted a herd of wild horses. The pilot, one who worked for Flynn, swept down over the brumbies, and they threw up their heads and fled in frantic escape at our approach, galloping beneath us, stretching out and hammering the earth, manes flaming back, muscles rippling. The pilot ducked the chopper close enough that I could almost reach out and touch their shoulders, the sweat running down, the horses spreading across the blond grass of the plains. I could not hear the thundering hooves for the sound of the propeller, but I felt the intensity and storm of their flight.

I had never seen horses this way, not astride but from just above, floating, as if I were galloping among them and had to watch out for the hooves and tangled manes. We pulled away from the brumbies, and they receded to miniature on the wide plain, dark flames on brown savanna.

The pilot gave directions over the two-way while Ivan, Max, and Tanner worked below on the motorbikes. They had trouble with some bulls who turned and charged the bikes. They slipped ropes over the massive beasts by running and dodging on foot, in danger of being pummeled to death, and eventually got the animals tied to trees.

Over the two-way: "Hey, we're out of head ropes, think you could drop us some down?"

The pilot veered off toward Miles, who was following a small mob in his open bull catcher. We landed in a flurry of weeds and dead grass a short distance away, and I ran to where Miles was already pulling ropes from the back of the truck.

Up in the air again, we swept back over to the bull fiasco. The ringers struggled to get another bull tripped and tied without being pulverized on their bikes. We dropped the mass of tangled ropes, and from above I saw the strewn motorbikes, men running, and the bull in a cloud of dust as he succumbed to ropes and fought against bowlines holding him to the stout trunk of a gum tree.

The pilot lost one cow who darted into a thicket of trees, so dense we couldn't get the chopper down between the branches. As we left, I saw Miles hitting the thicket full speed with the bull catcher. Splinters of tree trunks snapped up from the impact as the thicket brought the orange catcher to a full stop and swallowed it from view. A few cattle knuckled under from the stress of running with the helicopter, and little calves followed the pads that crisscrossed beneath us. We flew above wallabies, swamps and their water lilies, and meandering waterways. Cattle moved in a long smoky line in front of the helicopter. Storm clouds billowed up again, pulsing the heat with their mass. Rains sprinkled the bulldust, water balling up in the fine powder.

That night, back at the camp, I felt the rush of air and smelled rain coming in the distance.

Identity

I WAS LOSING THE SENSE of who I used to be, finding my identity disintegrating into the place, into hibiscus flower, kookaburra, cattle dust dreaming. If it is true that no one can travel on a path that isn't his or her own, then I had been drawn to the far corner of this place to accept a challenge of my birthright, to be anointed and hallowed and forever see the world in a new way.

In shifting camp, I officially joined the mustering crew, was taken into its fold, for better or worse. Adopted as one of them, I could engage more fully in the transformation, but I also gave up the sanctuary of protection—a house of my own and my status as one of the station crew.

~~

Night at the mustering camp and I walked off a ways—across a dried dam, over a fallen fence, and through the scrub tea trees, until I found a flat place of grazed grass and dried cow manure on which to sleep. Absolute happiness resided in two things—a shower and a cot Claire had given me so I could sleep a few inches above the slithering taipans. The shower even had hot water; the crew had lit a fire beneath a small water drum. The fire smoked, logs flickering and coals glowing, and the water inside the rusted drum gurgled. Inside a small tin enclosure, open to the stars, a showerhead with one lever issued scalding water. There was no cold-water lever, just the one pipe that emptied the boiling liquid held in the drum to sear us clean. The enclosure also had a wooden platform to stand on, a chair on which to set my clothes, and a small mirror dangling on a wire. This was bush luxury.

Steam rose and gauzed the stars and the silhouettes of long gum leaves. It was like a traditional smoking, burning leaves to cleanse the spirit, but the smoke was steam, and it pulled through my pores the remnants I was unable to release. I did not bother to look at myself in the mirror, knowing my reflection would never be as wild as I felt. Instead, I breathed in the humidity, infused by night and eucalyptus, and exuberant with the wet steamy dream that would drift me into sleep. I didn't give the taipans much consideration after the bliss of the hot shower, though I did set up the cot instead of curling up among the dried lumps of cow manure. I thought it wise to honor a creature that knew the squiggling, invisible trails.

～～

Miles had given the crew the next afternoon off, and we all packed up to go fishing. Miles stayed behind to talk with Angus, and was quite upset when we returned because Angus wouldn't listen to him. No one appreciated how hard Miles was working to make the cattle quiet, like an honorable and good stockman should, like he had in his blood to do, the product of generations of good stockmen. Angus had ordered that we use only the choppers the following day, no horses or bikes, to save on time and chaos. I didn't understand whose time he was saving, since we were all there anyway, without much to do except muster.

The rest of us had driven out to fish at a small water hole on Spencer Creek. I took the hand line and walked along the shore for several hundred yards, to a rock overhang.

Stephen had taught me that the secret to catching barramundi was finding structures, rocks or trees or submerged snags in the water, behind which the huge fish lie in wait, hidden from predator and prey, from the crocodiles and from the small fish they ambushed, snatching them unaware from the briny current.

He knew the creatures of the northern waters well. Stephen had called the office at the station once, asking for me, just to tell me about two freshies—freshwater crocodiles—in the lake at Ibis Downs. He said he had trained them to come when he threw a rock in the water.

I dropped the hook, baited with a piece of bloody beef, into the black water. I walked along with my line because the green ants kept crawling up my pant legs, biting with a burning fervor. I felt a tug and a small weight on the hook, then coaxed in a thirty-inch saratoga, large enough that the hand line cut into my palms when I hauled the monster, slowly flopping, out of the water. Tanner left his pole to help me, and when he returned, a fish had pulled his entire setup, rod and reel, under the water. He swore up and down and wouldn't leave it alone since the rod was almost brand-new, worth $150. He was going to dynamite the creek, and on top of that he hoped the fish choked on the hook. Ivan was so plastered that he fell asleep next to the truck. When Tanner laid my huge slimy fish on his face, all he did was groan.

We drove back to camp at night to find Miles moping. I walked off to set up my cot and returned to the arguing of inebriated men. Tanner wasn't drunk, but he was arguing anyway. Instead of eating my fish, I slipped off to bed without eating anything. The night would be my refuge.

Sleep came slowly, drifting down through the seine of outback stars. Crickets sounded through the hum of the generator. I didn't know which taipans visited the space beneath me in the night, which blessings they brought with them on their walkabout wanderings, their lean, air-tasting insistence, and their blood-clotting venom, lacing the world into existence again. I would wake only to a lovely lithe dawn.

~~

Morning in the mustering camp. Ivan pumped grease into his motorbike, Cole spread his toolboxes out to fix his four-wheeler, and Miles took the old yellow ute to water his dogs tied among the tea trees. He used rinsed-out tick poison jugs as water containers.

Miles started the generator at five, and two hours later we were almost ready to go. We had two electric kettles plugged in to make coffee and tea, but with the various lights on, as well as two-way radios and shock collars charging, the power kept tripping out. Cole and Ivan joined to work on the four-wheeler.

The camp felt chaotic, but everything had a place—spare tires, diesel drums, chainsaw, drums of empty beer cans and rubbish, saddles on a metal cot, hoses, and extension cords. Ross left in the grader before dawn, its yellow lights flashing. He had his own tin box in which to maintain his distance and privacy, and I rarely saw him.

I asked Ivan, "How you going?"

He said, "Ah, rough enough."

Cole always answered, "Yeah good, mate."

He and Vic coiled ropes and sorted out straps for the day's bulls. Cole buckled a bull strap around his waist.

Tanner walked in, swearing at everything. He even swore at his dogs when they came to him. Wind rippled the big green tarp, and Miles returned with a pack of dogs running beside the ute. The roar of the helicopters interrupted the noises of camp.

~~

I sat on the avgas fuel drum while the choppers flew in and the crew took their bikes out for the muster. Flynn landed and asked over the radio if I wanted to ride for a while and spot cattle. "I would love to," I said, when I should have said, "Right-o," or, "Yeah, mate." I wasn't quite getting the lingo down.

I got airsick that day, but not before hours of flying, cruising above sand ridges and lines of mangroves along the salt arms, trees so thick I could barely spot the cattle. Fall turned the earth red, blond, and brown as grasses dried and disintegrated into soil. Flynn had to set me down as the last cattle came out of the tea trees.

I remembered another time when I got sick after hours and hours in the chopper, and the pilot set me down amid the coarse grass of the plains. I sat down and leaned against a termite mound. The dirt had a rough texture, and the structure reached like a miniature castle with turrets above my head. I broke one open to see the many pockets and cities of insects. The termites added a waterproofing layer every wet season to keep the dirt skyscraper from slumping into a mud pile. Each species had a distinctively shaped mound, some small and round, some six feet tall and pointed like a bayonet. The helicopter would return. In the meantime, I was in the middle of the Australian outback, nauseated, leaning against a termite mound and a long way from anywhere—a picture absurd enough to make me smile.

When we arrived at camp, we drank tepid tea in the heat while the ringers took a truck to load up three bulls they had tied to trees somewhere in that coastal forest. I never did know how they navigated or remembered which coolibah of the thousand, all nearly identical, held their beast. Troy had arrived with his fiancée and eight-month-old son. I was a little surprised. I hadn't thought him attached to anyone, he seemed so indifferent. I also couldn't have imagined anyone who would put up with Troy, but sure enough, Wanda was there, sitting beneath the hot green tarp, smoking a cigarette. Little Robbie lay unperturbed in the pram beside her.

I hopped in the helicopter again for a short ride to yard the cattle, and then Flynn left for the flight back to Karumba. Sun slanted across termite mounds. A kite flew in outline against a cloud. Ivan offered Miles a cold beer on the ride out to pick up another bull, but Miles was on a diet and had stopped drinking for a while. Still, Miles said, "Of course, Joog," and Ivan handed it across.

Tanner tied up a bull who charged through camp, plowing within inches of the baby in the pram. They tied him to Ivan's truck and half dragged, half led the huge white Brahman out to the yards. Wanda got a picture of it first, the big avalanche of a beast sitting tied near the pram, the sleeping baby, and the folding table. Miles turned off the yellow ute out where we had to drag another bull onto the truck. Then he remembered that the starter had quit. He slammed the steering wheel in disbelief and swore. We rocked the old vehicle in the tight thicket of tea trees until Ivan got it started, and then they left it running.

~~

After lunch in the camp, I sat on a metal cot next to Miles' and Vic's hats, sunglasses on the crowns, listening to Cat Stevens playing on the portable CD player. Muddy puddles formed under the tarp where Cole had attempted to wet the dust with the heavy poly hose, but ended up just making a mud slurry around the table. Troy sat with his bad leg set across his good leg and, next to him, the clutter of a pan with grease from the morning cooking still in it, baby formula tipped over on a crate, and an electric jigger broken in three pieces. Miles slept on another metal cot, his tobacco bag sticking out of his front shirt pocket, his pull-on boots and spurs covered in dried mud from drafting in a pen where he'd left the sprinkler running and made a mudhole, the rest of the yards so dusty we had to squint all morning.

Rain clouds boiled and wind shook and squeaked the tarp against the welded pole overhead. Laundry flapped on the line. Wanda had cooked tea, cooked breakfast, made corned beef sandwiches and cleaned the table, so she was promoted to full-time cook. She sat doing crossword puzzles. A five-gallon tin of cooking oil sat next to the tea bags and sugar and powdered milk.

Miles finally got up and retrieved his hat for the afternoon work in the yards, where the cattle smashed through the crush, hit the portable panels, and ended up jammed in the back of the road train Angus drove up from the house. Troy came out to the yards and called Angus lazy—Troy, who did something only if he felt like it. Wanda brought the baby out in the pram with a piece of mosquito netting draped over the top and let Robbie out to crawl around every once in a while. But the scattered gear, manure, dust, and occasional bulls didn't provide a safe place for a baby to play.

Ivan, Cole, and I worked the crush. Cole slammed the head gate on a mad bull, crooning quietly to the massive beast, "It's not so bad." He gave the bull's trapped head a massage, scrunching the folded skin of his face, and the mean bull couldn't do a thing. Vic and Cole had offered Sutherland Corporation fifty bucks for each of their poddy calves—the ones without mothers who were likely to die anyway—and they said no, just knock them on the head. Vic couldn't do that, so she kept an orphan calf in the camp, telling him to duck when the rest of the station crew came around. She and Cole fed the poddy milk replacer in a cordial bottle with a nipple, and the little calf followed Cole around camp on wobbly legs.

At night, bottles of tequila sat on the table among beer cans and rum bottles, empty and full, cigarette smoke hazing the dangling electric lights. Wanda fried batter-dipped steak in a boiling lake of oil. Troy said they reckoned cigarette smoke wasn't good for babies, but it didn't worry him. Robbie seemed content enough, asleep in his pram beside the vice-laden table. Who was I to judge the inexplicable journeys of our lives? Perhaps the kid needed a rough upbringing to prepare him for survival out here.

Wind tipped over the generator during the night, covering the spark plugs in oil. In the predawn, Miles pulled up the four-wheeler to shine the headlights on it until Ivan eventually got it running again. Wanda didn't bother cooking anything for breakfast that day.

Angus came up in the road train and we loaded cattle in the heat and dust. Some of the cows lay down and refused to get up, some couldn't get up, and one red bull just lost heart. He refused to get off the trailer they had hauled him in on, so they dragged him off, and we had to drag him back onto the truck. Vic and Miles said they would meet us at the house yards, and I rode in the road train with Angus, marveling at the spacious air-conditioned interior that encapsulated us both from the billowing bulldust.

I unloaded most of the cattle by myself, running back and forth, dropping to my belly on the top planks to undo gates, raising and lowering heavy gates between trailers and decks, and working alone until Miles and Vic arrived. The red cleanskin bull had lain down again during the drive, and Vic, Miles, and I rolled him over and over to get him off the truck, his giant horns carving into the rubber mats, his head flopping. He did struggle up eventually, only to lie right in front of the pound gate, where cattle had to jump over him. He was a brokenhearted red beast. Vic said if we could drag him out to the paddock where he could see some space again he might recover, but for now he sank his head to the dirt, downhearted and depressed by his humiliation and stolen wilderness.

The rest of the ringers arrived with more bulls blowing snot and stirring up enough dust to obscure all vision. Ivan gave me a ride back from the Soda Camp Yards on his motorbike, and I held on as we flew through the air along the dirt stretch, without muscle or wings, just the lean ringer with his torn T-shirt and the road that reached long across the savanna.

Cohesion

THOSE WHO'D HAD ENOUGH of their own transformation arranged a departure subconsciously. Ivan was working a bull with Max, and he called over the two-way that he was trying to get the bull down and Max's ankle didn't look so good. Miles, Vic, and I rode horseback, blocking cattle near a bore, and Dustin drove the yellow ute with his broken arm. Cole came over on his four-wheeler, and we waited for word on the bull and the ankle. Tanner speculated that he was probably whining about a bashed-up ankle that wasn't even broke.

It was about the size of a football. We didn't have any first aid supplies with us, but Max thought they had some at camp. I told him how to tape it up, to get something cold on it and get some painkillers. The swelling called for a serious anti-inflammatory, compression, elevation, ice, and a splint-and-tape job, but none of that seemed likely to happen.

Max and Jenna and Dustin headed back to camp, Max saying he had been planning on leaving anyway, and he might just drive the nine hours back home. We didn't think he'd make it that far with a break like that. Tanner said he'd had ankle injuries worse than that, and the bones hadn't even been broken, "whining fuckin' kid." Ivan said to give Max a break.

"Fifty bucks the leg's not broke. If you win, I'll buy fifty bucks' worth of grog and help you drink it," Tanner said.

"All right." Ivan let it drop.

Cole left on the four-wheeler to find a red micky beneath the chopper. The pilot veered back, saying, "See you later, then," his voice echoing from our radios in their harnesses.

"Can you bring us back a carton of beer?" Miles asked, looking up into the sky.

"If I come back, how many cartons do you want?"

"A couple will do us, Jo." And then, "How many can you fit in the chopper?"

"A few."

"How about two of gold and two of red?"

The helicopter careened off into the lake of sky and left the day open. The cattle had calmed down enough to travel by that time.

We had one calf that Ivan picked up and put into the ute

beside Dustin because it was too young to travel far. "My poddies ride in the front of the truck," Ivan said, and then the calf smeared the seat with manure and jumped out the window. Cole lifted the struggling baby onto the seat again. Dustin managed to drive and shift and hold the calf back, all with one arm.

Tanner spoke over the two-way. "I spy, with my big eye, something that starts with C. It's on the opposite side of the mob from me."

Miles said, "Can't be a claypan because they're on both sides of the road."

"Cutie?" It must have been Ivan.

"Give us another hint, Jo."

"Lifeline or call a friend?"

"Lifeline, Jo, I ain't got no friends."

The voices came through the radio holstered on my chest, though we rode far apart on the edges of the moving mob. Each tipped his or her voice to the radio to talk, a dipping of the head, an interruption of the straight if relaxed postures, visible even at this distance. But I knew them by their voices too, and by the points they rode on the mob. I carried this net as a loose formation in my mind, something dynamic, holding all of us together because we rode together. The guesses came in, each of us waiting for the static to stop so we could press the push-to-talk button: cow, clearing, catcher, calamity, crow.

Vic said she saw two words together, starting with S and W, and the answer eluded all of us until Cole dismounted near a thin stream of water and tasted it: salt water. "Must be a high tide today," he said, for a rivulet of ocean to sneak this many miles in from the coast. A spring tide, wandering farther than its forerunners, that would eventually evaporate and deposit a thin coating of crystals on that chalky soil. Word games made the hours pass easily, though we sat in the saddles most of the day. The country separated us and wove us together, white cattle against bleached grass, the dusty track we followed, the horses' heads carried high even as the day drew to an end. Toward dusk,

Tanner rode the tail of the mob, coaxing the tired little calves with gentle kindness in a voice I almost didn't recognize, one that made me smile. "Hurry up now, the dingoes'll get you, the dingoes'll get you!"

At camp we unsaddled and turned the valve on the huge poly pipe to wash the horses' backs, the water rushing down their caked and sweaty sides and flooding beneath the tarp they had set up next to the donga. We rubbed cream into the sores on their backs where the other horses had bitten them or their coats had rubbed raw from the hard riding. Ivan brought me cold water and an orange because all they had was beer, and I preferred not to drink alcohol. A small token of tenderness to compensate for the rough situation.

Max took Jenna with him and drove with his crushed ankle all the way to Normanton. Then, despite the fact that there was a hospital there, he drove on for another eight hours, back to his own hometown. Tanner said he reckoned if Max's ankle was broke that bad, he wouldn't have driven the whole way. Ivan said it was probably broke. Miles weighed in with Ivan. We waited for a phone call, just to see who had won the bet; I don't think anyone was too concerned about Max. His mom called the next week though, asking about workmen's compensation, saying he'd had surgery and a pin put in his heel. Ivan said he reckoned surgery meant the thing was broke. Tanner wouldn't acquiesce. Miles said we should at least go look for Max's bull in the chopper, a bull he'd tied to a tree that no one could find; he would be tucked up pretty well if he weren't already dead.

The situation got worse when word filtered back from Max's hometown that Max had wrecked Ivan's ute after borrowing it without asking to go chase pigs. Jenna had been in the truck with him, and they had overturned; the truck was nearly totaled. Ivan didn't have much to say. He was the one who had brought Max out here in the first place, a kid he'd known for a while and wanted to give a chance out on the mustering crew, to get him a head start somehow. Ivan had paid for Max's way out, supplied him with food and grog, and now his truck was totaled.

~~

When Flynn next flew in to the mustering camp with the helicopter, he stuck his head through the window of Miles' yellow ute and saw the piles of beer cans on the floor, so deep that passengers had to shuffle their feet down into them or sit with their knees up. During the muster later, he asked Miles and Ivan over the two-way, "You guys been drinking plenty of water?"

Miles said, "No, haven't had time, Jo."

Before the day even began, one of Tanner's dogs had slipped his collar and killed one of Vic's. She was not in a good mood, and when she tried to load one of her tall thoroughbreds into the truck, he reared up in the race and flipped over backward. The saddled thoroughbred slammed his hooves between the pipe rails and struggled, upside down on his back against the narrow panels, threatening to break his legs with every kick. Then he would have needed a bullet too. The crew jumped forward to unbolt the heavy panels and drag them out of the way, dodging flailing hooves. Miles got a rope over the thoroughbred's head somehow and muscled the horse upright until he stood up, shaking and bleeding, but overall unharmed. Miles said, "What a way to start the day," but Vic just turned the horse around and marched him right back up the race and into the truck, then rode him for nine hours straight.

Troy and Wanda and the infant Robbie followed in another truck, hauling extra fuel for the helicopter. Ivan and Cole took the bikes out to work the sand ridges below the chopper. The trees in the sand ridge tangled in thickets with rubber vine between, each plant sprawling dreadlocks of twisting vines that were difficult to get through without being strangled or decapitated. Flynn called from the chopper, "Ivan, where're you?"

Ivan, unsure: "Ah, yeah, over near Cole somewhere."

The rest of us blocked cattle at a trough between pandanus palms and the flat of rubber vine. The cattle traveled well, and Flynn stayed far enough back in the chopper to keep them quiet. Then they scattered as we crossed a sand ridge, and we all rode hard to get them together again, losing only one cleanskin bull. Troy got the fuel truck stuck in the sand. He called over the radio, "Ivan, where're you?"

"I'm with the mob."

"Could you come back here for a sec?"

Ivan drawled out, "Looks like the McFuel truck is McStuck."

Tanner replied sarcastically, "I'm McShocked."

The mob walked the distance to the yards quietly. That one muster, directed entirely by Miles, had worked well, and Flynn spoke with a little more respect in his voice when he lifted and left, saying thanks again, he'd see us around, and the dust rose thick so that I could see only the first four of four hundred cattle.

After tea that night, Miles said I'd just have to get married and stay, and I could choose between him and Ivan—who would be groom and who would be best man. Miles, with his black beard, his too-big heart, his roughness, his frustrations, his white shirt not white anymore, his big hands. I said I would have to be drunk first, and he reached, not far, for the bottle of tequila. I had asked for that one. I loved all of them, enough to feel tears well up at times, but they would never know it. Anyway, Miles said, he wanted another beer, and was Ivan shouting? Meaning, was he buying? Ivan got up and pulled a few more beers out of the small cool box, one each for Troy, Miles, and himself, and rolled a cigarette.

Night hung wide and lonely around us. Who wouldn't want to fill the empty spaces inside with tenderness, reassurance, a sharing of the day in the night, skin to skin? Why spend so many nights alone, when they could have been so full and sweet? To lie against a hard chest, a body long and muscled, hands more gentle than their callused appearance would ever suggest? Instead, sweetness between us came in doses; small, almost unnoticeable gestures, moderated by hopelessness, unfulfilled desires, and extreme exhaustion.

Yellow light from the camp leaned out against the horse float, a few lumpy termite beds, and the top of the tree to which the clothesline was tied. A moon hung, almost big enough to write by, but writing could not pacify my feelings or absolve my weariness, and the splattering of outback stars felt inviting, as if they could lift me into the immense half dome of night. The generator would go off eventually, and the camp would settle in to the dust of the dark plain.

~~

Stephen Craye pulled up in the thick heat at smoko the next day, driving a new Hilux. The big boss had bought him the truck, complete with electric windows. Stephen said it was far above his station in life, but the boss had insisted, tacitly saying: You take care of us, and we'll take care of you. He came to sit under the tarp, his shades still on even in the shade, his clean clothes in stark contrast to ours. He rolled a smoke, and we threw around bits of conversation. Wanda had made pikelets that we smeared with margarine and cane syrup. He and Miles went for a drive to see the bores and cattle.

I felt a little drained of emotion when I saw him, not sure whom to think of as compassionate, right or wrong. But I remembered how Stephen had rescued me early on, driving the lengths of the station, pointing out the sandbars in the river where the crocodiles lay, huge ironwood trees where Aborigines had pulled sections of the outer wood off for shields and the cambium layer had healed over, leaving just the outline and indentation. He'd showed me another in the shape of a boomerang. But after Stephen tossed me into the intricate network of the crew, to struggle for my place among them, he had, by necessity, pulled back and changed his role of mentor and friend. I would never know what had possessed him to accept me in the first place.

Near Solomon Bore

AS WAS TYPICAL OF CAMP OPERATIONS, we mucked around until almost sundown, though we still had a killer to do. She was tied up clear on the other side of Solomon Bore, six or seven miles away. Ivan had the knives sharpened, and they threw a tarp in the back of the new Hilux and took all the other gear out—including the tire-changing tools, which we wanted when we got a flat tire on a mudflat behind the bore, almost dark, far from camp, most of us riding in the back with plenty of beer but no tools. On the way out, Garret had said Ivan could drive the station truck—which we all knew was a mistake as soon as he got behind the wheel and careened out of camp so fast that both Miles and Garret reached for their hats. Miles yelled for him to "fuckin' slow down, Jo," and Ivan did, a little, reaching out the open window for us to hand him a beer. Cole rode shotgun to direct him back to the cow he'd tied up during the muster.

He said she was fat, but after a day and a half tied to a tree, she wasn't going to be tender. Crossing a dried swamp too fast, we heard a sudden hissing. One of the tires had a puncture in the side, and it was big enough to be spewing air.

I leaned over and saw the gash, the rim almost sitting on the ground. There was nothing around us but cracked clay and a few dead plants. Beyond, the ground rose up into sandy edges of shadowed forests and pale stretches of wide salt pans. Somewhere in the distance was the coast. We all clambered out, spilling beer cans onto the hard mud. We stood around the de-flated tire. Evening hung low, a haze of dust burning on the horizon. I dug around for the jack, but we couldn't find a spanner, and the truck had no tools, no pliers, and no shifters, only a hundred or so of Dustin's CDs on the front seat and eskies full of beer in the back. We were six miles from camp with night hovering and a cow tied up somewhere farther in the bush. Miles didn't have much to say. Ivan lit a cigarette and grinned. "Ah, yeah, things are good, but they could be better."

Miles' other truck was still parked three or four miles away, where they'd left it after pulling Troy and the fuel truck out of the sand. Vic and I decided to walk to get it, and let the rest of them do the killer. She would have been about dead anyway. Vic took two ciders, gave me one of them for the walk, and we set off through a flat of rubber vine. We knew where the truck was parked, far away down the edge of one sand ridge and across to the point of another, where it met the salt arm.

The sun set orange and alone. We walked fast in the cool of evening, light pink across ribbons of clouds and tall trees on the sand ridge. Vic talked as she walked, complaining, since she was in female company, about how the boys wouldn't take responsibility for anything. She was always the one to remind them of everything. They would probably drive on the flat tire and completely ruin the rim, she said (which they did, shredding the brand-new tire beyond repair), and they wouldn't care because it wasn't their vehicle anyway. She repeated all of her accusations again, swigging her cider mid-stride. We hurried in the pearl glow of twilight, the wings of it settling and folding. Moist air off the coast cleansed my nostrils of dust, and I could breathe again. I preferred wide expanses to the cow who would meet her end in the havoc of dusk, bad luck, lack of preparation, and drunkenness. Light faded and condensed into a single star. Blackness hung in solution. Other stars precipitated. A faint scent of eucalyptus bathed our journey and blessed the butchering on the far side of Solomon Bore.

We crossed toward the end of the salt arm and reached the ancient truck at dark. We climbed up into the monstrous machine. The engine turned over and the lights turned on. I hadn't wanted to get my hopes up. I wouldn't have minded if we had to walk all of the way to camp, but Vic revved the engine to build up air pressure and worked her way through the gears. Then we drove the narrow two-track back to where we had left the crew.

We met the rest of the crew in the pitch black of night, near the bore. They had gone ahead on the flat tire, shot the cow, slabbed her up, and were driving back, rim thumping on the ground. I looked over and saw, in the headlights, the bloody cow head watching from the back of the truck. They said they'd poke along; we could go for the tools.

Vic and I roared slowly back to camp in the huge truck. When we arrived, we called out the predicament to Wanda. She sat under the yellow light, working on her crossword puzzles. She said she might cook up some rissoles—patties of meat mixed with onions, garlic, breadcrumbs, and cheese—that she would fry instead of having cuts of meat off the beast, if we were going to be so late for tea. We located the four-wheeler and the repair kit and rode out against the rush of night and stars. Ivan got out of the truck; they were about out of beer. Vic and I changed the shredded tire.

At the camp, Miles and Cole stretched a chain between two posts and hung up the dripping meat for the night, dangling the cow head from the tall cabbage gum, where the dogs couldn't get at it. Smoke from the fire drifted past huge hanging slabs of beef. Miles, grilling meat over the fire, said he didn't know why anyone would eat rissoles when they could have a fresh bloody steak. He smeared a hand across his mouth and gnawed a greasy rib bone clean before pitching it to one of his puppies. The beef was just as tough and stringy and stressed out as all of us.

That night, the absurdity of the shredded tire, ruined rim, reckless ringers, empty beer cans, and dead cow swirled together, completely normal, and I wondered at how far I had come since I arrived.

She was dust from the dried muck of the wet season, and weeping bloodwood and blue coolibah. She hung upside down from the cabbage gum, watching the camp and the night. I lay alone in the dark, waiting for the generator to go off, as smoke twisted up into the stars.

Flames

DUSTIN ALMOST BURNED DOWN the house yards one morning. He had lit piles of hay string on fire in order to clean up a bit, but he neglected to stay and guard the sticky pile of melting plastic, which then ignited the conveyor belt used as a fence around one of the pens. Flames were a purifier; they ravaged and renewed everything they touched. They licked up the belt fences, ate at the hay piles, pushed cattle into a crowded corner, and smoldered deep into layers of dried manure. The flames sparked out to grasses on the perimeter, running up the stems in red flares. Beyond, forests of coolibah, bloodwood, and tea tree waited, aching to burn. On hot days, vaporized oils filled the air above the forests, pungent and ripe for a blaze. When the oils did catch, the blue haze carried fire like a crown. Fire snapped and surged across grasslands and sand ridges—landscapes born to be revitalized this way. The erratic leading front tore at the savanna, the dead and the living, charring and turning the remains to ash. Fire could sweep across the entire expanse of gulf country during the dry season, sizzling at the edges of mangrove swamp and tide.

Dustin and Claire were at the house alone because we were stationed out at Soda Camp, Angus and Ross had gone to town, Mike had gone to visit family, and Wade's family was still at his father's funeral. Dustin tried to put the fire out with the road grader and his one good hand. He smashed through panels and wire, scraped up burning manure, and cut a fire line into the paddock. Still, the fire burned several hectares before it settled down to smoke. We saw the dirty orange film in the sky at dusk, and word of the blaze filtered back, but by then nothing more could be done.

Miles broke off our engagement with that far pasture to help Claire and Dustin salvage what was left of the house yards and muster cattle that had escaped into the surrounding scrub. We packed up equipment, loaded horses and motorbikes, and made the long journey back to where we had started, months before.

We took bikes and four-wheelers to muster the holding paddock, where large swaths still smoldered—piles of hay and manure glowing and smoking, black soot coating everything. We had to fix some of the fence where Dustin had driven through it with the grader, just so the cattle wouldn't escape again, and Vic started swearing then. Instead of helping us, Dustin was in the workshop fixing up his bike, or maybe the one he'd bought from Max when Max broke his leg and took his leave. Dustin was admonished for having his head in the clouds when he should have been watching the fire he'd set, and for escaping when he could have tried to set things right.

We had a sooty muster, cows smashing through burned and sagging fences, dogs scorching their feet on the hot earth, ashes coating us. Vic, Tanner, and I rode four-wheelers and Ivan took a motorbike. Garret came out to help us as well, looking clean when he arrived and somehow managing to stay that way though the rest of us looked as if we had been rolled in black ash by the end of the day.

We returned in the dark—charred—crossing the stilled savanna to Soda Camp as night fell and pulled its charcoal cape over all. We were weary, draping into plastic chairs and cots beneath the tarp, too tired to make any food. Vic was still upset, but no one cared too much. Tanner grumbled and no one listened. Miles moped and we didn't offer to comfort him. We all carried the blade of blame in easy reach, but it had lost its edge by that time, and no one bothered to sharpen it.

Vic went to bed early. Tanner tipped his seat back against the support pole, and the hanging light drew the shadow of his hat down across his face where his mouth still swore, but we couldn't see the shape of his words. Miles sat heavily on the plastic chair, bearing a weight he could not shoulder with ease any longer. He had creases across his broad, dust-smeared forehead, and his black beard barely disguised a grimace of disappointment. His shirt was crumpled and streaked with dark stains.

Miles anchored us there in the center of that black plain, whether we understood it or not, and bore our troubles as well. Ivan opened the lid of the chest freezer and groped through the packages until he found a cold beer. He handed one to Miles and sat in another plastic chair, the yellow light anointing those of us still left. Cigarette smoke and beer dampened any lingering emotion or injury. The generator hummed to keep the lights burning that hole through the universe. Blackness caught at the corners, and night reached into infinity. The camp was a ragged nest on a blackened branch.

The moon rose, a slender silver half-ring above the dusty plain, and beyond, dingoes crossed beneath the forests, their feet on crushed leaves and hardened mud. At the fringes, the world fell apart and the camp was a spot of yellow light, around which the sky rotated with its indecipherable constellations. The moon would diminish.

We settled in, sooty, the fire in the yards long gone. In the burning, fire had somehow erased us and the months that had come before, so that try as we might, we could never return to what we once were. Fire would destroy the traces of our passing, take back all that we had sacrificed our days to claim. Exhaustion consumed us, as if we had also been the flames ourselves, wreaking havoc on that remote set of paddocks, mudflats, coastline, and sand ridges, until we quieted down to smolder and, in the end, burn out.

We were a Soda Camp dream, I decided, and this was the last story that would brand us, the farthest we could get from the rest of the world. We were all crusted with dried sweat and the grit of dirt and ash that stuck to it. We were more tide than the fingers of the salt arms, and getting ready to pull out.

I had grown used to the dried mud and manure of the camp, the scattered tea trees and the jagged horizon they left after dark. Strange birdcalls punctuated the night. The quiet thump of wallaby tails drummed on the hollow plain. White dust, like ash, would filter down after we left, muting the tones of the world until the next wet season.

Breaking Camp

MILES RECEIVED WORD from Stephen that the crew had gotten the mustering contract for Ibis Downs, so they would be headed there next. They just had to finish walking the weaners out to their respective paddocks, load up the feedlot cattle, and complete a few other odd jobs, and then they were to leave Stilwater. Miles was relieved; they all had work for a few more months anyway. The crew would move on to another place of wild cattle, another series of days and adventures, more chewy beef, instant coffee, broken trucks, horse wrecks, and expansive country.

As they broke down Soda Camp I was surprised at how quickly the chaos could be boxed, put in tin trunks, loaded, and cleaned up—as if the camp had never existed. We folded the huge tarps, packed everything away, and lifted the washing machine and freezer onto the truck. Wanda, Vic, and I packed up the kitchen, Vic smiling often with her long hair in a ponytail. She had a couple races lined up, and the work at Stilwater was lapping to a close, a tide pulling away.

We had more vehicles than people to get back to the station compound, so Cole hooked the molasses truck to the back of the big station truck, which was full of horses, and drove cautiously, trying not to take out the grids. We had dogs piled into crates—their hollowed nests abandoned among the tea trees—and gas cylinders, fuel drums, and rubbish bins packed in the back with them. Miles' bull catcher was roped to the back of Ivan's truck, and more horses were loaded in Tanner's truck.

I drove the old truck with a huge iron crate that almost slipped off the back on the bumps. The starter didn't function, the engine

stalled if I didn't keep the accelerator pressed in at all times, the clutch was loose and the gears stiff, and the truck slipped out of gear on its own in the bulldust pockets. Troy drove the yellow ute with the horse float behind me, driving with his good hand and good leg, and giving me a push start when I stalled. I stalled three or four times when shifting gears, even with the accelerator pressed all the way down, but I got it into second, popped the clutch, and had enough momentum to get started again.

The caravan made it back to the house against all odds. Ivan was happy from a few beers, but the rest of the ringers had horses to unload. Cole took his four-wheeler to the mechanic's shed to weld his busted bull bars back on, and I could hear the snap of the arc welder and whine of the grinder.

We descended on the compound all rowdiness and dust, some of the ringers trying unsuccessfully to curb their profanity since they were back in civilization. The crew piled empty beer cans in a barrel, unloaded enough gear to get through the night, tied off the pack of yowling puppies, and fed the herd of horses. Afterward, they all went fishing, and I returned to my house with its pelicans floating across the lagoon.

I unfolded into the chair overlooking the water, completely dusted, my mind a savanna with mudflats. I washed my two pairs of jeans and two shirts in the washroom. I usually wore one set, washed it at night, and wore the second while it dried. Such a pattern had taken me through the months, but out at the mustering camp I had just let the dirt get thick. The jeans hung drying from a cord stretched across the end of my veranda, water dripping down to wooden slats and below, where cane toads hunkered in streaked light. I washed too, but did not come clean, stained too deeply by the white salt pans, the charcoal and the bloodwood sap.

At the kitchen later I found Claire cooking tea. I had given her a departure date before I left for Soda Camp; my legal stay was coming to an end, and I had booked a return flight from Australia months earlier, allowing myself enough time to get from the station in the remote northeast to the city of Perth in the farthest southwest corner of the continent, where my flight departed. She said she had reserved a spot for me on the mail plane the following Friday. There was a note of tenderness in her voice, not so much for her emotions, I assumed, as for mine. Her life on the station would stitch on farther, and if not there, then not far away, held within the loose borders of the gulf country for the rest of her living years. She was of the place. I had no such affiliations here, no bonds to claim, and nothing I could hold on to to keep from drifting away.

Ross and Dustin and Angus all came up for dinner and we sat on the veranda after tea, talking of who owned which properties, the smoke from Angus' cigarette drifting across the table. Tanner came after the crew returned from fishing, Ivan even later. He was covered in dirt, charcoal, and mud, his pants torn, and Angus asked where he had been. Ivan grinned and drawled, "Ah, the tide was out, the mud was in." His eyes were red and his words slurring, but he had us in hysterics, and then he almost ran over the road train driver on his way back to the donga on his motorbike. Claire wondered what he was doing, driving in that shape. We had returned from the wild, but it hadn't left us altogether.

The next day at smoko, Claire cooked pumpkin scones especially for Miles, and we ate them in the shade of the red shipping container—Vic, Cole, Miles, and I—while eight hundred weaners waited, halfway drafted. We left the sprinklers running during smoko so that we returned to a mud mess, and Miles worked in the yards barefoot, his rough persona not matching his little white toes.

Garret and Tanner went to fix fence in a holding paddock, the same one that Dustin had fixed the previous day, and returned with twelve barramundi. Tanner got out his video camera to get a clip of himself posing with big dead fish. Garret didn't want to get his hands dirty, but Cole found a couple of knives and showed me how to fillet them, and we moved the camp table into the shade of the donga, where we had them finished in an hour or so.

In the evening I caught a ride in the tractor with Dustin. We went up to feed the cattle in the yards. The new green tractor had a closed-in cab, with music and air conditioning, and I felt a little giddy, sitting on the edge of the seat near a control panel. Dustin drove about as fast as the tractor could go, both of us bouncing in the seat as if we were riding short swells.

We bounced along the elevated dirt road, dried swamp with its melon holes and bunchgrasses reaching out to the line of slender coolibah at the edge. I mentioned that I wanted to learn how to drive the huge John Deere with its sticker that said Sutherland Corporation. I meant at some point in the future, but Dustin hopped up immediately and motioned for me to take his place. He explained the buttons and gears, and I drove slowly, feeling tall, green, and air-conditioned.

I fed cattle several times with the tractor after that, Wade hopping in once to remind me about different levers when I couldn't get the bales centered just right on the hayforks. But that night, Dustin swung the tractor around behind the yards to a stack of round hay bales on a flatbed trailer. He raised the bucket with its row of long hay tines and drove forward, stabbing the top row. Two bales could fit, speared on the tines. He drove the metallic monster to dump the bales into the yards and I hopped the fence with a knife to slash away the string. I rolled another bale farther toward the middle of the pen, heaving my weight against the packed roll of pink grass, which left a trail on the pressed manure. Wheeling the huge bale took a concerted effort, as did rocking it upright again. I cut the net of plastic holding the loose grass together. Cattle swarmed the bale as I backed away.

That evening Stephen Craye came by my veranda for a few short minutes to say good-bye. He had returned for a brief visit and was off again to another station somewhere south, and I wished him safe passage and blessings on his way. Black water glinted in the lagoon, inky reeds at its edges. A sacred ibis landed not far from the acacia tree, and a blue-winged kookaburra took off into the silver light.

Wild Horses

As DUSTIN AND I DROVE out to do a lick run, Vic overtook us on the four-wheeler, saying her horses had jumped the grid and did we know what shape the fence was in when it reached the salt arm? "They were going flat out," she said, her hair whipping back from beneath her black hat. Dustin shifted into high gear out toward the salt arm, overtaking the horses who were wet and galloping, twenty of them in a brumby-like herd. We passed them and continued to the water, where we stopped at the bank, the salt arm full with the tide.

We had a minute before the thundering herd reached us. Then the horses pulled up, slowed to a trot as they neared us, white-eyed and breathing hard. They snorted at the water and bank, turned, and, in a cloud of dust and sleek bodies, galloped the other way. The ringers turned them back to the house eventually, but the long coastal plains carried the thunder of their hooves long into the night. Wind pulled their manes back in licking flame from strong shoulders—sun-glossed, sweat-soaked— the horses completing the salt-crusted expanse.

Salt Pans

ACROSS THE SALT PANS, thin bands of mangroves followed the rivers that made their way coastward in the distance. Dustin and I drove with windows down and music blaring, the endless expanse rushing toward us. Horizons melted and reappeared, and the lines dissolved between earth and sky, matter and gas.

Salt pans defied reason and eliminated boundaries, physical and psychological. They stretched on and on, mirages erasing the skyline. As we drove the line of a mirage advanced and retreated, a reflection of sky leaving islands of trees and small fingers of land afloat. Islands became land and then water and islands again. Floating water flamed silver and blue around them. No birds flew above the white salt, but the flats were a tattered wing that burned at the edges, and the mangroves along the river did little to define the flight.

Places undid themselves that far from anything. The scope was one lens fringed in trees or the flat skyline, a concave, pale blue glass above, hue and saturation changing near the edges. Plains had nothing to hide and no cover to offer. They reached and evaporated, distances left to imagination. The path to insanity lay in trying to make sense and give reason to expanses that dissolved into nothingness. In this place, the fantastical and the real had what seemed a more proper relation, one blending into the other, emerging and converging with no distinction. Waters of the gulf flooded in during the wet season and retreated in winter. Desiccated mud carried memories of water, and it replayed the scenario again and again as we drove. Rivers, lined in mangroves and hillocks of bristly grass, reached wide and blue to the gulf. There, bordered by a river and green mangroves, salt pans ended and sea began, and one expanse blended into another.

Brumby Colt

DUSTIN RESCUED A BRUMBY COLT that he found tangled in a fence line, and brought him home to the old yards next to the house. He tried to clean the wounds and give him a bucket of water, but the colt never recovered. Garret and Tanner maintained that he'd probably run the colt into the fence and now was trying to nurse him back to health. The horse was a lost cause from the start—wobbly legs with festering wounds, a rough coat, and wild white eyes. I didn't even cross the lawn and driveway to see the injured foal before Dustin took the .22 and put him out of his misery.

Script

Dawn burned a long orange line above the black script of bloodwood as we saddled the horses.

Redemption

We had two long days of riding at the end. The first of them was hard and fast, mustering a few cattle that had been missed from thick tea trees, the young heifers wild and circling, the dogs holding them along the fence and bringing back any that broke from the mob. Once we broke out of the scrub, wide grassland opened before us. I felt wild, my horse caked in dried sweat but still stepping out, the battery on my two-way almost dead, Cole's already dead, so that he could hear us but couldn't transmit. When Vic spotted a heifer that had escaped her the day before, Ivan brought the heifer in, but Vic begged a go at her, and her puppies wrestled the cow back into the herd, the heifer's ears and throat streaked with blood from their chewing.

The herd moved across the grasslands, their shadows rippling as if they were of the grasses themselves. The pattern of cattle sketched a horizontal calligraphy, paralleled by the length of the horizon. Low-angled light gleamed against horse flanks with flares of copper and bay, the mob itself in a liquid formation. We rode at different points of the herd for hours along the fence line, passing a bloodwood bigger than any I had ever seen, dark sap stains running the length of the trunk. The sun split rays through dust and tall trees, as if the herd and tired riders were a sacred procession and the day holy.

I needed my other horse for the ride the following day, so Miles gave me a ride out to the small herd of them on the back of Ivan's motorbike. He waited until I caught my brown gelding and then headed toward the house, a few miles away. Darcy's mane had grown just enough for me to grab hold; he was tall, but I swung onto his back and headed across the dead grass, riding through moments of salt pan and sea wind I didn't want to end.

On the last ride, we walked the cattle fifteen miles, and it took a good part of the day. Troy followed in the cruiser with water, extra dogs, and the lunch esky. The hours gave way steadily in the rhythm of the rub of saddle leather, the even gait of my big chocolate-colored horse, dust in clouds, the river of white, red, and brown backs ahead of me. We rode through a forest of bloodwoods and boxes, coolibahs and tea trees, and quinine with gold coin leaves and stout trunks.

That morning, Tanner's big white horse had reared back and pulled his reins loose from the rail. Tanner took a dog chain and, swearing, hit the horse several times with it. Troy, who was leaning on the rails, said, "You just have to laugh."

Ivan said, "Reckon it's all you can do." Then, grinning, "Good value, good value." And later, "Hey Troy, go throw a couple stones at Tanner's horse—see if you can stir him up, eh?"

Vic, Miles, and Cole rode young horses who were exhausted by the end of the day. Cole's little mare was "boogered," so tired she could barely walk. We reached the far water hole that had been the destination, the cattle piling in along the edges to drink. Cole, Vic, Troy, and Tanner stayed to do a bit of fishing. Troy said he'd seen two freshwater crocodiles there earlier.

That evening, I put my saddle back on its rack and took Dustin's tools to pull the shoes off Darcy because no one else would be riding him. He waited patiently, and it didn't take long to trim him up and shape the hooves. They would get ground down out among the sand ridges. I rode him bareback, slowly, across the plain and out to the herd that ran loose near the salt arm. Wind caught at my hair and the horse's mane. In a few days it would all be memories. I would not see those horses again. The months of hard riding, etched into the passing of time, would be worn away across other seasons. For the stretch between the station corrals and the salt arm, though, his back rocked beneath me, and he dropped his head in the tranquility of late afternoon. Sun glinted off his coat, casting our shadow on the rutted plain. I doubted if anyone would catch him to ride anytime soon; more likely he would turn wild like the rest of the unused station horses, perhaps jump the grid and join the brumbies. I slid down off his back to the powdered clay, pulled off the bridle, and set him free. He watched me turn and walk away, carrying the bridle with its caked and frothy bit.

The cells have a memory of their own, imprinted and carried on through several cellular generations. They record the journeys of the body and mind, carry emotion and experiences. I would remember those horses like many I've ridden, intimate hours of muscle and supple strength, give of the heart, the tremendous effort to meet my desires or the demands of the work, hour after hour, day after day, until I couldn't separate the rhythm of the horses' gaits from my own walking. I felt their daring and risk. I felt their loyalty and effort inside my chest. I would remember the way I became them on the wide plains and between tea tree veils. The strike of hooves, the glide and gallop, the power and pace and grace of the animal, *equus,* and the millennia of riding ingrained in the cells of each.

The horses I rode in Arizona and in Australia lingered with me, as would horses I was yet to ride and come to know intimately on other continents. I would come to know them on the blackest night by their movement and conformation alone, their unspoken means of communication, more clear to me than that of most people I encountered. I remembered my two dark geldings for the wildness within them and could feel, years after, that I was riding one or the other across the unfurled bolts of distant savannas.

~~

We had the eight hundred weaners to brand the next day and so we worked flat out, covered in dust and blood. When the sun set, there were still lines of cattle. The noise of them bawling and mooing was an overwhelming symphony. I was trying to tag a line of cleanskin mickies in the race and one kicked me through the rails, hard enough to leave a huge blue and purple hoof-shaped pattern on my skin. One slammed Ivan with a horn, and he had to sit against the fence for a few minutes, none of us attentive or quick enough to dodge the injuries.

Vic and I threw calves all afternoon. We were good at it by then, bodies hardened so they didn't give out as quickly. Vic did most of the castrating, and we worked intimately. I kneeled at each calf's head, in blood coagulating from the dehorning, in dirt and piles of horn nubs, grabbing one silky ear after another, more than a few of them already shredded, torn, and infected from the bites of wild dingoes. Vic held the small castrating blade in her mouth between calves.

The weaners we pulled hit the old tire hard, Vic and I almost flung back from each one we pulled over. Tanner and Cole stepped in to help there, Ivan working the gate and helping Vic lift the cradle after each calf. Smoke from the brands, blast of the furnace, crows on the wooden rails, edge of the sky hazy from a fire somewhere to the north: we worked until nothing was left to smolder.

Farewell

THEY HAD A BARBECUE FOR ME the night before I left. I didn't even realize it until I saw the feast Claire had prepared, and asked who was coming for tea. She said everyone, and I felt the tears then, a flood released, the tide heavy. As she cooked, I sat under the barbecue structure with her and Ross' wife, Mary, who had come in from Mareeba. Then I walked barefoot in the dark down to the donga, to tell Miles that dinner was almost ready. He said they'd be along shortly. They all had beers and hadn't even taken showers yet. I laughed and said fine, but I didn't believe him. But they did come, showered and shaved and in clean clothes.

Angus, Ross, Claire, Mary, and I sat in the outside light beforehand, and Angus, pouring rum into his beer can so that it foamed all over the concrete, said he could play a tune on a lemon leaf. Someone collected him a twig of lemon leaves, and he curled one inside his mouth and blew a buzzing tune until we couldn't stop laughing: "On Top of Old Smokey" and "Red River Valley." Ivan came up and said he'd give it a go, but he couldn't get more than a bunch of buzzing spit to come out.

During dinner Ross tapped his beer can on the table and said he wanted to make a speech. He and Miles were about the same size, but with his silver hair, Ross claimed the respect and authority of an elder, at least that night on the veranda. He stood up and said they'd all thoroughly enjoyed having me, they'd miss me, and thanks for the hard work. Then he sat down with his beer can, frothy from the emphasis, and Claire brought a box out from the kitchen. She gave it to Ross, who presented it with both hands across the table to me. It was a silverbelly, a felt Akubra stockman's hat, which Claire had purchased in Karumba. Mike had burned it with the Stilwater brand. Ross passed around a black felt pen so everyone could sign it. The hat covered my eyes, even with my hair stuffed up under it, but I was smiling. Angus gave a speech too. He said it took a lot to be accepted, and I had been. They all cheered and ate and opened more cans of beer. Mango trees and the line of palms beyond the kitchen held the night with its banded stars steady. I stayed up until everyone but Vic and Miles had said good night.

I slipped into the blackness of the lawn and mango leaf-cut constellations, unsure how to think of leaving them, my own solitary journey beckoning again. The journey into the un-known would cut the world around me away and leave me with the eerie feeling of a world lost entirely, one that existed only be-cause certain circumstances and people had aligned. I would be washed of the dust and corral dirt and manure and blood, but the feelings would remain within. I remembered taking a bath in a faraway bore that first time on Stilwater, when I went fish-ing with Stephen and Luci; water like a baptism before I would be hauled through the sacred rites of dust and sweat and cattle and blood—mine, the ringers', the cattle and horses'—until I felt that the earth itself needed such a sacrifice, and we, to be bound with the place, needed the same.

I would slip away like a tide that pulls in and pulls back to the roll of the surf. I had rocked onto Stilwater, and the place and people had penetrated into my consciousness. I had morphed to become part of them and more of myself, to change and be changed and then be pulled to some other faraway shore, neither myself nor my companions nor the place unscathed.

Tide

HOW HAD I CHANGED THEN, I wondered, after months of insight into the netted lives of human survival and dreams? I emerged as if from a cocoon spun between the surreal and the real, between the expected and the actual. How had we all changed, even the place itself? Would the bloodwood forests and tall termite turrets remember me as I remembered them, the stories written into the striated bark and plastered layers of dirt, waiting for rain?

The coast of Stilwater certainly inhabited me, changing, responding to season, enduring cyclones and cycling through the dry season. Certain memories, mental and sensual, would emerge again and again, unexpected and real enough to leave me shaking, but centering me in the world all the same. I was both witness and wilderness, swinging violently between being a sympathetic and not-so-sympathetic participant and observer. Coming to understand this was difficult—realizing the innate tendencies we have to become desensitized to the destruction, damage, and ugliness we must harden ourselves to and embrace. But it also revealed the wild still pulsing within all of us, beckoning, living at the edges from which it will overtake all in the end. I had to reach the end of the continent, clear to the water's edge, to know the limits of myself and to realize how little I knew of places, of the wild, and of people.

Certain of my cells still exist as the tea tree and gum savanna. I cannot escape my own transformation, so I am bound, eternally, to the place and its perennial patterning, even as uprooted as I feel from its shores. I still feel the people as well; I write some of them letters, though I have lost contact with most.

Waiting for the final mail plane, the wind tossed palms in front of the kitchen as I contemplated the huge map of the station on the wall, its long coastline, the paddocks drawn in, the erratic wanderings of the Powder and Solomon Rivers. A wallaby hopped along the short fence on the lawn. Green mangoes lay fallen on the ground. Corellas clung in white flocks on the naked tea trees. In the dark of early dawn, Angus had teased me again with my own mantra: "Another beautiful day, eh? How am I going to know if the day is beautiful or not when you're gone? Can't even see the bastard yet."

I cleaned my little house quickly and went up to the yards, where I climbed the rusty rails and the crew paused in the branding and loading to give me hugs and bid me safe travels. I heard the engine drone as the small aircraft landed and came to a stop near the house. Angus took me out to the plane and exchanged mailbags with the pilot. I handed my small backpack across. I turned back toward the house, lifted my own hand to wave, and then climbed over the wing and into the front seat.

We cruised down the dirt strip, the plane throbbing as its wheels bounced on the dirt, and then we lifted out over the brassy sheen of the coastal plains. I watched a small herd of horses lift their heads, my own dark geldings who would grow old and die, and I felt shaky. We flew above the winding salt arm and over plains and sand ridges, heading toward the Solomon.

The season on Stilwater, like a lifetime, ebbed to an end. The heat of mango season would descend. Rains would come and drench the entire gulf country for months, storm after storm, lightning streaking down from the thunderheads, heat so thick it dripped from the skin of sky. The few people who were left would sink into their own form of solitary madness, the roads washed out, landing strip underwater, floods lapping beneath the kitchen and houses.

Flynn often said I should return just to see the country in flood, land like a sea, the sea shaded with the red mud the river carried, suspended clear into the gulf, the color of green the ground turned afterward, bursting with vigor, and then the way it dried to pale gold and the soil cracked in the memory of its loss. Even then I knew Stilwater would not be the same station, the same glittering coastline lined with river she-oaks and mangroves, long plains that patterned far beneath the helicopter like clouds, like the surface of boiling water, and lines of sand ridges, palms, tea trees, nonda trees, and, closer, tracks and mud messes left by the pigs in the swamps, the green ants wrapping the broad leaves of the wild pear trees together and plastering thin seams of white glue to make hanging huts that broke when brushed against, releasing torrents of green bodies. Crocodiles would move inland and seaward, water lilies would open purple palms to the sky, the mangoes would rot and sweeten, and pelicans would cruise above the length of the long white coast.

The Sutherlands had indicated that they would be re-evaluating their strategy with the property. The cattle would likely turn wild again; with the crews gone and the money from above slowing to a trickle, there wasn't much to keep the place from regressing to its previous state. The tornado of that one winter—one season of crazed effort to mend the fences and grade the two-tracks and catch every last cow, of attempts to ascribe order to this place—would be one small knot in the line of time. Sea eagles would return to build their nests in the snags along the shore. And certain stretches of savanna, certain clearings within the forests of gum, might remember the scuffles and life and death that had happened there, a distant thought disappearing into the expanse of the outback.

The gulf reached, glittering, to the horizon. Soon I would be gone altogether, Stilwater already small below me. I was not finished with my wandering or my inner imperative to investigate the world, but I would never be able to return here as the person I had been. Tanner wrote me a letter, months afterward, saying he was thinking of becoming a saddle maker, that he still remembered my sweetness and was really trying to be more positive. He wrote me a few letters over the years, and I wrote back to him of my own adventures, until the distance eventually dissolved all communication. I sent them all the photographs that I had taken from the helicopter, but not long after those same photographs would seem a lifetime away, as if someone other than myself had taken part in the experience.

Months later, Alan called to say that Gene Sutherland and his wife had been killed in a plane crash, along with two pilots. They had been on their way to Brisbane. A tragedy, he said. He had known them both and worked for them in the south for years. Even then, the news shook me, as if I had heard another ending to a story still unfolding, and could suddenly feel again the pervasive presence of the complete wild. I was one small part of the script, haunting still, because soon after I left, everyone else left as well, except Wade and his family, who lived alone on the expanse of Stilwater through at least the next wet season.

I tried to place the topography of the plains until we passed beyond Stilwater's farthest boundary. I was leaving country that I had ridden and memorized, each water hole, stretches of grassland and trees. In a way, I had fulfilled my part in recreating the station, as a songline will, mapping the world into existence by one's path across the landscape. But beyond that boundary, I had no memories, and there my song ended. The melody would continue, changing owners, and I would pass off my responsibility to those who rode across the next stretch of savanna. I knew only a few lyrics of the land that had held our epic for a season. As we did, I released my last tendril of longing, and then I leaned back and simply looked out the windows at the sparsely forested gulf country. I knew in my mind the hook of the coastline, and I imagined the strange track that would be mine across it, unnoticeable, leaving little or no trace of my passing except in memory. I did not mind traveling lightly on the earth, with few possessions to encumber my flight.

I do remember that it took me a long while to find my feet again after leaving Stilwater. I wandered aimlessly as if only my body had been transported, while my mind and spirit remained on Stilwater, riding still in the coastal scrub. I had wrestled and wiggled my way so deeply into the continent that I felt as if my skin were folded around a forest of bloodwood and coolibah and bouncing wallabies. I felt as if my own boundaries had expanded, the space within me stretched wider, and time no longer held the same tight rein on my existence. Long after I left, I was still part tea tree and salty coast, dust and cattle mob, deep night and dusk of silver sky, leather and horse muscle, slamming horn, splintered wood, and hot tea. But it was the horses I would miss the most, the tangled black manes of my geldings, their warm breath and sleek necks, their tossing heads, and their willingness to work across the days.

Tears came easily and I let them flow, but the experience of that place left scars I could feel a decade later, writing and rewriting the memories. I felt sick on that plane too, the disorientation of leaving suddenly a landscape that had written and rewritten the days, and transformed the person I thought I knew.

We landed at the next station, handing across another mailbag, and then stopped shortly thereafter to refuel at an Aboriginal settlement. I vomited on one of our stops, out on the airstrip, and then curled up among the mailbags and stacks of newspapers. We flew on to properties I did not know, small dirt strips, and then there was the whir of landing, stepping out to unload the mailbags, lifting again into the blue above the northern peninsula country, lifting as I had landed, in the dry season, high above and beyond the lens, the small stretch of a thousand square miles of wildness that would forever haunt me, that would wrap my story into countless others that created, transformed, and crossed the stretch of distant coastal forest and savanna that was Stilwater.

Acknowledgments

THIS WORK WOULD NOT HAVE BEEN POSSIBLE without the love and support of my family and close friends: Thank you to Don, Rebecca, Kanin and Cody Routson, Jaime de Grenade, Beth Horan, and Karen and Bill Pearson for holding the net as I leaped, and for your constant presence in my life. Thank you to Dennis and Deb Moroney for my early years on the ranch, for teaching me the livestock skills necessary to survive on an outback cattle station, and for a long friendship. Special thanks to Vince and Joan Kontny and Barbara Parker for providing the stories that first inspired my Australian dreaming and, later, for providing the plane ticket. To Jill, who met me upon arrival. To Mark and Gillian Bryant for introducing me to the outback, for the loan of the horses and knowledge, and for the letters over the years. Thanks to Mick Petroff, Mick and Yvonne Hayes, Mick Flemming, and Peter and Mark Menegazzo for your part in facilitating this grand adventure. To the folks at Inkerman: Nancy and John Grostelo, Dan, Kirstie, Lane, and Grace Doyle, Ben, Dave and Allison, Rex and Blondie, Janelle, Vandy and Cooper, Coby and Ryan, Grant Butler and Paul McMahon. And to the mustering crew: Lee Streeter, Ben Moss, Graham Quinn, Mel and Brian Condon, Trevor and Linda Bennett, Conan and Vivian. I would like to extend a deep gratitude to Gary Nabhan, Allison Deming, Patrick Thomas, and Daniel Slager. The journey of writing, though much longer than my stint at Stilwater, has itself transformed me.

RAFAEL DE GRENADE grew up on a farm in the foothills of the Santa Maria Mountains, outside Prescott, Arizona. Living on the land fostered an intimate connection to family and place, cultivated a deep-rooted work ethic, and inspired a passion for the relationship between humans and the rest of the natural world. She began working on mountain ranches in north central Arizona at age twelve, riding, branding, and shoeing horses and gathering cows. This diverse and place-based education helped her to develop a deep understanding of the farm and the Southwest, and of her place as a land steward, artist, scientist, and writer. She earned a BA in Environmental Studies from Prescott College, and an MFA in Creative Writing and a PhD in Geography from the University of Arizona. She has traveled widely, seeking to understand the complexities of the people-place relationship in the context of a globalizing world. Rafael lives with her husband, Jaime, and daughter, Soraya, in the Southwest and in Chile.

The Editor's Circle of Milkweed Editions

We gratefully acknowledge the patrons of the Editor's Circle
for their support of the literary arts.

~~

Mary and Gordy Aamoth
Cliff and Nancy Anderson
Elizabeth Andrus
Maurice and Sally Blanks
Bridget Bly
Mary Bly and Alessandro Vettori
Noah Bly and Becky DaWald
Karen Bohn and Gary Surdel
Tracey and Jeff Breazeale
Emilie and Henry Buchwald
Robert and Gail Buuck
Robert Chandler
Barbara Coffin and Daniel Engstrom
Libby and Tom Coppo
Betsy and Edward Cussler
Edward and Sherry Ann Dayton
Mary Lee Dayton
Mary Dolan
Julie DuBois
Mary and Joseph Fleischhacker
Martha and John Gabbert
Charles and Barbara Geer
Joanne and John Gordon
Ellen Grace
William and Jeanne Grandy
Moira Grosbard
John Gulla and Andrea Godbout
Jocelyn Hale and Glenn Miller
Amanda Hawn and Nate Larsen
Liz and Van Hawn
Elizabeth and Edwin Hlavka
Joel Hoekstra and Eric Jensen
Barbara A. Jabr
George R.A. and Emily Johnson
Kathleen Jones

Leroy Kopp
Constance and Daniel Kunin
Jim and Susan Lenfestey
Kathleen and Allen Lenzmeier
Nivin MacMillan
Chris and Ann Malecek
Susan Maxwell
Walter McCarthy and Clara Ueland
Robert and Vivian McDonald
Mary Merrill and William Quinn
Elizabeth Moran
Sheila Morgan
Chris and Jack Morrison
Kelly Morrison
    and John Willoughby
Robin B. Nelson
Wendy Nelson
Ann and Doug Ness
Jörg and Angie Pierach
Patricia Ploetz
Margaret and Dan Preska
Pete Rainey
Deborah Reynolds
Cheryl Ryland
Daniel Slager and Alyssa Polack
Schele and Philip Smith
Stephanie Sommer
    and Stephen Spencer
Bruce and Julie Steiner
Larry Steiner
Joanne Von Blon
Edward Wahl
Cynthia Walk
Eleanor and Fred Winston
Margaret and Angus Wurtele

Interior design by Connie Kuhnz
Typeset in Minion Pro
by BookMobile Design & Digital Publisher Services